W9-CNQ-558

Rogers Cadenhead

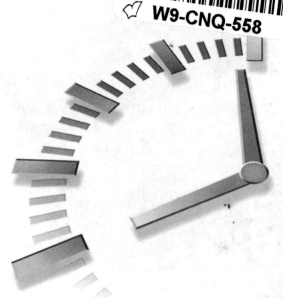

SAMS
Teach Yourself

Microsoft®
FrontPage® 2002
in 24 Hours

SAMS

201 West 103rd St., Indianapolis, Indiana, 46290 USA

Sams Teach Yourself Microsoft® FrontPage® 2002 in 24 Hours
Copyright © 2001 by Sams Publishing

All rights reserved. No part of this book shall be reproduced, stored in a retrieval system, or transmitted by any means, electronic, mechanical, photocopying, recording, or otherwise, without written permission from the publisher. No patent liability is assumed with respect to the use of the information contained herein. Although every precaution has been taken in the preparation of this book, the publisher and author assume no responsibility for errors or omissions. Neither is any liability assumed for damages resulting from the use of the information contained herein.

International Standard Book Number: 0-672-32104-1

Library of Congress Catalog Card Number: 2001091415

Printed in the United States of America

First Printing: June 2001

04   03   02   01   4   3   2

Trademarks

All terms mentioned in this book that are known to be trademarks or service marks have been appropriately capitalized. Sams Publishing cannot attest to the accuracy of this information. Use of a term in this book should not be regarded as affecting the validity of any trademark or service mark.

Microsoft and FrontPage are registered trademarks of Microsoft Corporation.

Warning and Disclaimer

Every effort has been made to make this book as complete and as accurate as possible, but no warranty or fitness is implied. The information provided is on an "as is" basis.

ACQUISITIONS EDITOR
Betsy Brown

DEVELOPMENT EDITOR
Jan Snyder

MANAGING EDITOR
Charlotte Clapp

PROJECT EDITOR
Leah Kirkpatrick

COPY EDITOR
Mike Henry

INDEXER
Aamir Burki

PROOFREADER
Tony Reitz

TECHNICAL EDITOR
Dallas G. Releford

INTERIOR DESIGN
Gary Adair

COVER DESIGN
Aren Howell

LAYOUT TECHNICIANS
Gloria Schurick
Ayanna Lacey

Contents at a Glance

Contents

About the Author

Rogers Cadenhead is a writer and Web developer who has written 11 books on Internet-related topics, including *Teach Yourself Java 2 in 24 Hours* and *Sams Teach Yourself Microsoft FrontPage 2000 in 24 Hours*, but not *Teach Yourself Microsoft Bob in a Holiday Weekend*. He maintains this book's official Web site at `http://www.cadenhead.org/frontpage/`.

Dedication

To my wife, Mary Christine Moewe, for the first 14 years of forever. We'll always have Arlington, Denton, Fort Worth, Denver, Peoria, Dallas, Jacksonville, Palm Coast, and St. Augustine.

—Rogers Cadenhead

Acknowledgments

I'd like to thank the team at Sams Publishing, including Mark Taber, Jan Snyder, Mike Henry, Dallas G. Releford, and Betsy Brown. With a group like this working to make the book good, I'm proud to have my name on the cover so I can claim a disproportionate share of the credit.

I also must thank my wife Mary and sons Max, Eli, and Sam. You've given patience, support, humor, and love to someone who spent enough time at a computer to qualify as a plug-and-play device. I love you at least 200 percent above the recommended daily allowance.

Finally, I'd like to thank Microsoft Bob.

Tell Us What You Think!

As the reader of this book, you are our most important critic and commentator. We value your opinion and want to know what we're doing right, what we could do better, what areas you'd like to see us publish in, and any other words of wisdom you're willing to pass our way.

You can e-mail, or write me directly to let me know what you did or didn't like about this book—as well as what we can do to make our books stronger.

Please note that I cannot help you with technical problems related to the topic of this book, and that due to the high volume of mail I receive, I might not be able to reply to every message.

When you write, please be sure to include this book's title and author as well as your name and phone or fax number. I will carefully review your comments and share them with the author and editors who worked on the book.

E-mail: webdev@samspublishing.com

Mail: Mark Taber
Sams Publishing
201 West 103rd Street
Indianapolis, IN 46290 USA

Introduction

Microsoft FrontPage 2002 prevents you from learning.

That might sound like a knock against the software, but it's actually one of its strongest selling points.

A person who becomes skilled at FrontPage 2002 can publish on the World Wide Web without learning any of the following:

- Hypertext Markup Language (HTML)
- Cascading Style Sheets (CSS)
- Dynamic HTML
- JavaScript
- Common Gateway Interface programming
- Active Server Pages

You don't need to learn any of these Web design languages and technologies because FrontPage 2002 does all it for you. When you work on a Web site in FrontPage, you edit it in a visual point-and-click environment that's similar to Microsoft Word. Web design features that are the stock in trade of professional Web designers can be implemented in FrontPage with a few mouse clicks.

FrontPage, now in its fifth major release from Microsoft, is also a tightly integrated part of Microsoft Office, the most popular productivity suite in the world.

You might be familiar with FrontPage 2000, FrontPage 98, or another older version of the software. FrontPage has always been one of the most popular Web editing tools because it makes creating a Web page as easy as typing a letter in Microsoft Word.

FrontPage 2002's inclusion in the Office suite shows how important the World Wide Web has become. Putting yourself and your company on the Web is an everyday part of life today. People are using this medium to shop, learn, communicate, play, and teach. A network that once was occupied by a few thousand scholars, students, and military officials is now as ubiquitous as television. People who don't even own computers are familiar with Internet companies such as Amazon.com, Yahoo!, and eBay. Thousands of new Web sites are launched each day by a variety of publishers—corporations, small businesses, organizations, and individuals.

Whether you are a business owner launching her Web presence or a high school student publishing his literary efforts for a global audience, you can benefit from FrontPage's sophisticated editing, publishing, and site maintenance capabilities.

FrontPage 2002 makes it simple to master the complex tasks required of a Web publisher, but you must first master the software itself. The fastest way to do this is with *Sams Teach Yourself Microsoft FrontPage 2002 in 24 Hours.*

During 24 one-hour lessons, you'll develop hands-on skills with each feature of FrontPage 2002:

- Creating new Web sites quickly with templates, themes, and wizards.
- Editing Web pages exactly as they will appear in a browser—a feature known as WYSIWYG, or "What You See Is What You Get."
- Turning on and off features of FrontPage 2002 depending on the Web browsers used by your audience.
- Adding interactive capabilities such as surveys, discussion forums, and feedback pages.
- Editing image files within FrontPage instead of using an image-editing program.
- Tracking visitors to your Web site, one of more than a dozen new features introduced in FrontPage 2002 that are covered in this book.
- Connecting your Web site to a Microsoft Access database.
- Integrating your Web seamlessly with the other programs in the Office XP suite.
- Bringing existing sites into FrontPage 2002 without altering their appearance.
- Telling FrontPage 2002 what you want and letting the software figure out how to implement it through sophisticated Web technology such as Cascading Style Sheets, JavaScript, and Active Server Pages.

Creating a FrontPage Web site has never been easier. Whether you're using FrontPage 2002 at your office, home, or home office, *Sams Teach Yourself Microsoft FrontPage 2002* provides the skills you need to publish your own Web sites. By the time you've completed the lessons in this book, you'll be taking part in the same publishing revolution that spawned millions of pages, including well-known sites such as Yahoo! and ESPN.com and more unusual fare such as Derek's Big Website of Wal-Mart Purchase Receipts.

 Since Nov. 17, 1996, Derek Dahlsad of Fargo, North Dakota, has scanned in every receipt from his frequent shopping trips to Wal-Mart. Hundreds of people visit and leave comments about his purchases such as this: "I couldn't help but notice that you've bought 40WTBULBs on a fairly regular basis. May I suggest that you have your wiring checked." To keep track of Derek's Wal-Mart expeditions, visit http://lightning.prohosting.com/~receipts.

As you read this book, you'll also become well-acquainted with one of the first Web sites created with FrontPage 2002: this book's official site at `http://www.cadenhead.org/frontpage/`. It contains the following features:

- Updates to the material covered in the book.
- Solutions to the exercises at the end of each hour.
- Answers to questions commonly asked by other readers.
- A way to contact author Rogers Cadenhead with your own questions, comments, and corrections.

By the time you finish *Sams Teach Yourself Microsoft FrontPage 2002 in 24 Hours*, you'll be equally surprised by how much FrontPage 2002 can do for you. It can make Web sites much easier to create and manage, letting you focus on the content you want to publish and the audience you want to reach.

PART I

Starting Strong with FrontPage 2002

Hour

Hour 1

Create a FrontPage Web

Today, somewhere in the neighborhood of one million books have been released about the subject of World Wide Web publishing. Wait—I just heard a report on the radio—there are now one million and five.

These books normally start with an introduction to the World Wide Web, a mass medium that was born in the early 1990s and has blossomed into an amazing way to receive and send information.

At this time, you probably have heard about the Web. Otherwise, there isn't much reason for you to be interested in FrontPage 2002, Microsoft's Web site creation software. (This kind of keen analytical insight is why I'm writing computer books today and have completely abandoned my previous career in salads, fries, and milkshakes.)

Although the Web might be old news to you, there's a lot of new news to report about FrontPage 2002. With the release of this software, Microsoft has made Web publishing a core part of its Microsoft Office productivity suite. Many features of past FrontPage versions have been improved or expanded. Many others are completely new.

All 24 chapters of this book are used to cover FrontPage 2002, arguably the most sophisticated Web publishing software on the market today. You'll learn how to use each important feature of the software in easy-to-handle one-hour lessons.

Each chapter focuses on tasks you can accomplish rather than procedures you must memorize. By the time a day's worth of these hours has been completed, you'll be an expert user of FrontPage 2002, publishing your own Web sites, attracting visitors, receiving feedback, updating your sites, and attracting more visitors.

The best place to start is with a copy of FrontPage 2002 somewhere in the vicinity of your computer.

Acquaint Yourself with FrontPage 2002

Microsoft FrontPage 2002, as with all elements of the Office XP productivity suite, was named after a year. After you begin to use the software, you might start to think that FrontPage was named for the number of different things you have to learn to use it.

FrontPage 2002 comprises all the tools you need to create, publish, and manage a World Wide Web site. Each of these tools is integrated into a single program, which is one of those good news, bad news kind of things.

The bad news is that there are a large number of things to learn about this all-in-one software package. Creating, publishing, and managing a Web site are all substantive tasks that have traditionally been handled by several different types of software: page editors, file transfer programs, hyperlink verifiers, and more.

The good news: You don't have to learn the quirks of several different programs or keep track of which program handles which task. In previous versions of FrontPage, the software's page editor and site explorer were separate programs. This could easily cause users to zig by running one program when they should have zagged by running the other.

Learning to use FrontPage is like learning to use Microsoft Word, the popular word-processing software that's also part of Office XP.

Although Word has hundreds of different features, the basic mechanics of creating and editing a document are fairly simple. You type text into a window, click a few buttons or menu options to format the text, and save your work. You can start using Word long before you have mastered its more sophisticated features.

More good news: For the most part, you can learn to use FrontPage 2002 the same way.

Have you ever used a word processor such as Microsoft Word to create a nice-looking business letter, produce an effective resume, or butter up an older relative to get into her will? If so, you have most of the skills you need to master FrontPage 2002 and create your own Webs.

> Although most people call a collection of related Web pages a Web site, Microsoft FrontPage refers to them as *Webs*. This term is used throughout the book because you'll be encountering it often when using the software and its built-in help system.

Discover FrontPage 2002's New Features

Before the release of FrontPage 2002, thousands of people were using earlier versions of the software to publish their Web sites. To get an idea of its popularity, FrontPage is referred to on more than 212,000 Web pages, according to the World Wide Web search engine AltaVista at http://www.altavista.com.

FrontPage 2002 is the fifth major release of the Windows version of the software (another product, FrontPage 1.0, is currently available for Apple Macintosh users).

Like most major software releases from Microsoft, FrontPage 2002 introduces significant new features. People who are upgrading to FrontPage 2002 from the 2000 edition will find the following improvements:

- Surveys—Poll your users on a variety of topics, automatically tally up the results and present them.
- Link bars—Add graphical menu bars to your Webs that are displayed vertically or horizontally, linking to each of the areas of your site.
- Inline frames—For the first time, FrontPage can be used to create frames that are placed entirely within another page.
- Visitor tracking—Learn more about how your site is being used, tracking the number of times pages are loaded, the browsers used to view it, and the hyperlink that was used to find your site.
- Web components—FrontPage 2002 includes more than a dozen new Web components such as bCentral page counters, MSNBC headlines, and links to Microsoft Expedia maps.

In addition to these new features, FrontPage 2002 is more tightly integrated into the Office XP productivity suite. FrontPage shares common user interface elements such as toolbars, shortcuts, and menus with other Office applications.

FrontPage 2002 also shares a common file format with the other applications such as
Excel and Word: HTML. Each Office program can save its documents as Web pages.
These pages can be loaded by FrontPage for editing without losing any of their information. A Word document can go from Word to FrontPage and back to Word, never losing
its font selections or paragraph formatting.

If you're already familiar with past versions of FrontPage, the most significant thing
you'll be adapting to is the software's strong connection to the rest of the Office suite.

Run the Software for the First Time

FrontPage 2002 presents all of its features in a single interface. You will be able to create, edit, and publish a Web without leaving FrontPage. You can keep hyperlinks up-to-
date, manage files, and even create a task schedule to organize your Web publishing
projects.

The FrontPage 2002 graphical user interface is shown in Figure 1.1.

FIGURE 1.1
*Running FrontPage
2002.*

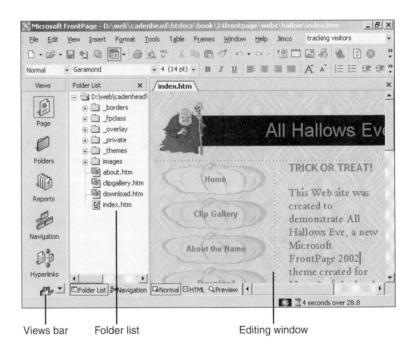

In Figure 1.1, FrontPage 2002 is being used to edit a page that's part of a Web. The three
main sections of the interface consist of a Views bar, Folder list, and editing window.

The FrontPage user interface takes on six different appearances depending on the view you've selected. *Views* are different ways that you can explore a Web as you work on it in FrontPage.

Views are chosen by using a set of icons inside the Views bar identified in Figure 1.1. The view you select determines the kind of work you can do to the Web, and the following icons can be selected:

- Page—Edit a Web page
- Folders—Explore a Web's file folders and files
- Reports—View reports related to a Web
- Navigation—Navigate a Web's organizational structure
- Hyperlinks—View the way a Web's pages have been hyperlinked
- Tasks—Plan the upcoming tasks in a Web's development

All work that you do within FrontPage revolves around the Views bar.

The Folder list shown in Figure 1.1 lists all files and folders associated with the current Web. Clicking one of the listed Web pages opens that page in the editing window.

> The Views bar and Folder list can be closed to make room for other windows on the FrontPage 2002 interface. Choose View, Views Bar to close the bar and choose View, Folder List to close the Folder list. You can use the same options to open these windows after they have been closed.

The editing window functions like a word processor's editing window. You can add, edit, and delete Web page elements such as text and images.

There are two toolbars running along the top of the FrontPage 2002 interface, as shown in Figure 1.2.

Standard toolbar   Formatting toolbar

FIGURE 1.2

Using the Standard and Formatting toolbars.

The Standard toolbar and Formatting toolbar are used primarily when you're editing a Web page in the editing window. These toolbars are *dockable*, which means that you can move them around the FrontPage 2002 interface if you don't like where they have been placed.

To dock a toolbar, grab it with your mouse and drag it to the left, right, top, or bottom edge of the FrontPage 2002 interface. If you place the toolbar on the left or right edge, it will be displayed vertically instead of horizontally.

If you place a toolbar away from the edges (or off the FrontPage interface entirely), it will float in its own window. You can move a floating toolbar around by grabbing its title bar with your mouse.

If you can't find a way to grab a dockable toolbar in a Windows program, look on the toolbar for a line that separates two buttons—the Standard toolbar in FrontPage 2002 has several of them. Click your mouse on top of one of these lines, hold down the button and move the toolbar around. When you release the button, the toolbar will be placed at that spot.

Take Different Views of a Web

Most of the work you do in FrontPage 2002 will be accomplished in the Page view. Each of the other five views is more specialized.

The Folders view opens a Windows Explorer–style list of the files and folders that make up a Web. You can use it to do any of the things that Windows Explorer is used for: opening, moving, renaming, and deleting files. You also can see the title, size, and modification date of each page in a Web.

The Tasks view is used to create and manage a to-do list of the tasks associated with your Web. If you're working on a Web alone and want to keep track of your progress, or collaborating with others who need to see what you've been doing, the Tasks view provides a built-in project manager. Task management is covered during Hour 15, "Keep Your Web Up-to-Date."

View Reports About a Web

The Reports view, shown in Figure 1.3, opens a list of reports that tell you more about your Web.

Each report in this view has a description that explains its purpose. Eight of the reports list files included in the Web based on a specific criteria.

The report that lists unlinked files is useful to determine when one or more Web pages are not connected to the rest of your Web. These pages can't be reached by a person who goes to the main page of your Web and uses hyperlinks to visit every page in your site. Unless there's a reason not to make these pages a part of the Web, you can use this report when either deleting the files to save space or adding links on those pages.

1

FIGURE 1.3

Viewing reports about a Web.

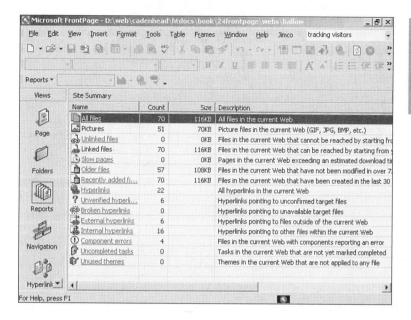

Another useful report lists slow pages, which are defined as pages that would take 30 seconds or more to download using a 28,800-baud Internet connection (also called a 28.8).

One of the things you must keep in mind as a Web developer is the way your audience connects to the Internet. Most people are using a 28.8 or 56.6 modem to dial up an Internet service provider, load their Web browser, and start viewing pages, although this is changing as ISDN, DSL, and cable modems become more popular.

The 30-second report considers all parts of a Web page: text, images, interactive programs such as Java applets, and anything else that is downloaded when the page is viewed in a browser.

Is 30 seconds a long time to wait for a page to load when you're surfing the Web? The half-minute wait is generally a reasonably good benchmark for when you should start worrying whether a page contains too much text, graphics, and other elements.

The slow pages report can be customized to use a connection speed other than 28.8 and a time other than 30 seconds. You can set a different speed and different time: Choose Tools, Options to open the Options dialog box, and then click the Reports View tab to bring it to the front (see Figure 1.4).

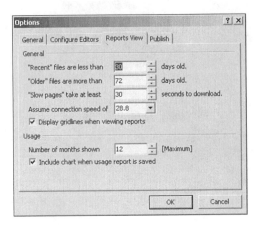

FIGURE 1.4

Customizing several Web reports.

The Reports View dialog box also can be used to change the number of days that constitutes a recently added or older file in a Web—two other reports you can run.

Five reports that you can see in the Reports view concern the hyperlinks used in a Web. These reports enable you to find links that will cause a "file not found" error if they are used. You can report on bad links that are a part of your Web and bad links to other addresses on the World Wide Web.

To see a fully up-to-date hyperlinks report, you must choose Tools, Recalculate Hyperlinks before selecting the report. FrontPage will check all links, including external ones to other Web addresses if you're currently connected to the Internet. This can take five minutes or longer, depending on how many other Web addresses are contained in hyperlinks on your Web.

When you find a bad link, you can update it directly from within the Reports view by clicking the line in the report that displays this link. This can be a huge timesaver if your Web contains a large number of hyperlinks, because it's faster than loading each page into the editing window and finding the erroneous link.

View the Structure of a Web

The last two views of FrontPage 2002 are the Navigation and Hyperlinks views, which provide two different ways to look at your Webs in a visual manner.

The Hyperlinks view displays the relationship between a page and all Web addresses that it hyperlinks to, whether they're part of the same Web or available somewhere else on the World Wide Web. This view is shown in Figure 1.5.

By clicking the + icon on any page in the Hyperlinks view, you can see all of its hyperlinks. You also can move a page to the center of the Hyperlinks view by right-clicking the page's icon and selecting Move to Center on the shortcut menu that appears.

FIGURE 1.5

Viewing the hyperlinks in a Web.

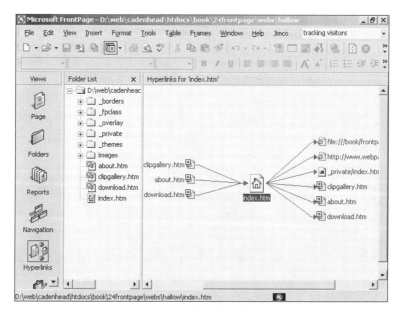

Pages can be opened for editing, deleted, and opened in a Web browser for viewing from the Hyperlinks view.

The Navigation view is used to establish a Web's navigational structure. Figure 1.6 shows the Navigation view for a Web.

FIGURE 1.6

Navigating the structure of a Web.

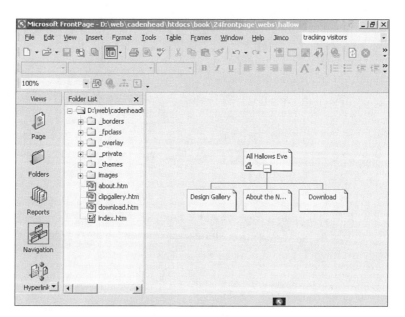

Each icon in the Navigation view represents a page in the Web. You might think that this view is redundant, because hyperlinks already establish the way a Web is navigated.

FrontPage 2002 supports the use of link bars—a group of common hyperlinks that can be placed on all pages of a Web for easy navigation. These bars can be made up of graphics or text.

Almost all large Webs have a common navigational structure. A sports site could have a link bar that enables visitors to go to specific hockey-, baseball-, football-, and basketball-related pages. A political news site could have a link bar with links to elections, allegations, resignations, condemnations, and legislation.

Putting a link bar on each page of the Web makes it easier for people to go directly to the information they want from your Web. Link bars also can include a link to the Web's home page and establish an order in which pages should be viewed.

Figure 1.7 shows a page of a Web with a vertical link bar that has four links: Home, Design Gallery, About the Name, and Download.

FIGURE 1.7

A Web page with one graphic and one text navigation bar.

Links added to a page through a link bar do not show up in the Hyperlinks view. You'll have a chance to work with link bars during Hour 20, "Use FrontPage Components."

Workshop: Explore the FrontPage 2002 User Interface

This hour's workshop is to familiarize yourself with the FrontPage 2002 interface.

Before you can do that, you need a Web to work on. The fastest way to create one is to use one of the default Webs that FrontPage 2002 knows how to build by itself.

To begin creating a Web, choose File, New, Page or Web (see Figure 1.8).

FIGURE 1.8

Creating a new Web.

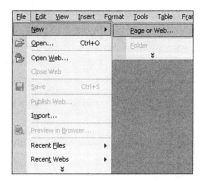

The New Page or Web task pane shown in Figure 1.9 opens in FrontPage 2002. This pane lists the new Webs and pages you can create, some pages and Webs you recently edited, and other options.

FIGURE 1.9

Viewing FrontPage Web templates.

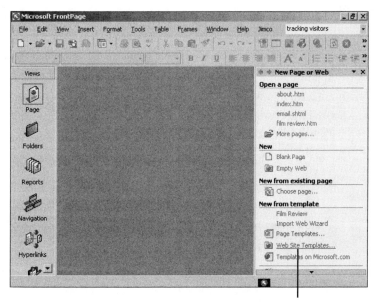

Web Site Templates hyperlink

To create one of the default Webs FrontPage knows how to develop, click the Web Site Templates hyperlink.

The Web Site Templates dialog box opens, listing each of the Webs FrontPage 2002 can build (see Figure 1.10).

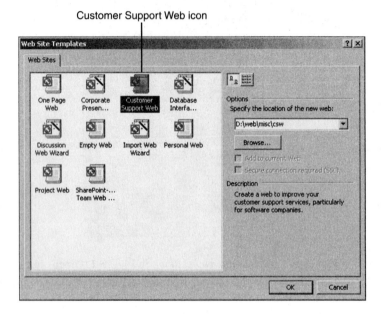

Customer Support Web icon

FIGURE **1.10**

Choosing a Web to create from a template.

Double-click the Customer Support Web icon to create this Web and all its folders and pages on your hard drive. FrontPage 2002 creates this Web using a template, which is a blueprint for a Web and all the files it contains. The customer support template is designed for Webs that support a company's products.

To see what this Web looks like, double-click the page index.htm in the folder list and choose File, Preview in Browser. (There's also a Preview in Browser button on the Standard toolbar.)

Use this new Web to answer each of the following questions:

1. What's the title of the discuss.htm Web page?
2. How many files of the Web are pictures?
3. How many hyperlinks does the page faq.htm contain?
4. How many hyperlinks does the entire Web contain?
5. What happened to the site on Wednesday, July 26?

Solution

There are several ways to come up with some of the answers to this workshop. The following solutions are either the fastest to accomplish or the most definitive:

1. Title of `discuss.htm`: In the Folders view, you can see that the title of this page is "Customer Support -- Discussion." This title is displayed in the title bar of a Web browser when the page is loaded.

2. Number of pictures in Web: According to the Reports view, none of the files in the Web are pictures.

3. Number of hyperlinks in `faq.htm`: If you open the Hyperlinks view and make faq.htm the center page, you'll see that it links to nine pages. This is a different total than you'd get by loading the page into the editing window and counting the links by hand, because the Hyperlinks view does not include link bars.

4. Number of hyperlinks in Web: There are 159, according to one of the items of the Reports view.

5. What happened on July 26: The customer support Web was placed online, according to `whatsnew.htm`.

The last solution is more labor-intensive than the others. Using what you learned during this hour, you could either look at each page in the Web in the Page view or preview the Web in a browser and visit each of its pages until you came across a reference to July 26.

A faster method is to use the Edit, Find menu option available in many of the programs of Microsoft Office XP.

Those programs have Edit, Find menu options that can search through entire documents to find specific text. FrontPage 2002 has one that can search an entire Web, making it impossible for "July 26" to hide.

Summary

If you've accomplished all the tasks from the first hour, you now have a copy of FrontPage 2002 somewhere inside your computer. This copy has been used to create a Web and explore the FrontPage interface.

All work you do in FrontPage 2002 begins by selecting a view—the six different ways to look at a Web. The Views bar contains icons for each of these options: Page, Folders, Reports, Navigation, Hyperlinks, and Tasks.

Moving from view to view, you can do everything that's needed to create a Web, keep its content up-to-date, and easily fix things such as broken hyperlinks.

This hour presented a bird's-eye view of the views in FrontPage 2002. You'll be swooping down for a much closer look at this interface in each of the 23 hours to follow.

In case you're counting along at home, the number of books published about the World Wide Web is now one million two hundred and twelve.

Q&A

Q What modem speed should my Webs be designed for?

A The answer depends largely on the kind of Web you're producing. Most Web publishers who are going after the widest possible audience take care of the person on a 28,800-baud connection. Alienating them with a lot of slow-loading pages narrows the audience considerably.

Some publishers organize a Web into pages for slower connections like 28.8 and pages for faster ones such as cable modems and T1 lines. It's more time-consuming, but you can experiment with more graphics and interactive page elements without worrying as much about the time-to-load report.

Q I am confused by the illustration of the Folder list—I cannot get it to appear as it does in the book. Folders appear but files all appear to the right in a Contents window. How do you get folders and files in one list?

A There are two ways to view files and folders. The one you are describing is the Folders view. Figure 1.1 shows something else—the Folder list. You can see this list no matter what view you are in. Choose View, Folder List to open or close the Folder list. I usually keep the Folder list open at all times while working in FrontPage 2002.

Exercises

Challenge your knowledge of the FrontPage 2002 graphical user interface with the following exercises:

- Create another new Web using a different template such as Personal Web or Project Web. Explore each of the views with this Web, especially Navigation and Hyperlinks, to see how different it appears from the Web you created during this hour.

- Using the customer support Web that FrontPage created, give your company a name. Make sure that each page of the Web contains this name and preview the whole site in Internet Explorer.

For solutions to these exercises, visit the book's official Web site at http://www.cadenhead.org/frontpage/.

Hour 2

Use Templates to Quickly Create a Web

Historians believe that one of the most remarkable achievements of mankind is the completion of the Great Wall of China, the 1,500-mile fortification built by some 300,000 laborers in the third century B.C.

Personally, I've always had more respect for the guys who started the thing. Looking out on miles and miles of unspoiled mountains, a group of workers had to put down the first stone, knowing that millions more must be stacked before their job was over and employee benefits were fully vested. As someone who faces paralyzing indecision in a buffet line, I can't imagine what it was like to place the Great Wall's first brick.

As you get ready to create your own Webs in FrontPage 2002, the program might look as imposing as a line of Chinese mountains in need of a wall. Knowing where to start, and what to do, can be a daunting task when you've never used the software.

FrontPage 2002 makes the task less daunting through the use of *templates*, built-in Webs that the software knows how to create by itself.

Templates enable you to develop a complete Web in a few minutes, and then spend your efforts customizing that Web rather than creating it from scratch.

Although they won't work with all Webs, templates are a huge timesaver when they are suitable for your projects. During this hour, you'll create a Web in a matter of minutes, an accomplishment made possible through the use of a template.

Discover FrontPage 2002 Templates

Templates are standard Webs or Web pages that FrontPage 2002 can build upon request. The software includes several dozen different templates, and they match some of the most common ways that publishers use the World Wide Web.

The built-in templates include a personal Web, a corporate Web, customer feedback Web pages, and site search pages.

During the previous hour, you used a template to quickly create a Web you could experiment with. The customer support Web included numerous hyperlinks, a link bar, and other features common to FrontPage Webs.

To create a new Web with a template, choose File, New, Page or Web (see Figure 2.1).

Figure 2.1

Creating a new FrontPage Web.

The New Page or Web task pane opens in FrontPage along the right edge of the interface. In this pane, click the Web Sites Templates hyperlink. A dialog box opens listing the templates that are available, along with a list of wizards.

Wizards are helper programs that simplify a task by breaking it down into discrete steps. In FrontPage 2002, wizards can create a Web or Web page based on the answers you provide in a series of dialog boxes.

Figure 2.2 shows a dialog box listing the templates and wizards that you can use to create a new Web.

Browse button

FIGURE 2.2

Selecting a template for a new Web.

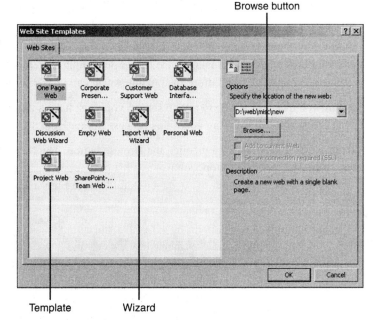

Template   Wizard

All Webs and Web pages start from templates, even if you don't want FrontPage 2002 to do any work for you. If you're creating a Web that should not contain any built-in pages, choose the Empty Web template. If you're creating an empty page, the Blank Page template should be selected in the task pane.

Select a Web Template

Before you can create a page in FrontPage 2002, you should create a Web that will contain that page. Because all Webs start from a template, you must choose one to start a project.

The following templates can be used to start a Web:

- *Empty Web*—A Web containing no pages
- *One Page Web*—A Web with a single blank page
- *Personal Web*—A Web for personal information
- *Customer Support Web*—A Web that enables a company to offer customer support for one or more of its products
- *Project Web*—A Web devoted to a collaborative project, with pages for member information, project status, a schedule, group discussions, and an archive

When choosing a template, you must also choose the location where the Web will be saved. Webs can be saved to a folder on your system or to a World Wide Web server.

If you save a Web to your system, you must save it again on a World Wide Web server to make it publicly available. This is also called publishing a Web. A Web must be made available on a Web server before the outside world can visit it.

Before you can save a Web to a Web server, you must have a username and password for that server. You'll learn more about this process during Hour 14, "Publish Your Web."

To save a Web on your system, click the Browse button. The New Web Location dialog box opens. Click the Desktop icon to see a list of places where you can save a Web on your system, including your My Documents folder (see Figure 2.3).

Create New Folder button

FIGURE 2.3

Selecting a location for a new Web.

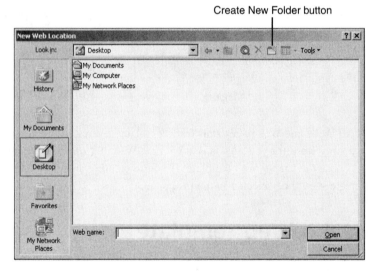

Use the dialog box to find a folder where the Web should be stored. This folder should be used only to store files related to your Web. Click the Create New Folder button shown in Figure 2.3 to create and name a new folder.

Choose the folder and click Open. The folder you have selected will appear in a field on the Web Site Templates dialog box. Click OK to create the Web.

Although it adds an extra step, you should save all Webs to disk and publish them on the Web separately. This prevents you from losing any files in the event that the Web server crashes or the server's administrator deletes your site.

After a template and location have been selected for a new Web, FrontPage 2002 creates all pages contained in the Web, and any subfolders that are needed. Each of the built-in templates includes _private and images subfolders.

Figure 2.4 shows how FrontPage appears when a new Web is created. The pages, folders, and files in the Web are displayed in the Folder list.

FIGURE 2.4

Editing a newly created FrontPage Web.

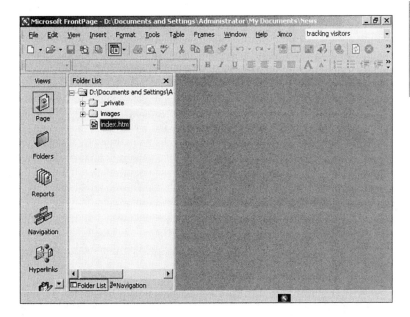

The images subfolder holds any graphics files that are part of the Web. The _private subfolder, which initially contains no files, can be used as a place for files that should be hidden from visitors to your Web. If you create a Web that collects information such as a visitor's name and mailing address, the _private subfolder is a good place to keep it away from prying eyes.

Despite its name, the _private folder is actually as public as everything else when your Web is created. You must use FrontPage security features to hide the folder's contents, which is possible only on Web hosts that are equipped with FrontPage Server Extensions.

If the template contains any pages, the main page of the Web will be named index.htm.

The filename `index.htm` is one of several names that are commonly used for a Web's main page—also called its *home page*. Others are `index.html`, `default.htm`, `default.html`, `home.htm`, and `home.html`.

Customize a Template

After a new Web has been created from a template, you can begin making changes to customize the Web.

If you're creating a home page for yourself or someone you're exceptionally familiar with, the Personal Web template is a good starting point.

This five-page template includes the following elements:

- A main page with space for an introduction
- A page to display photos
- A page to describe several hobbies and interests
- A page to list your favorite Web sites
- A page for visitors to contact the Web's author

A link bar provides links to each of these pages, as shown in Figure 2.5.

FIGURE 2.5

The hyperlinks page from the Personal Web.

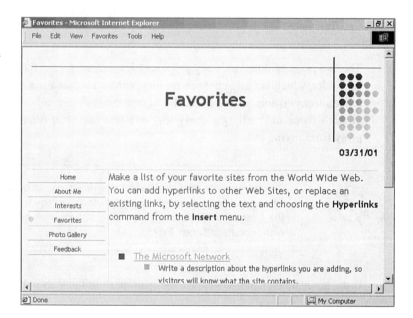

By choosing Page view to load each of these pages in the editing window, you can edit several different things: text, hyperlinks, link bars, timestamps, and page banners.

Edit text by placing your cursor anywhere within the text and using your keyboard. You also can employ features common to most word processors: text highlighting, cut-and-paste, and the Formatting toolbar.

Some things on a page look like text but are actually something else, such as hyperlinks or timestamps.

As you move the cursor over different parts of a page, the cursor changes depending on what it's placed on. FrontPage 2002 also might display a ScreenTip—a short box of informative text—that describes how you can modify that part of the page.

Link bars, timestamps, and page banners are all *components*—special page elements that add functionality to a FrontPage 2002 Web.

The main page of this Web, `index.htm`, contains a timestamp component immediately after the text "This page last updated". The timestamp displays the date that the page was last edited, and changes automatically each time changes are made to the page.

The timestamp component makes it easy to tell visitors how current the information on a page is. You don't have to enter the date using text and change it manually during each page update.

Placing the cursor above a timestamp causes the cursor to change to a hand-and-page icon. Double-click the timestamp and a dialog box will open enabling you to edit how it is presented. This dialog box is shown in Figure 2.6.

FIGURE 2.6

Editing a timestamp component.

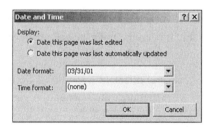

Each FrontPage 2002 component is edited using a dialog box like the one shown in Figure 2.6.

The timestamp component can be modified to display a date, a time, or both. You also can choose the format that the time and date are displayed in.

If you make a change to a timestamp component and it is not immediately reflected in the Web page, press the F5 function key or click the Refresh button. The Refresh button works like the one on a Web browser, which causes a Web page to be completely redrawn.

Another component that you can modify is the page banner, a heading atop a page that can serve as its title.

Each page in the personal Web template has a banner at the top. By default, the banner is graphical—text appears over a simple graphic file.

To change a banner, double-click it to bring up the Page Banner Properties dialog box, as shown in Figure 2.7.

FIGURE 2.7

Editing a page banner component.

You can change the text of a banner and determine whether it should be displayed as a picture or text.

Any changes to a page's banner will be made to that page's icon in the Navigation view, changing the text of link bars that link to the page. A page banner serves as a title for that page.

The Personal Web also includes several different hyperlinks. Some of these are part of the link bar, a FrontPage component that uses the Navigation view to determine which links should be displayed.

Other hyperlinks can be edited directly. The favorite.htm page of the Personal template contains three of these hyperlinks. One leads to The Microsoft Network, another to Expedia.com, and a third to MSNBC.

Each hyperlink consists of two things:

- The Web address that the link leads to
- The part of a page that should be clicked to visit the link

Hyperlinks can be associated with any element of a Web page, including text, graphics, or a combination of both. The Web address is also called a *URL*, an acronym that stands for *Uniform Resource Locator*.

The Web address associated with a hyperlink can be anything on the World Wide Web: pages, graphics, MP3 files, or other documents. It also can be a page or file contained within the Web itself.

Text that is being used as a hyperlink can be changed with the keyboard like any other text on a page.

Changing a hyperlink's URL is different than editing a component. Place your cursor on the hyperlink, right-click, and select Hyperlink Properties from the shortcut menu that appears. The Edit Hyperlink dialog box opens, as shown in Figure 2.8.

FIGURE 2.8

Editing a hyperlink's Web address.

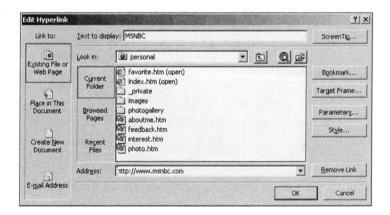

The Edit Hyperlink dialog box looks like the one that appears whenever you're opening a file in Windows. If you're linking to another page or file in the current Web, you can select it using this dialog box.

If the link is to an address on the World Wide Web such as http://www.teevee.org or http://www.google.com, enter this in the dialog box's Address field.

After changing the address, you can test it in a Web browser: Choose File, Preview in Browser. If the URL links to an address on the World Wide Web, you need to connect to the Internet before trying it out.

Workshop: Create Your Own Personal Web

You now should be able to create a personalized Personal Web, your first real Web in FrontPage 2002.

Use the Personal Web template to create a person's home page. The person in question can be you, someone you're familiar with, or someone you hope to become familiar with—after she sees the Web that has been created in her honor.

This Web should have each of the following:

- An introduction on the main page that describes the person in a few sentences
- An interests page that describes three of the person's interests
- A hyperlinks page that links to three of the person's favorite Web sites

If you have photos of the person, you should use some of them on the photo page that's part of a Personal Web.

Also, change the page banner of the interests page to Hobbies instead of Interests. This change will require some changes to the text of that page, and it also should appear on the link bar throughout the Web.

While you're working, you might accidentally delete a component or hyperlink you're working on. You can add a new one to replace it using one of the following menu commands:

- Choose Insert, Date and Time for a timestamp
- Choose Insert, Page Banner for a banner heading atop the page
- For a hyperlink, highlight text on a page and choose Insert, Hyperlink

The final thing you should do is to personalize the text on each of the pages, removing anything that doesn't make sense. Use interesting, energetic language to describe the subject of this Web, especially if you're developing it in someone's honor.

> If you're creating a personal Web to honor someone, please stay away from phrases such as "Your No. 1 fan," "We were meant to be together," and "If I can't have you, no one else will." Also be sure to obey any mail that has the words "restraining order" in it.

After making all these changes, preview the Web in a browser. Before previewing the pages, FrontPage 2002 will give you an opportunity to save anything that hasn't been saved yet.

Solution

An example of a Web that was produced for this workshop can be found on this book's official Web:

`http://www.cadenhead.org/frontpage`

Each hour of the book has its own page on this Web, offering workshop solutions, corrections, clarifications, and answers to reader questions.

Figure 2.6 illustrates the main page of this workshop's solution: Misery Loves Company, the home page of Annie Wilkes.

FIGURE 2.9

The Personal Web of Annie Wilkes.

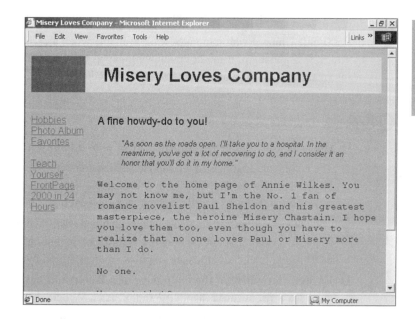

2

Using FrontPage 2002, Annie was able to quickly create a personal home page for herself. Templates free up time that can be spent on other pursuits, such as rescuing your favorite romance novelist after a car accident and holding him hostage until he brings your favorite character back from the dead.

Most of the changes required to customize the Personal Web template can be handled with text editing in the Page view.

Because there already are three hyperlinks on `favorites.htm`, these hyperlinks can be modified to suit the person for whom you're creating the Web.

If you changed the page banner on `interests.htm` so that the text is Hobbies, you might have run into problems displaying this change in a Web browser.

To fix this, load the page in Page view and press the F5 key or the Refresh button to redisplay the page. This is a common oversight when you're changing components, and the first thing you should try when a page doesn't look right during a browser preview.

Summary

Templates are a great way to reduce the amount of time it takes to develop a Web. When they are applicable to a project you're working on, they're a great timesaver. Your efforts are spent customizing a template instead of starting from a bunch of empty Web pages.

There is always something to be said for doing everything by hand, of course.

If 1,500-mile Chinese wall templates were available when a certain project was started by Emperor Shihuangdi, it might be known today as the Good Wall of China. Centuries of international tourism would have been greatly reduced.

Q&A

Q How can you change the appearance of a Web template?

A The colors and graphics in a template such as Personal Web are controlled by its theme. Themes, as you will discover during the next hour, are a way to establish a consistent and pleasing visual appearance for a Web.

The theme of a built-in template can be changed easily within FrontPage. You can change everything about the way the Web looks, including its background color, background image, component graphics, text color, and hyperlink color.

Q Earlier, you said that the main page of a Web could have different names, such as index.htm, default.htm, and index.html. Which should be used?

A The one you choose depends on how the Web server that hosts your Web is configured. Some servers look for index.htm or index.html when someone tries to pull up the Web without naming a page, and others look for default.htm, home.htm, or another page name. For example, if someone visits http://www.cadenhead.org, the server will actually look for http://www.cadenhead.org/index.shtml. This occurs because the Web server is configured to add index.shtml to any address that doesn't include a page reference.

FrontPage 2002 calls any new page index.htm. You can easily rename this file in the Folders view to conform with your Web hosting provider.

Exercises

Challenge your knowledge of FrontPage 2002 templates with the following exercises:

- Expand the Personal Web that you created during this hour by adding short reviews of all three sites listed on the hyperlinks page. Put each of these reviews on its own page and move the URLs to these new pages.
- Using a portal such as Yahoo! at http://www.yahoo.com, find a Web site that matches each of the things listed on your personal Web's hobbies page. Add hyperlinks on this page linking to these sites.

For solutions to these exercises, visit the book's official Web site at http://www.cadenhead.org/frontpage/.

2

HOUR 3

Apply a Theme to an Entire Web

Half the battle in any Web project is to create the information that will be displayed on the pages of your site. FrontPage 2002 makes this easier through the use of templates, which can generate pages—and even entire Webs—for you to customize.

The other half of that battle is to make that information look good.

There was a time when the World Wide Web was almost entirely text. The information contained on a Web was more important than the different ways that browsers displayed it. That time ended a few minutes after a new Web page element was introduced—the image file.

Most Web users expect sites to be easy to use and visually interesting. FrontPage 2002 makes this part of Web design easier through the use of themes, packages of coordinated graphics that can be applied to your Webs.

During this hour, you'll learn how to apply themes to Webs and individual Web pages. You'll also customize a theme, making changes to fit your own project.

Sample the FrontPage 2002 Themes

As a Web publisher, one of your most important tasks is to establish the visual appearance of your site. This is determined by each of the following, among other things:

- The color of text and hyperlinks
- The color or image used as a background
- The fonts used
- The images and link bars

Another choice you must make is whether these things should vary from page to page or be consistent throughout an entire Web. Using the same visual elements makes it easier for a visitor to know they're still on your Web. It also can make a Web easier to navigate, if you've kept the layout consistent and used link bars.

FrontPage 2002 enables you to establish the visual identity of a Web by assigning a theme to it.

Themes establish the visual appearance of a Web or a Web page by defining its colors, fonts, text, and images.

Select a Web Theme

A *theme* is a collection of colors, link graphics, and banners that gives a FrontPage Web a consistent visual identity. More than a dozen themes are included with FrontPage 2002, and many more are available on FrontPage sites on the World Wide Web.

You can apply a theme to a specific page in a Web or to the entire Web.

To use a theme, open a page for editing and choose Format, Theme (see Figure 3.1).

FIGURE 3.1

Using themes in a FrontPage Web.

The Themes dialog box opens (see Figure 3.2), enabling you to preview the themes that are available and choose one for the page (or for an entire Web).

FIGURE 3.2
Choosing a theme.

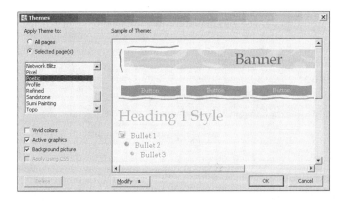

The themes in FrontPage 2002 are given short names that help describe their appearance. Expedition is a theme that looks like a wildlife safari company's brochure. Topo features graphics inspired by maps. Blank, although not actually blank, is relatively plain.

Select each theme to see a preview of it in the dialog box's Sample of Theme pane. The Poetic theme is shown in Figure 3.2.

The first choice you must make is whether to apply your chosen theme to a page or your entire Web. Apply a theme to only the current page by choosing the Selected Pages option at the top of the Themes dialog box. Apply a theme to the entire Web by choosing All Pages instead.

Themes are one of the easiest features to experiment with in FrontPage 2002. If you apply a theme to your Web and don't like it, you can easily wipe out the change by choosing a different theme. You also can remove all themes by choosing (No theme) in the Themes dialog box.

The next decision to make is whether to select any of the following options:

- Vivid colors
- Active graphics
- Background picture
- Apply using CSS

The Vivid colors option determines whether the theme will use a variety of bright colors or a white background and darker colors.

If a theme uses vivid colors, it will have a bright background color such as light green or yellow and other colors that work well on that background.

If a theme does not use vivid colors, the background will be white and all other colors will be darker, making them easier to read.

This color choice will not be as significant if you use the theme's background image. This causes a graphic to be tiled—repeated over and over like tiles on a kitchen floor—underneath the contents of a page. The difference between vivid and darker colors is less noticeable over a background image.

Choosing Active graphics adds some animation effects to the theme. One common feature of an animated theme is a link bar with buttons that change in response to mouse movement. These are called *hover buttons* in FrontPage 2002, because the buttons change when a mouse hovers over them.

FrontPage creates this effect through the use of one of the scripting languages that it supports: JavaScript or VBScript. All the scripting is handled internally by FrontPage, so you don't have to be familiar with these languages to make use of them on your Webs.

As with all features offered through scripting, hover buttons are not supported by all browsers. Versions 3.0 and later of Microsoft Internet Explorer and Netscape Navigator support these buttons. On browsers that don't support them, a non-animated version of the graphics will appear.

The last option you can enable with a theme is to apply it using *CSS—Cascading Style Sheets*. Style sheets are a standard for how pictures and text are presented on a Web page. They enable the basic visual elements of a page—its text, colors, fonts, and formatting—to be defined separately from the information the page contains.

Because a theme is a representation of a Web's visual appearance, it makes sense to define it through the use of Cascading Style Sheets.

However, an important thing to note about Cascading Style Sheets is that it has been inconsistently implemented by the browser developers. Although a standard for Cascading Style Sheets has existed since December 1996, Microsoft and Netscape offer different and occasionally incompatible implementations of style sheets in their browsers.

If you apply a FrontPage theme using Cascading Style Sheets, it should be fully supported by the current version of Internet Explorer. This is the first version of FrontPage that offers support for style sheets, and its implementation is most compatible with Microsoft's Web browser. You should test the Web in other browsers to make sure that their users are able to successfully view the site.

Assign a Theme to a Web

During the last hour, you created a Web using the Personal Web template. Although you might not have realized it at the time, you were using a theme. The Personal Web, like all built-in templates, has a default theme that it applies to all pages in the Web.

Depending on the person for whom you were creating that Web, the theme might not have been quite what you were looking for.

> As you're selecting a theme, you might notice the (Install Additional Themes) option in the Themes dialog box. Select this to install several dozen additional themes on the CD from which you installed FrontPage 2002.

As the first project of this hour, load the personal Web that you created and apply a new theme to all of its pages.

Because it's so easy to experiment with themes, preview the Web in a browser in three different ways:

- With active graphics
- With non-active graphics and a background image
- With vivid colors and no background image

Figure 3.3 shows last hour's Annie Wilkes home page with a different theme.

FIGURE 3.3

Trying a new theme on a personal Web.

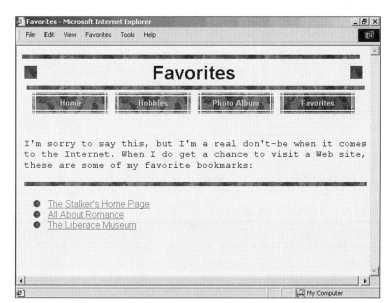

Modify a Theme

As you have seen, themes are a quick way to establish the appearance of a Web. Whether your Web contains 5 or 500 pages, the same minimal amount of work is required to apply a theme.

If none of the built-in themes suit the Web you're trying to create, you can develop your own.

To create a new theme, you can begin by modifying an existing one. Start by selecting the existing theme as if you're going to apply it to a Web, and click Modify in the Themes dialog box. Three new buttons will appear: Colors, Graphics, and Text, as shown in Figure 3.4. Each of these enables you to change part of the selected theme.

FIGURE 3.4

Modifying an existing theme.

Selecting a Color Scheme

The Colors button is used to pick the five colors that make up the theme's color scheme. These colors can be selected in three different ways:

- Selecting from a list of available schemes
- Using a color wheel
- Manually assigning a color to each Web element that can be placed on a page, including headings, text, and hyperlinks

Many of the listed colors correspond with existing themes, so you can borrow them for your new theme.

Figure 3.5 shows the Modify Theme dialog box with the Color Schemes tab at the front.

The color wheel is used to pick a set of five related colors. Picking a red area of the wheel creates a color scheme that is predominantly red, for instance.

FIGURE 3.5

Selecting a theme's colors using existing color schemes.

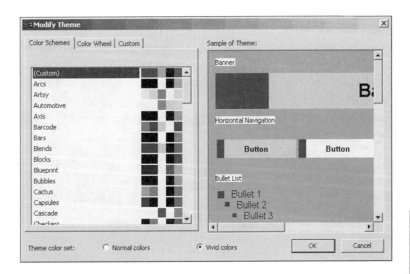

The scheme changes as you move to different places on the wheel, making it easy to meander around until you find something you like.

Another thing you can do that greatly affects the scheme is to adjust the brightness level of the entire wheel. If you're looking for a gloomy range of colors, you will need to darken the entire color wheel first.

Every change you make while selecting colors is reflected in the Sample of Theme pane, as shown in Figure 3.5.

One thing that isn't obvious about selecting a color scheme is what the five colors are used for. The color in the middle is the page's background color. The other colors are used in a variety of different ways, as you'll see in the Sample of Theme pane.

The third way to select colors for a theme is to assign them manually. Instead of picking a five-color scheme, you assign specific colors to specific Web elements such as the page background, active hyperlinks, and body text. This is more time-consuming, but it provides total control over the colors employed in the theme.

After you have made changes to an existing theme, you can save them in the Themes dialog box by clicking Save As and giving the theme its own name. This is preferable to clicking Save because it doesn't wipe out the existing theme.

Selecting Text and Graphics

The Text button of the Themes dialog box is used to associate fonts with body text and the six different heading sizes that are used on Web pages. A dialog box opens, enabling you to select any font that's installed on your system, as shown in Figure 3.6.

FIGURE 3.6

Selecting fonts to use in a theme.

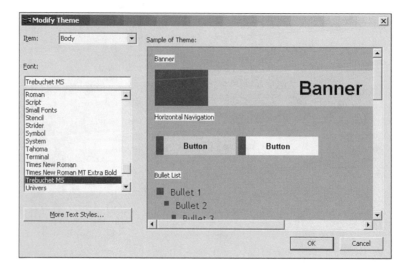

Fonts are a very system-specific element of Web page design. If you use a font on your Web that isn't present on a visitor's system, his browser will default to a standard font such as Arial, Helvetica, or Verdana.

If you're developing a Web that will be seen only on a company's intranet, you can use any font that you know will be present on the machines that have access to that Web.

> If you're a corporate Webmaster, you can always order your colleagues to install a font. This might seem a little cheeky, but it's time someone showed why the word "master" is part of the job title. Harbormasters control traffic on a waterway. Jedi masters control potent Forces. Is it too much to ask that Webmasters have sovereign power over fonts?

Anything bound for the World Wide Web probably should stick to fonts that are the most widely supported. The built-in themes in FrontPage 2002 use the following fonts: Arial, Book Antiqua, Century Gothic, Helvetica, Times, Times New Roman, Trebuchet MS, and Verdana. The safest of these fonts to use are Arial, Helvetica, Times, and Verdana.

If you're concerned that a font won't be present, you can specify one or more alternative fonts when modifying a theme. Instead of picking a single font, enter a list of fonts separated by commas, such as "Verdana, Arial, sans serif" or "Times New Roman, Times, serif." Web browsers will look for each font in the list and use the first one that's present on the system running the browser.

The final way to create a new theme is to modify an existing theme's graphics.

Every theme has graphics files associated with 11 different page elements, including the background image, page banner, and both horizontal and vertical navigation bars. Some of these elements have several different graphics files associated with them—hover buttons have files for each image that appears on the button.

Changing graphics requires strong working knowledge of how the different page elements function.

To change the graphics associated with a theme, click Graphics from the Themes dialog box. The Modify Theme dialog box opens, enabling you to select graphics and see how they look in a Sample of Theme pane, as shown in Figure 3.7.

FIGURE 3.7

Choosing new graphics for a theme.

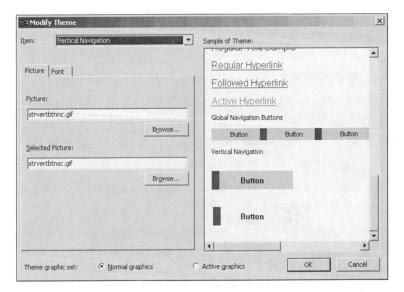

One of the simplest graphics to change is the background picture. This graphic is displayed beneath Web pages when the theme is applied with the Background Picture option selected.

Click Browse to choose a new graphic file. If this file is located anywhere on your system, you can find it using the standard Windows file open dialog box. If the file is located on the World Wide Web, you can find it using the image's URL.

Regardless of where you find the file, FrontPage 2002 will make a copy of it for use with the theme. FrontPage will use a copy instead of the original whenever the theme is applied to a Web.

> One thing FrontPage 2002 doesn't do for you is secure permission to use the graphics it can grab from the Web. Portals such as Yahoo! have dozens of links to sites that offer background images you can freely use on Webs. Search for text such as "Web page backgrounds" or "background archive."

Workshop: Customize a Theme

The last project for this hour is to express your patriotism by developing a patriotic theme devoted to a country and the colors of its flag. If you're not feeling patriotic at the moment, your project is to express someone else's patriotism.

Take one of the existing themes and save a copy of it as Patriotic or a comparably inspiring name. Any of the themes can be used for this purpose, though some of the more generic themes such as Blank are probably the best choices.

Using this new theme, make each of the following changes:

- The predominant color of the theme should match the darkest color of the country's flag.
- The background color should match the lightest color of the flag.
- Hyperlinks should match a third color of the flag.

Some artistic license might be required if you're patriotic about a country with a one-color or two-color flag.

After setting the colors, select two new fonts that suit the theme—one for body text and the other for each heading. These fonts should be relatively common if you're going to employ the theme on your own Webs. Otherwise, you can take more liberties.

Solution

Figure 3.8 shows a version of the Patriotic theme created for the Republic of Palau, an island chain that's home to 16,000 people in the Pacific.

The first step was choosing a theme to start with—Network was selected because it is relatively plain, making it easy to customize.

FIGURE 3.8

A page featuring a new Patriotic theme.

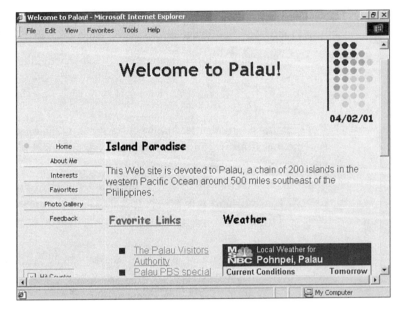

Before making any changes, Network was saved under a new name by clicking Modify in the Themes dialog box and clicking Save As. A dialog box opened where Patriotic could be selected.

The flag of Palau is a bright yellow circle on blue. Light blue was selected as the background color for pages, yellow was used for banners, and dark green was used for hyperlinks.

The fonts on the page also were customized: Comic Sans MS was used for headings and Arial was used for body text.

Summary

During this hour, you learned how to use FrontPage 2002's built-in themes to establish the graphic appearance of a Web. FrontPage has themes suited to a variety of purposes: corporate sites, personal home pages, hobbies, and more.

If the software's built-in themes did not fit a project, you learned how to create your own theme by customizing an existing one.

Themes define several different aspects of a Web, including its background picture, link bars, and the color of text, headings, and hyperlinks. They can make use of advanced Web design features such as JavaScript to cause buttons to change in response to mouse movements on a page.

If you can develop your own graphics, plug them into new themes for an easy way to establish the appearance of a page or an entire Web.

If you're not graphically inclined, themes are a good way to hide this fact.

Q&A

Q I'm creating a new theme. I chose a background color as part of a color scheme, but it always shows up as white when I'm using the theme. What's causing this?

A The background color of a theme is affected by whether you've opted to use vivid colors when you apply it to a Web. If you have not chosen vivid colors, FrontPage 2002 will use a white background with a more muted version of your color scheme.

To put your missing background color to use, reapply the theme with the Vivid colors option selected.

Exercises

Challenge your knowledge of FrontPage 2002 themes with the following exercises:

- Create a new theme inspired by your favorite holiday, picking colors and fonts that are suited to the occasion.

- Create a new Web that you can use for some theme-related experimentation. Pick a theme for this Web that has animated graphics and is applied through Cascading Style Sheets. Try this out with each browser on your system to see whether it displays successfully.

For solutions to these exercises, visit the book's official Web site at http://www.cadenhead.org/frontpage/.

Hour 4

Let Wizards Do the Hard Work

One of the things you learn quickly about FrontPage 2002 is how much work it can do without you. As you saw in past hours with templates and themes, FrontPage can create an entire Web and its graphic appearance with a few menu commands.

FrontPage automates even more complex tasks through the use of wizards.

Wizards, as you probably encountered using other Microsoft software, are programs that ask a series of questions about a project you're trying to complete. Your answers control how the program does its work.

During this hour, you will use a wizard to load an existing Web site into FrontPage for editing.

Employ a Web Wizard

You've already used a complex wizard with FrontPage 2002—the Installation Wizard that set up the software on your computer for the first time.

Wizards in Microsoft FrontPage 2002 can be thought of as templates with brains. They are used to create Webs and Web pages that are too variable to be handled with a template.

By breaking down a task into a series of simpler steps, wizards make it possible to create complex Webs—such as a 20-page professional site, a discussion forum, and a customer support site.

There are two kinds of wizards in FrontPage 2002: Web wizards, which create entire sites, and single-page wizards.

As you learned when working with templates, wizards can be selected when you're creating a new Web or adding a new page to an existing Web. Click File, New, Page or Web to open the New Page or Web task pane (see Figure 4.1).

FIGURE 4.1

*Creating a new page
or Web.*

Click the Web Site Templates hyperlink to see the Web templates and wizards you can use when creating a new Web. The Web Site Templates dialog box opens, as shown in Figure 4.2.

FIGURE 4.2

Selecting a wizard or template for a new Web.

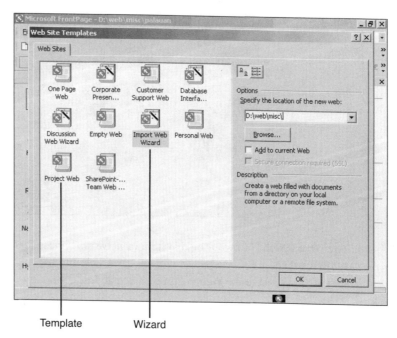

Template   Wizard

Import an Existing Web

One of the FrontPage 2002 wizards will bring an existing Web and all its files into FrontPage. The Import Web Wizard enables you to take advantage of FrontPage's features on a site that wasn't originally created with the software.

To import a Web, choose the Import Web Wizard icon in the Web Site Templates dialog box. FrontPage provides a default folder name and location in the Specify the location of the new web text box. To change this, enter a different location in the text box or click the Browse button to open the New Web Location dialog box and choose a folder.

After you have chosen a location for the Web, click OK. The Import Web Wizard opens, as shown in Figure 4.3.

There are two ways to import a Web:

- From a source directory or files on your own system (or another system connected to the same network)
- From an address on the World Wide Web

The address of the Web you are importing should be entered in the Location text box.

FIGURE 4.3

Importing a Web into FrontPage.

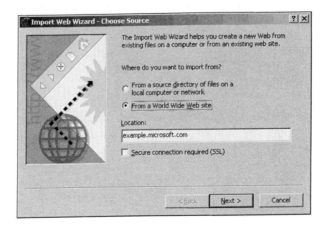

To retrieve a Web from your own system or network, choose that option in the Import Web Wizard and a Browse button will appear. Click it to use the File Open dialog box to find the folder where the Web is currently located.

When you are importing a Web from your own system or network, select the Include subfolders check box to make sure that the Web includes all parts of the Web.

Click Next to continue. The Web and all its pages are copied to the folder you have chosen for the new Web, leaving the original intact.

To retrieve a site over the World Wide Web, you specify its Web address—the same thing you enter in a Web browser to view the site—and click Next.

The next question the wizard asks is how much you want to retrieve from the site, as shown in Figure 4.4.

FIGURE 4.4

Choosing the elements of a Web to import.

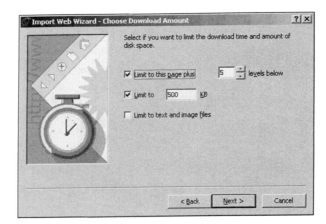

The download can be limited in three ways:

- Reducing the number of levels that are downloaded
- Limiting the Web to a maximum disk size
- Limiting the retrieval to text and image files only

Restricting the number of levels prevents FrontPage 2002 from digging any deeper when it visits the pages of a Web. Each level represents a page—if FrontPage goes from the main page to a "What's New?" page and then to a specific news item's page, it has traversed three levels into the site.

Limiting the disk size and the type of files downloaded might cause FrontPage 2002 to retrieve only a portion of the Web.

After choosing how much of a Web to import, click Next. The Import Web Wizard will be ready to load the pages and files associated with the Web. Click Finish to import the Web.

After you retrieve a Web, you can begin working on it as with any other FrontPage 2002 site that you create.

FrontPage 2002 will download the pages of the site, all of its images, and other files that are part of the same Web. It will even re-create the folder structure of the site—if the site stored all graphics files in an images subfolder, the subfolder will be maintained when the site is re-created on your system.

FrontPage 2002 will also retrieve any other pages that are part of the same Web. If there is a main home page and 20 other pages, each of these will be downloaded along with all its images and other files.

4

One thing this wizard won't grab is programs that run behind the scenes on a Web site: search engines, feedback forms, and the like. The wizard saves output of these programs, rather than a working copy you can run as part of your own Web.

By default, FrontPage 2002 keeps the formatting of existing Web pages intact when they are imported into a Web. As you start making changes and using FrontPage features such as link bars on the Web, this might necessitate changes to existing features. You'll have to test imported Webs thoroughly to make sure that they function as intended.

As with other retrieval features of FrontPage 2002, the Import Web Wizard makes it easy to incorporate existing Web content into your work. One thing it doesn't do is ask permission before making use of the content of other Web publishers, so you'll have to be careful to secure permissions when using images, pages, and other material downloaded directly from the World Wide Web.

Create a Corporate Web

Another useful wizard for quick Web development is the Corporate Presence Wizard, which can be used to establish a company's official Web.

If you're developing a site for your own company or for a client that isn't on the Web yet, this wizard guides you through the process of developing a professional Web. You'll be able to choose products or services that should be spotlighted, solicit feedback from customers, incorporate the corporate logo into each page, and other business-related tasks.

To select this wizard, choose File, New, Page or Web and click the Web Site Templates link in the New Page or Web task pane. The Web Site Templates dialog box opens (it was shown earlier in Figure 4.2).

Choose the Corporate Presence Wizard icon, pick a location for your Web, and click OK.

When you select this wizard, you'll answer a series of questions on 13 different dialog boxes. To make the most effective use of the wizard, you should know each of the following things about the Web before you start:

- The products or services that will be promoted on the Web
- Whether feedback will be solicited from visitors, and how it should be saved
- Whether the Web needs its own search engine
- The company's mission statement, if one should be displayed on the Web
- Other kinds of information, such as catalog requests, that will be collected
- All contact information about the company along with the e-mail address to use for the company and for Web-related inquiries

If you don't know some of these, you can add them later, after the wizard has created the Web. As a general rule, though, you'll be much closer to completing the Web if you gather all the necessary information before calling the wizard.

Figure 4.5 shows the first dialog box that's used to tell the wizard what kind of corporate Web to create.

Figure 4.5

Selecting the main pages of a corporate Web.

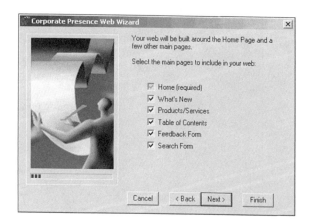

As with all FrontPage 2002 wizards, the corporate wizard includes a lot of explanatory text that describes what it is capable of creating. If you're still in the wizard and you change your mind about a previous answer, you can use the Back button to return to the dialog box and revise it.

One of the dialog boxes asks exactly how many products and services you will be describing on the Web. A page will be created for each of these, along with a main page connecting all of them with hyperlinks.

If you're not sure whether to include a feature in your corporate Web, err on the side of excess. You can usually take things off a Web more easily than you can add them later. It's a gastronomic shame that the human waistline doesn't follow the same principle.

For each product, you can determine whether to display an image or pricing information. Each service can be described along with the relevant capabilities and account information. You'll also be able to associate information request forms for each product and service, so prospective customers can use the Web to ask for more details about the company's offerings.

These aspects of the new Web are determined with the dialog box shown in Figure 4.6.

After you answer all of the Corporate Presence Wizard's questions, it creates the Web.

The wizard creates each of the main pages that you requested—pages for products, services, and other features, and the start of a navigational structure for the Web.

4

FIGURE 4.6

FIGURE **4.6**

Customizing the products and services pages.

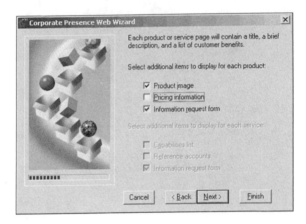

Another thing the wizard will do is add comments to each page offering tips on what you should add to that part of the Web.

These comments show up in Page view, displayed in a lighter color than the body text of the page and preceded with the word "Comment." Comments are not displayed when the page is loaded by a Web browser, so you can leave them on the page while you're working on the Web.

> To add your own comment to a page, click the menu command Insert, Comment. A dialog box will open, and the comment you enter into it will be added to the page at the current cursor location.

The Corporate Presence wizard has numerous features that make it easier to establish a company's Web. One example: The wizard asks for some common information that should be available about any company: its mailing address, phone number, fax number, e-mail address for customer inquiries, and the like. These things can be automatically placed on different pages, and when something changes, FrontPage 2002 updates every page where it appears.

For example, if your company has to relocate because no one ever taught your original architect about flood plains, you can change the address: Choose Tools, Web Settings, and then click the Parameters tab to bring it to the front of the Web Settings dialog box (see Figure 4.7).

After this change is made, it will be updated on every page where the parameter appears. You don't have to edit each of the pages individually. The Corporate Presence Wizard offers several shortcuts that make creating and maintaining a company's Web easier.

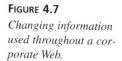

FIGURE 4.7

Changing information used throughout a corporate Web.

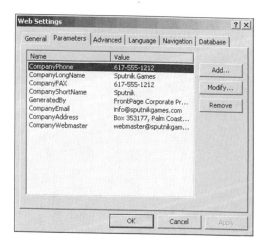

Workshop: Create a Corporate Web

This hour's workshop is to create the official World Wide Web site for a fictitious company.

If you're not feeling particularly fictitious today, you can use the following work order as the basis for your Web:

```
MEMORANDUM

From:   I.M. Overpaid, V.P. of New Media and Interoffice Mail
Addr:   21st Century Cheese
    1 Milking Way
    Combined Locks, WI 54113
Phone:    (920) 555-JACK
Fax:    (920) 555-BRIE
To:     That person with the cubicle near the coffee machine who
surfs the Web all day on company time
```

Recently, it has come to my attention that our competition, Dairy Godmother, has created their own World Wide Web site with the intention of going public. They've received very favorable coverage in both *CheeseWeek* and *American Dairyperson*, and are now being described as "the big cheeses of the Fox River valley."

I would like you to create the official World Wide Web site for 21st Century Cheese. Our customers should be able to visit the site to learn more about each of our brands:

```
Mo' Betta' Feta
Hit the Road Jack
Live Brie or Die
Gouda for You
Significant Udder
```

```
They also should be able to contact us with suggestions, and our
address and other contact information should be prominently
displayed.

I have been told that Web sites are highly complex projects that
take skilled professionals weeks, if not months, to create.

I expect to see the site online by two weeks ago last Wednesday.

Sincerely,
I.M.
```

Use a FrontPage wizard to create the Web presence for 21st Century Cheese or a fictitious company of your own creation. Be sure to include the kinds of information requested by Vice President Overpaid even if you're working for an entirely different company, and answer all of the questions about the business asked by the wizard. Some of these you'll have to make up on your own, such as the e-mail addresses for the company and the e-mail inbox for information requests.

If you're working on I.M. Overpaid's assignment, under no circumstances are you to use the expression "cut the cheese" on the company's Web. For a full explanation of the company's reasoning, see Section 14-D of the 21st Century Cheese Employee's Manual, "Why Hank Got Fired."

Solution: Using the Corporate Presence Wizard

Figure 4.8 shows the main page of a 21st Century Cheese Web.

In addition to the information found in Vice President Overpaid's work order, the following choices were made using the Corporate Presence Wizard:

- Three main pages: Home, Products/Services, and Feedback
- Two things on the home page: Introduction and contact information
- Number of products: 5
- Number of services: 0
- Product details: Pricing information and a request form
- Feedback requests: Full name, mailing address, e-mail address
- Page contents: Page title, links to main pages, e-mail address, and page modification date
- Theme: Arcs

FIGURE 4.8

Establishing a company's presence on the Web.

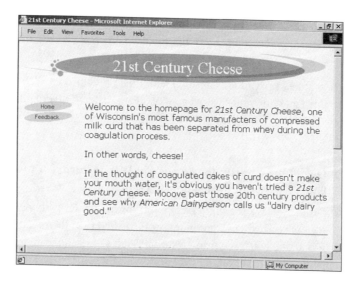

The Web shown in this solution can be found on this book's official Web:

`http://www.cadenhead.org/frontpage`

Visit the Hour 4 section of the site to find a link to this version of 21st Century Cheese.

4

There also might be links to other fictitious companies created by readers of this book, provided that any of them take this very broad hint and contact the author after publishing their own workshop solutions on the World Wide Web.

Summary

During the first four hours of this book, you learned how to take advantage of three time-saving features of FrontPage 2002: templates, themes, and wizards.

Templates are default Webs and Web pages intended for use in your own projects. The template gets you part of the way on a task you're working on, and you finish it by customizing the template.

Themes are built-in graphic styles that you can apply to either a Web page or an entire Web. They define the background, colors, image buttons, and fonts that are used, and you can quickly establish a consistent look-and-feel for a Web using themes.

Wizards are interactive programs that create templates based on your answers to a series of questions. You can create more complex Webs with wizards than are possible with templates, including a corporate Web, a discussion Web, and an interactive form page.

By using these three features, you're able to solve one of the problems any Web designer faces: how to go from an empty file folder to an entire Web, complete with pages, images, hyperlinks, and a navigational structure.

These features save a lot of development time on your own Web projects. Whether you share this fact with your own version of Vice President Overpaid is entirely up to you.

Q&A

Q One of the wizards, the Discussion Web Wizard, isn't introduced during this hour. Where can I learn how to use it?

A Discussion Webs are interactive forums in which visitors can read and post their own messages. They are more sophisticated than the other Web wizards offered in FrontPage 2002, requiring a special Web server that can handle these kinds of Webs. You'll find out how to work with these wizards during Hour 18, "Enable Discussions on Your Web."

Exercises

Challenge your knowledge of FrontPage 2002 wizards with the following exercises:

- Using a portal such as the Open Directory Project (`http://www.dmoz.org`) or a search engine such as Google (`http://www.google.com`), find a company's official Web site that doesn't appear to be more than 20 pages in size. Use the Import Web Wizard to bring this Web into FrontPage 2002 and use the Folders view to explore its structure.

- In the corporate Web you created for this hour's workshop, add a complex and intimidating legal disclaimer to the bottom of every page.

For solutions to these exercises, visit the book's official Web site at `http://www.cadenhead.org/frontpage/`.

PART II

Designing Web Pages with FrontPage 2002

Hour

HOUR 5

Manage a FrontPage Web

If you have never used FrontPage before acquiring version 2002, you might be a little unclear about what the software means when it calls something a "Web."

On the World Wide Web, a Web is analogous to a Web site—the pages, images, programs, and other files that you view in a browser as you navigate through it.

During this hour, you'll learn about the life cycle of a FrontPage Web. You'll see how a Web is created and deleted.

You also get your first chance to create content in a Web, turning a Microsoft Word document into a Web page.

Create and Explore a Web

In FrontPage 2002, a Web is a site that FrontPage knows how to edit, publish, and perform maintenance on. In all other respects, a FrontPage Web is like any other site that you have used, no matter what software created it.

All Webs must be FrontPage Webs in order for FrontPage 2002 to work on them.

You can edit individual Web pages in a Web without turning it into a
FrontPage Web, but if you use any of the site management features,
FrontPage will open a dialog box asking to convert the Web. If you decline,
you can't make use of those features.

A FrontPage Web is created in two ways:

- Creating a new Web using a FrontPage template
- Importing an existing Web using the Import Web Wizard

After either of these tasks has been completed, you can work with these FrontPage Webs
in the same manner.

Past versions of FrontPage loaded existing Webs and retranslated the HTML
of the pages so that it was consistent with how FrontPage creates HTML.
This resulted in some compatibility problems with tables and other page elements that change appearance depending on the way their HTML code is
organized on the page. By default, FrontPage 2002 leaves existing HTML
unchanged, giving you much better success in importing Webs successfully.

To create a Web, choose File, New, Page or Web (see Figure 5.1).

FIGURE 5.1

Creating a new Web.

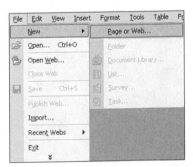

The New Page or Web task pane opens alongside the FrontPage 2002 editing window,
listing page templates, Web templates, and existing pages you can open.

The Empty Web template is used to create a new FrontPage Web that doesn't contain any pages yet. To create a new Web, click the Empty Web hyperlink (see Figure 5.2).

FIGURE 5.2

Choosing the kind of Web to create.

Empty Web
hyperlink

The Web Site Templates dialog box opens with the Empty Web icon selected. To create a FrontPage Web, you must specify a location where the Web will be saved.

The most common place to save a Web is in a folder on your own system. This enables you to work on the Web before publishing it on the World Wide Web or your company's intranet.

To save your new Web in a folder on your system, enter the path and name of the folder in the Specify the location of the new Web box and click OK (see Figure 5.3).

When you create a new Web, FrontPage 2002 places files and folders at the specified location that it uses to maintain the Web. The first time you create a Web, the Folder list opens, displaying the folders and pages in the Web (see Figure 5.4). If it is not visible, choose View, Folder List.

5

FIGURE 5.3

Storing a Web in a folder on your system.

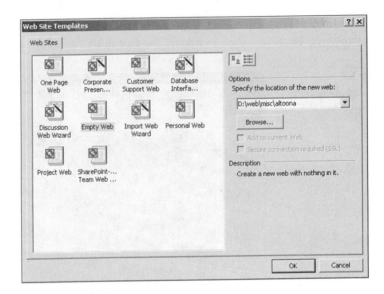

FIGURE 5.3

Storing a Web in a folder on your system.

Click the Browse button to open the New Web Location dialog box, which enables you to explore the folders on your system and choose one where the Web can be stored.

FIGURE 5.4

Working on a new Web.

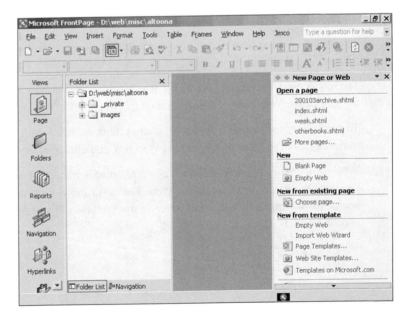

Import Files to a Web

The World Wide Web is a conglomeration of different media. Although pages consist of text documents, these pages can include a variety of different file types, including the following:

- GIF, JPG, and PNG graphics files
- WAV, MIDI, and MP3 sound files
- AVI, MOV, and MPG movies
- Java applets
- ActiveX components

A convention of FrontPage is to create an images subfolder where a Web's images can all be stored. If you're working with other types of media, you might want to create folders for them as well—such as java for Java applets and sounds for any sound files you're using.

To incorporate these media into your FrontPage 2002 Web, you should first make them a part of the Web:

1. With the Web open, choose File, Import (see Figure 5.5).

FIGURE 5.5

Importing a file into a Web.

5

The Import dialog box opens, listing the files you have selected to import into the Web. You haven't imported any yet, therefore the list is empty (see Figure 5.6).

2. Click Add File to select a file. The Add File to Import List dialog box opens.

3. Locate the file you want to add, which can be in your folder or at a Web address (if you are currently connected to the Internet).

   After you have selected a file to import, it will show up in the Import dialog box.

4. Click Add File to select another file to import or click OK to add the listed file (or files) to your Web.

Add File button

FIGURE 5.6

Choosing a file to import.

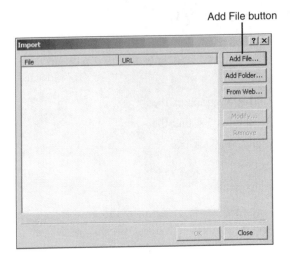

Imported files become part of the Web. Whenever you copy the Web to a new folder or publish it to the World Wide Web, that file will be included.

There is a way to add a file to a Web and avoid publishing that file. Right-click the file in the Folder list and choose Don't Publish from the shortcut menu that appears.

This book's official Web site has a Microsoft Word document that will be useful in a project later this hour. Import it into the empty Web you created earlier.

First, copy the file from the World Wide Web to your system:

1. Visit the book's Web site at `http://www.cadenhead.org/frontpage/`.

2. Open the Hour 5 page.

3. If you are using Internet Explorer 5, right-click the Microsoft Word Newsletter hyperlink and choose Save Target As from the shortcut menu that appears.

   If you are using Netscape Navigator 4, right-click the Microsoft Word Newsletter hyperlink and choose Save Link As.

4. Save the file in a folder on your system such as My Documents. Do not save the file in the same folder as your Web.

Next, import the file into your Web:

1. Open the Web.

2. Choose File, Import. The Import dialog box opens.

3. Click Add File. The Add File to Import List dialog box opens.

4. Open the folder where you saved the newsletter file. Select the file and click OK. The Import dialog box lists the file.

5. Click OK. The file is added to your Web. In the Folder list, you can drag the file to a new folder to change its location within your Web.

Delete a Web

You can delete a FrontPage 2002 Web in two different ways:

- Delete only the parts of the Web that control how it is edited in FrontPage
- Delete the Web entirely

To perform either deletion, open the Web and display its folder list (if this list isn't visible, use View, Folder List). Right-click the name of the Web—the top line in the folder list—and select the Delete command. A dialog box that enables you to delete FrontPage material or the entire Web opens.

Both of these actions are permanent, so you should handle them with due diligence—a phrase I picked up from stock traders that seems to mean "anything bad that happens as a consequence of my advice is entirely your fault."

Deleting an entire Web wipes out the folder containing the Web, all its subfolders, and all the pages, images, and other files that comprised the Web.

Deleting the FrontPage 2002 material of the Web deletes only the files and folders that FrontPage uses behind the scenes to manage the Web. Everything else—pages, images, and other files—is not removed.

A Web with none of its FrontPage material can still be viewed normally with a Web browser, but you won't be able to open it for editing in FrontPage. You can open individual pages in the Web for editing, but you can't apply a theme to a Web, add shared borders to several pages, or any other feature that involves an entire Web.

If you ever change your mind after deleting this part of a Web, you can bring it back: Choose File, Open Web and open the folder that contains the Web. FrontPage will ask whether you want to convert this folder into a FrontPage Web.

Using Imported Content in a Web

FrontPage 2002 is tightly coordinated with the other programs in Office XP, Microsoft's product suite. As a result, you can easily incorporate data produced with one program into another.

For example, you can make documents created with Microsoft Word a part of your FrontPage Web. There are two ways you can do so.

The easy way is to import a Word document in your Web and leave it in that format. Visitors to your Web who can view Word documents will be able to view the file by loading it with Word.

When you leave a document in Word format, you won't be able to edit it with FrontPage. Instead, when you try to open it normally—by double-clicking the file in the Folder list—it opens in Microsoft Word.

You can also convert the contents of a Word document to a Web page. Import the document, right-click it in the Folder list, and select Open With from the shortcut menu that appears (see Figure 5.7).

FIGURE 5.7

Editing a Word document in FrontPage.

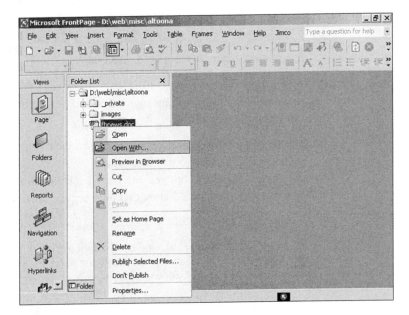

To try this out, open the Web that contains the Word document you imported earlier this hour. If for some reason you couldn't reach the book's Web site to download the file, any Word document on your system can be used for the same purpose.

The Open With Editor dialog box opens, listing the programs you can use to edit the document. Choose FrontPage and click OK.

The first time you do this with a document, FrontPage might not have a converter available to display the file correctly. A dialog box will appear asking whether you want to install one. Because you are converting the document into a Web page, click No.

When you use FrontPage to edit a Word document, a new page will be created that contains the contents of the document (see Figure 5.8).

FIGURE 5.8

Creating a Web page from a Word document.

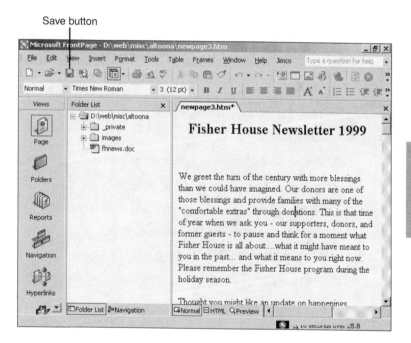

To save the page, click the Save button shown in Figure 5.8 or choose File, Save.

Workshop: Create a Web from Scratch

For this hour's workshop, create a FrontPage Web that contains a document converted from another word-processing format, such as Microsoft Word or text.

Solution

The first thing to do in this workshop is to find a file suitable for publication in a Web.

Windows has numerous files you can use—search for files ending in .DOC (for Word files) or .TXT (for text files).

To create a Web and add a text file to it:

1. In FrontPage, choose File, New, Page or Web. The New Page or Web task pane opens.
2. Click the Empty Web hyperlink. The Web Site Templates dialog box opens with the Empty Web icon selected.
3. Choose a location for your Web and click OK. The Web is created.
4. Choose File, Import. The Import dialog box opens.
5. Click Add File. The Add File to Import List dialog box opens.
6. Find the file you have chosen for use in this Web. Select it and click OK. The file is listed in the Import dialog box.
7. Click OK.

The selected file is added to your Web in its current format.

To convert the file's contents to a Web page:

1. If the Folder list is not visible, choose View, Folder List.
2. Right-click the file and choose Open With.
3. If FrontPage asks you to install a converter, click No.

A new Web page is added to the Web containing as much of the file as FrontPage could convert.

Summary

During the past hour, you followed FrontPage Webs from their creation to their deletion. You should be comfortable giving life to new Webs and taking away that life when you want to reclaim some disk space.

Because FrontPage offers built-in support for opening folders, importing files, and moving them around, you don't have to leave the program to handle these tasks.

In the coming hours, you will see more reasons why it's convenient to use FrontPage as a site-management tool.

Q&A

Q I copied several files into the folder that contains my FrontPage Web. Why aren't they displayed in the Folder list?

A If you added the files while the Web was open in FrontPage, you need to make the software look over the Web again to see what files it contains. Select the location of the Web in the Folder list (the first item) and choose View, Refresh, or press the F5 key.

This should cause the missing files to appear in your Web, even though they have never been imported. If it doesn't, close the Web and reopen it again.

Exercises

Challenge your knowledge of FrontPage 2002 Webs with the following exercises:

- Take a Web—preferably one you can afford to experiment with—through the following life cycle: creation, removal of the FrontPage Web without deleting it, making it a FrontPage Web again, and deletion.

- If you have created one of your own Webs prior to using FrontPage, convert it to a FrontPage Web.

For solutions to these exercises, visit the book's official Web site at http://www.cadenhead.org/frontpage/.

5

HOUR 6

Create a Web Page

During this hour, you'll face something that has been avoided until now:

The blank page.

Filling an empty page is a challenge that the World Wide Web inherited from its ancestors in the written family: books, magazines, and newspapers. Graven stone tablets also could be included in that list, but Moses produced them by dictation, so that's a different challenge altogether.

Absent of divine commandment, you'll be filling blank pages with the basic elements of the Web: text and hyperlinks. You'll work with text in several different ways, changing its font and colors, aligning and formatting paragraphs, and turning text into attention-grabbing headings.

You also will associate text with hyperlinks that connect a page to other documents on your own Web and the World Wide Web. While you are working with pages, you'll also learn to title a page.

Create and Title a Page

To create a new Web page in FrontPage 2002, choose File, New, Page or Web (see Figure 6.1).

FIGURE 6.1

Creating a new Web page.

The New Page or Web task pane will open alongside the FrontPage editing window, listing pages and Webs you can create along with existing pages you can open.

Every Web page in FrontPage 2002 begins as a template. If you want to start from scratch on a new page, click the Blank Page hyperlink to choose that template (see Figure 6.2).

Blank Page hyperlink

FIGURE 6.2

Creating an empty page.

When you select a new page template, the page appears in the editing window.

If the current Web does not have a theme applied to it, the new page is completely blank. Otherwise, the theme's background, fonts, colors, and other formatting details are applied to the page.

The new page is initially given a unique filename such as new_page_1.htm or new_page_2.htm. When you save it for the first time by clicking File, Save, you are asked to give the file a name.

If the Folder list is visible while you're in the Page view, you also can use it to rename files: Right-click a file in the list and choose Rename from the shortcut menu that appears. To make the Folder list appear or disappear, select View, Folder List.

If you close the current Web without making any changes to the new page, FrontPage 2002 discards the page. Otherwise, the software will remind you to save when you close the Web or preview it in a browser.

Add Shared Borders to a Page

Another thing added to a new page upon its creation is any border that it shares with the rest of the current Web.

FrontPage 2002 enables you to create border areas that are common to all pages on a Web. To see what shared borders are currently being used in a Web, click Format, Shared Borders (see Figure 6.3).

FIGURE 6.3

Viewing a Web's shared borders.

The Shared Borders dialog box will open (see Figure 6.4). A FrontPage Web can share top, bottom, left, and right borders, although sharing all four doesn't leave a lot of real estate for the rest of each page. They are often used to provide room for things such as link bars, site logos, and copyright notices.

Check marks on the dialog indicate which shared borders are currently part of the page you are editing. Add or remove check marks to change how the page uses borders.

The changes you make can apply to the current page or to all pages in the Web.

Many of the built-in FrontPage themes use the left border for a link bar that appears on every page of a Web. A do-it-yourself fireworks site should probably consider a shared

6

bottom border with a note disclaiming the publisher from any legal responsibility in the event of unexpected limb loss.

FIGURE 6.4

Editing a Web page's shared borders.

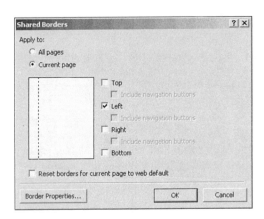

The Shared Borders dialog box can be used to add and remove these borders.

A shared border can contain anything that a Web page can hold, such as text, pictures, link bars, and hyperlinks. You edit a border from any page that shares it.

If a page includes a shared border, it will be displayed in editing view, separated by a dotted line (see Figure 6.5). These lines won't show up when the page is viewed in a browser.

FIGURE 6.5

Editing a page with a shared border.

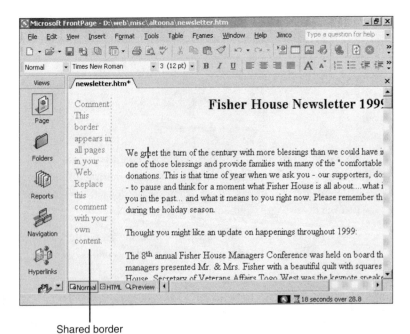

Shared border

When you first add a border, FrontPage 2002 inserts a comment that describes the border. Delete this comment when you add something to the border.

Any change made to a border area on one page is instantly reflected on all pages that share the border.

Title a Page

Every Web page is entitled to a title. Although FrontPage 2002 will assign a default title, it's usually something along the lines of New Page 6, which isn't terribly helpful to people using your Web.

A page's title appears in the title bar of most Web browsers—the topmost edge of the window containing the browser. (Nonvisual and all-text browsers render it differently.)

To title a page, right-click the page in editing view and select Page Properties from the shortcut menu that appears (see Figure 6.6).

FIGURE 6.6

Editing the properties of a page.

The Page Properties dialog box opens. There are six tabbed pages that can be used to alter the page properties. The General tab will be in the front (see Figure 6.7).

Enter a title for the page in the Title field and click OK.

FIGURE 6.7

Setting a new title for a page.

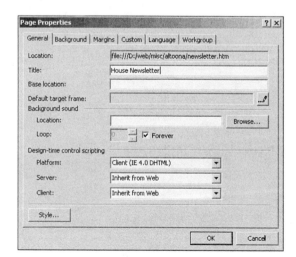

6

When you title a page, FrontPage 2002 uses this text for the page's banner and link bars, if you set up these components or they are part of a theme. It also is suggested as a file-name for the page when you first save it.

Choosing a succinct, descriptive title is important for two reasons: it helps people use your Web, and it helps others find it.

The title of a page is the most prominent thing shown in a search engine when results are listed. For example, the AltaVista search engine (`http://www.altavista.com`) lists the title of each page followed by a few lines of text pulled from its contents.

The title might also be used to determine how a Web is ranked during a search, so if you place "Totally Nude Furniture" in a page title, you'll get more visits from people search-ing for that topic than you might otherwise. (You'll also get more visitors who were expecting something other than unfinished rocking chairs.)

Add Text to a Page

To add text to a Web page, open it in the editing window, place your cursor anywhere on the page, and begin typing. The characters will appear at the currently selected cursor position, whether you are in a shared border or the main part of the page itself.

After you have entered some text on a page, you can highlight a selection of the text and use FrontPage's formatting options on it.

The easiest way to do this is to use the buttons on the Formatting toolbar (see Figure 6.8).

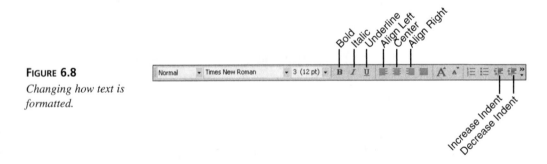

FIGURE 6.8

Changing how text is formatted.

The Formatting toolbar contains the following buttons:

- Bold—Makes the text appear in boldface
- Italic—Italicizes the text
- Underline—Underlines the text

- Align Left—Lines up all selected text and other page elements along the left margin of the page
- Center—Centers the selected page elements
- Align Right—Lines up the selected elements along the right margin
- Increase Indent—Indents the selected elements more than they are currently indented
- Decrease Indent—Reduces the indentation of the selected elements

Most of these buttons are common to word-processing software, especially the B, I, and U icons used for boldface, italic, and underline, respectively.

FrontPage 2002 can help you learn the purpose of each button on the Standard and Formatting toolbars. If you hover your cursor over a button for a few seconds, FrontPage displays a ToolTip naming that button.

When you are working with text on a Web page, you should let text wrap around the right margin at all times and press the Enter key only when you finish a paragraph. On most Web browsers, the text appears in block style, with each paragraph beginning at the left margin and a blank line separating paragraphs.

Pressing the Enter key causes a paragraph break to appear, even when you're arranging images and other page elements along with text.

The main reason you should not worry about the right-hand margin is that it varies depending on the browser and system being used to view a Web page. Someone on an 800-by-600 resolution monitor is going to see much more text per line than someone on a 640-by-480 monitor. A person who has enabled large text for easier reading will greatly reduce the number of characters that appear on a line. These are just two examples of the variability of Web presentation.

If you're using FrontPage 2002 to publish a Web page for the first time, you must become accustomed to the lack of control you sometimes have over a page's appearance.

Unlike a medium such as print, where a page looks exactly like the designer intended it to look, the Web is a fluid medium where pages can rearrange themselves to fit the space they have available to them.

To see this in action, connect to the Internet, load your favorite Web site, and resize your browser window so that it takes up a portion of your desktop instead of the whole thing. Figure 6.9 shows a page from one of my favorite sites, TeeVee, in two different browser windows.

6

FIGURE 6.9

*How page presentation
varies in different
browsers.*

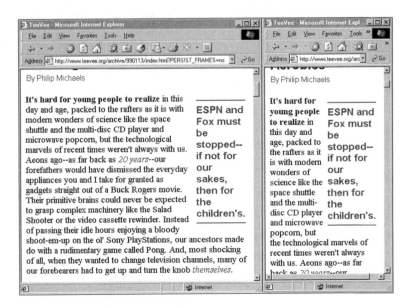

FIGURE 6.9

*How page presentation
varies in different
browsers.*

The text of the page wraps differently depending on the space that's available to it.

Every paragraph break on a Web page causes a blank line to appear in most browsers, including Netscape Navigator and Microsoft Internet Explorer. To begin text at the left margin without a paragraph break, you can insert a line break by selecting Insert, Break and choosing the Normal Line Break option from the Break dialog box.

There's a shortcut for adding a line break without leaving the keyboard—hold down the Shift key while pressing Enter.

Line breaks can be used to ensure that text appears on different lines without a paragraph break separating them. They're also useful when you're aligning images and other page elements.

One of the main ways to get some control over the appearance of a Web page is to use tables—boxes that can hold text, images, and other parts of a page. You'll learn how to create tables during Hour 7, "Organize a Page with Lists and Tables."

Turn Text into a Hyperlink

Documents on the World Wide Web are connected to each other through the use of hyperlinks. When you click on a link, your browser opens up the Web page or other type of file that has been associated with the link.

Hyperlinks can be associated with anything you place on a page: text, images, Java applets, QuickTime movies, MP3 sound files—you name it. If my Uncle Kirby ever goes through with his plan to wire an Internet port at an appropriate body juncture, you'll be able to create a hyperlink to him.

Text hyperlinks are displayed in a way that sets them apart from other text on a page. In most browsers, they are underlined.

> For this reason, underlining other text that isn't a hyperlink is frowned upon. Users will click the underlined text and wonder why it isn't functioning as a hyperlink.

To create a hyperlink, highlight the part of the page that should be associated with the link and choose Insert, Hyperlink (see Figure 6.10).

Highlighted text

FIGURE 6.10

Inserting a hyperlink.

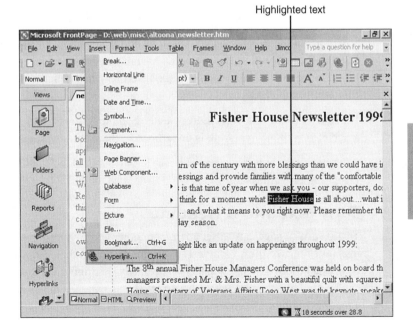

The Insert Hyperlink dialog box is displayed (see Figure 6.11).

Hyperlinks can be associated with files on your system or an address on the World Wide Web. If the file is another page in your Web, use the Insert Hyperlink dialog box to find and select the file, then click OK.

FIGURE 6.11

Adding a hyperlink to a page.

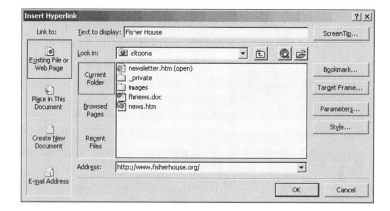

A Web address is also called a *URL*, which stands for Uniform Resource Locator.

A hyperlink to a URL should contain the full URL preceded by protocol information such as http:// or ftp://. Some examples are http://www.samspublishing.com, http://www.google.com/unclesam, and ftp://ftp.netscape.com.

If you're linking to a file on your system, add it to your Web first: Choose File, Import, find the file, and add it. If you don't, the link will not be usable when the page is published to the World Wide Web. Use the Insert Hyperlink dialog box to find and select the file, and then click OK.

If you are linking to a Web address, enter it in the Address field and click OK. The text associated with the hyperlink is underlined in the editing window.

After creating a hyperlink, you can edit it by right-clicking the link and selecting Hyperlink Properties.

Turn Text into a Heading

Text on a Web page can be set apart from other text by turning it into a heading. Headings range in size from 1 (largest) to 6 (smallest), and they can be used for the same purpose as a headline in a newspaper—succinctly describing the text that follows. They also can be used as subheads with a larger article, as enlarged quotations, and for other attention-grabbing purposes.

The easiest way to turn text into a heading is to use the Style pull-down menu on the Formatting toolbar, which is shown in Figure 6.12. This menu has several different options for formatting text, including choices for six heading sizes from 1–6.

FIGURE 6.12

The Style pull-down menu.

The actual size of a heading is browser-specific, but as a general rule, you can rely on the 1-to-6 ranking system.

Headings can be associated with hyperlinks and used in most other ways as if they were text. One exception is that a heading must occupy its own paragraph.

To see this in action, highlight a single word in a paragraph and turn it into Heading 1 text. Everything else in that paragraph will be turned into that heading also, occupying a very large chunk of the page.

Change the Font and Color of Your Text

When you add text to a page that has a theme applied to it, the text will have the font and color assigned to body text in that theme. If no theme has been applied, the text will be displayed in the default font and color of the Web browser used to load the page— usually a Times Roman, Arial, or Helvetica font.

To override the font or color choice for text, highlight the text and click Format, Font (see Figure 6.13).

6

FIGURE 6.13

Changing the font of text on a page.

The Font dialog box is shown in Figure 6.14. You can use this dialog box to select a new font and color for the selected text. Click OK to make the change and see how it looks in the editing window.

FIGURE 6.14

Selecting a font for text.

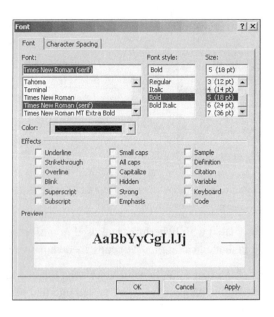

You can choose any font that's present on your system, but if it isn't present on the system of the person viewing your Web, a default font will be substituted for it.

As with font selection for themes, you should stick to common fonts such as Arial, Helvetica, Times, and Verdana because they are likely to be present on most systems. FrontPage 2002 also relies on Book Antiqua, Century Gothic, Times New Roman, and Trebuchet MS in many of its themes.

You also can specify a font and several alternatives in a list separated with commas, such as "Times Roman, Times, serif" or "Courier New, Courier, monospace". Type this list in the Font text box.

The size of a font can be designated on a scale from 1 (smallest) to 7 (largest). The point size associated with each of these sizes is a rule of thumb rather than an exact measurement. Although the font will be displayed at that size within FrontPage 2002, it's another thing that differs according to the browsing software being used and how it is configured.

A font's color can be selected with the standard FrontPage 2002 color selection dialog boxes. You also can apply several different effects to the text:

- Strikethrough—Text will be marked with a line through it, ~~like this~~.
- Blink—Text will blink on and off.
- Superscript and subscript—Text will be shrunken and appear either above or below other text on the same line.
- Hidden—Text will be part of the page but not displayed.
- Strong—Text will be displayed with strong emphasis (in most browsers, this causes it to appear in boldface).
- Emphasis—Text will be displayed with emphasis (italics in most browsers).

Several of the other text effects are used to define the kind of information the text represents. They are presented differently in different browsers, and are not as commonly used today as effects that describe how text is presented.

The following are descriptive effects you can use:

- Variable—A variable name describing a place used to store information in a computer program
- Keyboard—Something that a user should enter with a keyboard
- Code—Source code of a computer program
- Sample—Sample output from a computer program
- Citation—A citation crediting the source of information in an essay or similar paper

Workshop: Write Your Autobiography

The project you undertake next is the authorship of your life story, background, and achievements. Because there isn't too much time left in the hour, I hope you're either succinct or extremely modest.

To get ready, create a new Web with no pages in FrontPage 2002 and give it a name such as "common." This Web will serve as a convenient holding place for pages that you can import into other Webs.

Create a new page with your name as the title and bio.htm as the filename. Use this page to answers each of the following questions:

- Where were you born?
- Where do you live today?
- What schools did you attend?
- What is your career and some of the jobs you have worked?

6

- What are your greatest professional achievements?
- What are your best personal accomplishments?
- Who's in your immediate family?

Answer each of these with enthusiasm—even if you have to fake some of it. My own career in academia had some low points I'd rather not discuss until the restraining order expires.

Use left-aligned headings to divide the body text into several different sections such as Personal, Professional, and Educational. (If one of your sections is Criminal, you might want to answer with a little less enthusiasm.)

Change the margins of each section of text so that there is some blank space between the text and the edges of the page.

As the last element of the assignment, add at least five hyperlinks: one back to index.htm and four to sites on the Web. If your schools or jobs have their own Webs, they would be good links. Your hometown and birthplace also should have Webs—if not, the portal Yahoo! (http://www.yahoo.com) has pages devoted to thousands of cities and countries.

Solution

After putting your life story into hypertext, you should have a better grasp on the basics of Web page creation. You also might have learned something about yourself, but that's entirely accidental.

Neither the author of this book, Sams Publishing, its employees, or its affiliates is responsible for any personal growth caused by this publication. Any incidental growth that might occur should not be interpreted as a reason to file this book in stores under Self-Help rather than Web Publishing.

The trickiest part of the project was the requirement to set text apart from the margins of the page. That's achieved by using the Increase Indent button on the Formatting toolbar.

You can test your page out by clicking the Internet Explorer icon on the Standard toolbar. FrontPage 2002 will make sure that you have a chance to save the page before it's loaded by a browser.

Summary

As a writer myself, I can attest to the power of the blank page. Regardless of the medium, there are few things on earth that can inspire more fear in writers [editor's note: other than editors].

After this hour, you should have some tools for keeping the blank page at bay.

Text, headings, and hyperlinks make up the largest part of the World Wide Web. By combining the three, you can create entire Webs that reach an audience of thousands.

Of course, that audience is going to wonder why you're not using any feature of the World Wide Web introduced after 1994.

You'll correct this perception in the next several hours as you work with lists, tables, and forms.

Q&A

Q I'm not a computer programmer. Why would I want to use text effects such as Variable, Code, and Keyboard?

A You probably wouldn't. Those effects date back to the first version of HTML, the language used to create Web pages, and they aren't used on many pages today—even when things such as variables and source code are displayed on a page. Most browsers display these effects simply as boldface, italicized, or underlined text, so the Bold, Italic, and Underline buttons can be used instead.

FrontPage 2002 includes these effects primarily for users who are accustomed to them. You can probably avoid them entirely, especially if none of your own pages is on a technical subject.

Q During this hour, the serif and monospace fonts were mentioned. I've never encountered these when selecting a font. Are they new?

A Those fonts are generic, catch-all fonts that a Web browser matches to a real font that's present on the system. There are five of these: serif, sans serif, cursive, monospace, and fantasy. The Web browser will choose the default font for each of these styles, which is most commonly a Times font for serif, Helvetica for sans serif, Courier for monospace, something like Zapf-Chancery for cursive, and Western for fantasy. A good way to use these fonts is to put them last in a comma-separated list of fonts—such as "Verdana, Helvetica, sans serif".

6

Exercises

Challenge your knowledge of FrontPage 2002 page creation with the following exercises:

- Load a Web you created during a previous hour and make some changes to how text is formatted. Add indented text and reformat the headings to a different size.
- Create a Web page containing a list of 10 of your favorite Web sites, with a hyperlink on each name that contains the address of the site.

For solutions to these exercises, visit the book's official Web site at `http://www.cadenhead.org/frontpage/`.

Hour 7

Organize a Page with Lists and Tables

Today, entire stores are devoted to the subject of containers. You can spend hours figuring out ways to hold and store things you've never actually heard of, or things you're not actually using anymore.

I own more floppy disk containers today than floppy disks. If there's ever a run on the things, no one else will be more prepared.

With any luck, you'll feel the joy of containment—or should that be *contentment*—about the subject of this hour.

Lists and tables are two ways to contain something on a FrontPage 2002 Web page.

You'll learn how to package text and other information together into lists—groups of related items set apart from everything else with special symbols.

You'll also learn how to package anything on a Web page into tables—boxes that can hold text, images, Java applets, and even more tables.

Create Numbered and Unnumbered Lists

Text on a Web page is grouped into paragraphs that are normally displayed with no indentation and blank lines separating them.

Another way to organize text is to turn it into a list.

Lists, as the name implies, are groupings of related items. Each item is a paragraph of text or even a combination of text and other page elements.

Web pages can display two kinds of lists:

- Numbered lists, where each item is prefaced by a unique number
- Unnumbered lists, where each item is prefaced by a character

The text you just read is a two-item unnumbered list. The "•" character is similar to the ones commonly used on Web pages, which are also called *bullets*.

To turn lines of text into a list, select the text and click either the Unnumbered List or Numbered List button on the Formatting toolbar (see Figure 7.1).

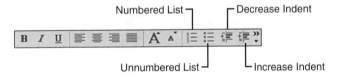

FIGURE 7.1
Formatting text in a list.

Numbered lists are in sequence, starting with the number 1 and counting upward. Unnumbered lists are displayed with bullets next to each item.

Lists can be placed inside other lists. Figure 7.2 shows a Web page that contains several lists nested within each other.

To place items in a list inside another list, highlight the items and click the Increase Indent button twice.

To take items out of another list, highlight the items and click the Decrease Indent button twice.

You can create lists as many levels deep as needed.

The bullets that are displayed next to items in an unnumbered list provide a visual clue about which list they belong to. If an unnumbered list is placed inside another, the two lists will have different styles of bullets.

FIGURE 7.2

Displaying lists inside other lists on a Web page.

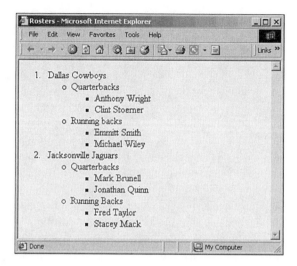

If you put a list on a page that sports one of FrontPage 2002's built-in themes, graphic bullets that are coordinated with the overall theme are used.

To change how a list is presented, place your cursor on a list item, right-click, and select List Properties from the shortcut menu that appears (see Figure 7.3). The List Properties dialog box is displayed.

FIGURE 7.3

Configuring a list.

You can specify a different starting number for a numbered list and change the appearance of bullets in an unnumbered list.

FrontPage Webs designed for current browsers can use *collapsible outlines*—bulleted and numbered lists that can change the number of displayed items. To make all or part of a list collapsible, enable the Enable Collapsible Outlines box. If you want the items to be collapsed when the page is first loaded, click the Initially Collapsed box in the List Properties dialog box (see Figure 7.4).

7

FIGURE 7.4

Enabling collapsible outlines in a list.

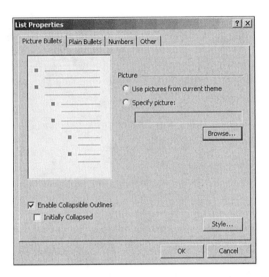

Items in a collapsible list can be clicked to show or hide any of their sublists. If the page displayed in Figure 7.2 was collapsible, you could click Dallas Cowboys to make all the lists under that item disappear. Clicking it a second time would make them reappear.

The collapsible outlines feature should be selected in FrontPage 2002 only if your target audience uses version 4.0 or later of Netscape Navigator or Microsoft Internet Explorer. To determine the audience for your Web, choose Tools, Page Options, and click the Compatibility tab to bring it to the front. You'll learn more about this during Hour 13, "Make Your Web Compatible with Multiple Browsers."

Create a Table for Tabular Data

One of the things that befuddles Web page designers is the fluid state of a Web page. Text, images, and other page elements move around depending on the way they're presented. The same page can look remarkably different in two different browsers on different computer systems.

Web designers can achieve more control over the appearance of page elements by placing them into tables.

Tables are rectangular grids that are divided into individual cells that are themselves rectangular. Information can be placed into each of these cells to line it up vertically or horizontally with the information in other cells.

If you're having trouble conceptualizing a table as it relates to a Web page, think of a wall calendar:

```
SUN MON TUE WED THU FRI SAT
 *   *   1   2   3   4   5
 6   7   8   9   10  11  12
 13  14  15  16  17  18  19
 20  21  22  23  24  25  26
 27  28  29  30  *   *   *
```

A calendar like this is a rectangular table containing a bunch of cells.

On a wall calendar, each day takes up its own cell in the table. The name of each day from SUN to SAT also occupies its own cell.

Tables are divided into vertical columns and horizontal rows. The wall calendar shown has seven columns and six rows.

The primary purpose of tables is to organize information that must line up into straight rows and columns. You can use tables to display data such as an expense report in easy-to-read columns.

Tables also are useful when structuring the content of a Web page. Anything that can be put on a Web page can be placed inside a table cell—even another table.

Most commercial World Wide Web sites use tables to lay out the contents of their pages.

As you work with tables, you'll see how this is useful.

Add a Table to a Page

To add a table to a page, choose Table, Insert, Table (see Figure 7.5).

FIGURE 7.5

Adding a table to a page.

The Insert Table dialog box opens (see Figure 7.6), enabling you to define the size and spacing of your table. Choose the number of rows and columns that it contains by changing the values in the Rows and Columns boxes.

The number of rows and columns in a table determines the initial number of cells that it contains. If you add a three-row by three-column table, it will contain nine cells.

7

FIGURE 7.6

Setting up a new table.

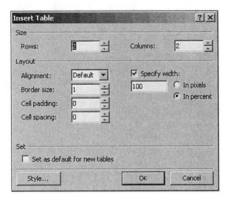

You will be able to easily add and subtract rows and columns from a table as you edit it, so the initial values are not important.

Tables can be limited to one row and one column, which creates a single-cell grid.

When you add a table to a page, it is placed at the spot of your cursor in the Page view. The table's borders and cell borders are visible, as shown in Figure 7.7.

FIGURE 7.7

Editing a page with a table.

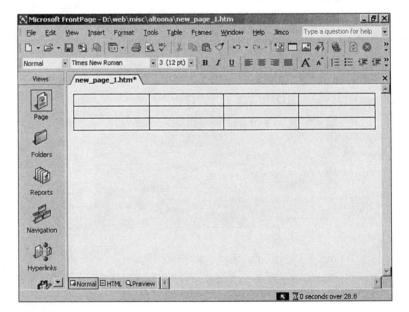

Add Data to a Table

After you have a table on a page, click your cursor to place it inside a cell and you can begin adding text, images, and other things to that cell.

Tables begin with all cells and rows the same size, and FrontPage 2002 attempts to keep them the same size while you're adding text. Words wrap around the right edge of a cell as if it were the right margin of a page.

If you add an image or something else that's too large to fit into it, rows and columns stretch to make room.

You also can make cells shrink to take up only the room they need: Place your cursor in the table and select Table, AutoFit to Contents.

Figure 7.8 shows a Web page that contains a table used to display the offensive statistics for several baseball players. The auto-fit feature has been selected for this table, so the leftmost row—which contains the last name of each player—takes up more space than the rows containing statistics.

FIGURE 7.8

Presenting a table for baseball statistics.

When you're adding things to cells, you can use the Tab and Shift+Tab keys to jump from one cell to another. Tab advances to the next cell to the right or the next row. Shift+Tab moves left or to the previous row.

An unusual thing happens if you press Tab when you're in the cell that's on the bottom row and the far-right column: FrontPage 2002 creates a new row and moves the cursor into the first cell in this row.

This enables you to keep adding new data to a table such as the player statistics table shown in Figure 7.8. If you don't know the number of rows you need, you can just start with a few and add them as you're entering data.

A new row or column can be added to an existing table: Right-click a cell adjacent to where the row or column should be inserted, and then choose Insert Rows or Insert Columns from the shortcut menu that appears.

You can delete rows and columns: Select the rows or columns to be deleted and then right-click a cell in the selected area. Click Delete Cells to remove the selected area from the table.

7

Resize a Table

By default, a table in FrontPage 2002 is sized in one of two ways:

- All cells take up the same size if they don't contain something that's too big for this to be possible
- All cells are resized to be as small as they can be and still hold their contents

You can resize a table so that its rows and columns have specific pixel widths.

To do this, place your cursor over any of the borders on the table. The cursor will switch to a double-sided arrow that points either up/down or left/right. This cursor indicates you can drag that border on the table to adjust the size of adjacent rows and columns.

> Setting specific pixel dimensions for a table is something that can easily detract from the usability of a page, especially if you're making it larger than 640 pixels wide or 480 pixels tall. Those dimensions match the monitor resolution for a large number of Web users, so bigger tables will require scrolling to be seen in full.

You also can resize a table so that it takes up a percentage of the space that's available to it: Right-click the table and choose Table Properties from the shortcut menu to open the Table Properties dialog box (see Figure 7.9).

You can resize a table, align it on a Web page, and change the way cells are displayed in relation to each other. It's shown in Figure 7.9.

FIGURE 7.9

Modifying the properties of a table.

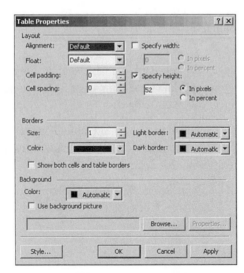

You can set the width and height of a table by pixels or by percentage. Choosing a width of 100 percent means that the table will take up all the space that's available to it—the entire width of the page, unless the table is inside another table that's restricted to a smaller size.

Height isn't normally specified as a percentage because Web pages are much more flexible in dimension from top to bottom than they are from side to side. Web users are accustomed to scrolling down a page to read it, whereas very few Webs require scrolling to the right.

When you set these dimensions for a table, you shouldn't use Table, AutoFit again or you'll wipe them out. Removing settings for height and width will cause tables to default to their normal sizing: all cells the same, or the minimum space needed for any cell.

The alignment options for a table are the same as they would be for anything else: left, centered, and right.

Three more things you can modify about a table are its cellpadding, cellspacing, and border values.

Cellpadding is the amount of empty space that surrounds the contents of every cell. If you increase cellpadding from the default value of 1, cells will grow bigger, although their contents will stay the same size.

Cellspacing is the amount of space in the grid between each cell. This makes the height and width of the grid lines bigger, if they are visible. Increasing it from the default of 2 causes the table to grow while cells remain the same size.

The *border* determines the size of the border that surrounds the table. If it is set to 0, the table border and all of its grid lines will disappear. The cells of the table will still line up correctly, but it won't be as apparent to your visitors that a table is being used.

Many of the things you change about a table can also be done to individual cells. When you right-click a cell and choose the Cell Properties dialog box, it looks almost identical to the Table Properties dialog box shown in Figure 7.9.

You can change the height, width, and alignment of individual cells. You also can remove the height and width values to revert the cell back to the default sizing behavior.

Tables and even cells can have their own background. To set up a background color for one cell or a group of cells, right-click the selected cell (or cells), choose Cell Properties, and use the Background Color drop-down box shown in Figure 7.9.

As with a page background, a table background can be a color or a graphics file that is tiled to fill the space. You work with page backgrounds during Hour 10, "Create and Edit Graphics for Your Web."

Backgrounds are selected in the Table Properties and Cell Properties dialog boxes.

7

Use a Table to Lay Out a Page

Although tables were introduced to HTML as a means for displaying tabular data such as the calendar and player statistics shown earlier, they were immediately appropriated for another purpose by Web designers: layout.

Tables are the way to rein in the fluidity of information on a Web page. By placing elements within tables and even nesting one table inside another, you can create page layouts that don't change substantively with every browser, monitor, and computer that's used to view them.

FrontPage 2002 uses tables for this purpose behind the scenes. Shared borders are implemented as cells in a table, and the page's content between all the borders also occupies a cell.

When tables are used to lay out a page, the border is usually set to 0 so the effect is transparent.

The main disadvantage of using a table for this purpose is that Web browsers can't display any part of the table until the entire table has been downloaded.

Ever wondered why so many professional World Wide Web sites have a banner ad that loads immediately while the rest of the page shows up sometime later that week? This happens because the banner is often outside the table that contains the rest of the page.

One feature of tables that's handy when you're laying out a page is the ability to combine cells. You can stretch a table cell so that it takes up the space normally occupied by several cells.

To do this, drag with the mouse pointer to select an area that covers all the cells you want to merge it with. The merged cell must be a rectangle, like any cell, but it can take up as many original cells as you want.

Right-click the selected area and choose Merge Cells to combine them into one new cell.

Figure 7.10 shows a new row atop the baseball statistics table. All four cells in the row have been selected, so the Merge Cells command will create a new cell that's four columns wide and one row tall.

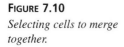

FIGURE 7.10

Selecting cells to merge together.

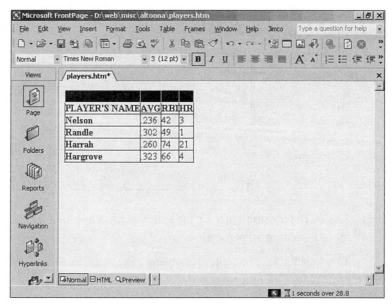

Workshop: Create a Monthly Calendar

This hour's workshop gives you a chance to revisit the topic of calendars by creating one of your own.

In a dummy Web or one of the ones you have already created, add a new page called `calendar.htm`. This page should contain the full calendar for the current month.

The calendar should include each of the following:

- Abbreviations for each day's name
- A row across the top displaying the month and year
- Each day's number lined up horizontally and vertically
- Different colors to distinguish weekdays from weekends
- A calendar color that's different than the page's background

Solution

With the exception of the row across the top, the workshop's calendar can be created as a basic table with seven columns and enough rows to hold the weeks, the day abbreviations, and the month and year atop the calendar.

The top row of the calendar is a single cell—either the rightmost or leftmost cell on the first row had to be merged with all the others.

Figure 7.11 shows a table calendar for January 2002.

7

FIGURE 7.11

Using a table to display a calendar.

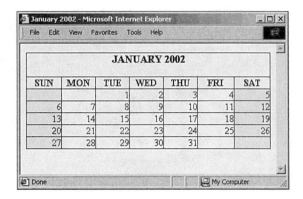

This calendar doesn't take up the entire width of the browser window because the table is set to a width of 90 percent.

To set the background color for several cells at the same time, select the cells, right-click, and choose Cell Properties.

Summary

Like a person coming home from a store with new containers, you now know two places to put stuff in your FrontPage 2002 Webs:

- *Lists*—Groups of related items set apart by bullets, symbols, or numbers
- *Tables*—Rectangular grids of cells that can hold anything Web pages can hold

Lists are primarily useful as a way to organize text within a larger document.

Tables are useful for presenting tabular data and organizing the layout of a Web page. FrontPage 2002 itself relies on the latter to implement features such as shared borders.

It is hoped that the presence of these containers will serve as an inspiration for you to find things that must be contained.

If not, contain yourself.

Q&A

Q I've highlighted a group of cells to delete, but the Delete Cells command can't be selected when I right-click the area. What's wrong?

A There are two ways to select a group of adjacent table cells in FrontPage 2002. One is to drag your mouse over the cells to highlight them in the same way that text is highlighted.

If this selection method doesn't allow the cells to be deleted, try the alternative. Hover your cursor at the outer border of a row or column you want to delete. The cursor will change to a thick arrow pointing at that row or column. Click once; the chosen area will be highlighted, and you can use the Delete Cells command on it.

Exercises

Challenge your knowledge of FrontPage 2002 lists and tables with the following exercises:

- Create a Web page that outlines a project you're planning to undertake, such as the first Web you are going to design after finishing this book. Use numbered lists for each major section of the outline and internal unnumbered lists breaking down those sections.
- Create a table that takes up an entire Web page and has around five rows and five columns. Give each cell a different background color, and then add tables inside several of these cells. Give those different background colors, too. Repeat the process until your work qualifies as an homage to the artist Piet Mondrian.

For solutions to these exercises, visit the book's official Web site at http://www.cadenhead.org/frontpage/.

7

Hour 8

Communicate on Your Web with Forms

One of the easiest mistakes to make as a World Wide Web publisher is to treat this medium like its older siblings: television, radio, and print. For the most part, those media are a one-way street because the audience can't immediately respond (with the possible exception of Elvis Presley, who once registered his displeasure with a television by shooting it). Nor can they do anything to change the presentation as it's occurring—no matter how many times I yell "Look out! Iceberg!", my favorite character in the movie *Titanic* still ends up in several pieces at the bottom of the ocean.

At its best, the World Wide Web is a collaboration between the people who publish sites and the people who visit them. As a Web publisher, you can collect information from the visitors to your pages, present it on your site, and use it in other ways to create a more engaging experience.

When you collect information on your FrontPage 2002 Web, you'll be using a Web page element called a *form*. Forms are made up of text boxes, lists, and other means of gathering information from visitors.

Today, you'll learn how to work with forms in the following ways:

- Using the Form Page Wizard to quickly create a new form
- Adding questions to a form
- Customizing a form
- Saving the information collected on a form to a text file or a Web page

Create a Form with the Form Page Wizard

If you've never created a form before, the easiest way to start is by asking the Form Page Wizard to do it.

Like other wizards in FrontPage 2002, the Form Page Wizard asks a series of questions to determine what you'd like to add to your Web:

- What questions do you want to ask?
- What kind of answers are acceptable?
- How should the questions and answers be formatted on the Web page?
- What should happen to the answers afterward?

When all of this has been determined, the wizard creates a new page in the current Web and adds the form to it. You can either use this page or transfer it to another page using copy and paste.

Call on the Wizard

The first step in using the Form Page Wizard is to add a new page to an existing Web by choosing File, New, Page or Web. The New Page or Web task pane opens (see Figure 8.1).

FIGURE 8.1

Choosing a page or Web to create.

Click the Page Templates hyperlink to open a dialog box that lists templates and wizards you can use to create a page.

In the dialog box, which is shown in Figure 8.2, choose the Form Page Wizard icon and click OK.

FIGURE 8.2

Choosing the Form Page Wizard.

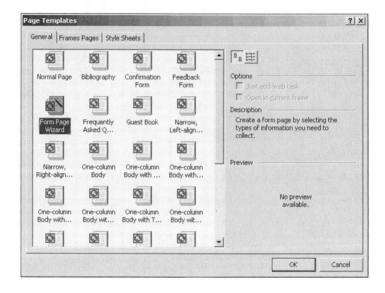

The Form Page Wizard asks you a series of questions about the kind of information you would like to collect from a user on your Web.

You collect information by asking the user questions.

When you begin using the Form Page Wizard, you will see a dialog box that contains no questions yet (see Figure 8.3).

FIGURE 8.3

Starting a new form.

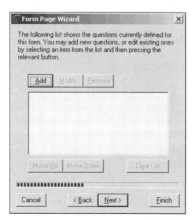

Click the Add button to add your first question to the form you are creating. Later, you will be able to remove or modify questions you have added, which makes it easy to change things on-the-fly as you're trying out the wizard for the first time.

The wizard requires two things to add questions to a form: a prompt and the type of input you are looking for. A *prompt* is a succinct line of text that asks a question or describes a group of related questions. The *input type* represents the structure of the information collected in response to the prompt.

Ask a Simple Question

Several of the wizard's input types determine how a single question can be answered. They include the following:

- date—A calendar date
- time—A time
- number—A numeric value
- range—A number from 1 to 5 that's used to rate something
- string—A single line of text
- paragraph—Text that can be longer than a single line
- boolean—A response limited to one of two options, such as yes or no, true or false, and on or off

Figure 8.4 shows the Form Page Wizard being used to add the question "Have you ever been convicted of a crime?" The input type for this question has been set to boolean, which limits responses to an either/or proposition such as yes or no. The string or paragraph input types could have been used instead, giving someone a chance to provide a more unstructured answer such as "Not since I quit using illegal drugs."

FIGURE 8.4

Adding a boolean *question to a form.*

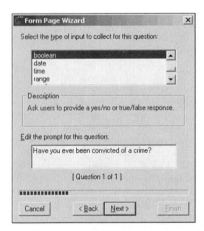

Each of these questions can be customized after the input type and prompt have been defined. You can limit date and time answers to specific formats, restrict a string answer to a specific number of characters, and make other decisions that affect how the form will be used.

After you have specified a question and input type, the wizard will ask for more information. One of the things you must provide for each question is the name of its *variable*, a name used to keep track of a user's answer. Each variable is given a name that can be used to retrieve or modify its value.

A variable's name should describe its purpose. You can use any combination of letters, numbers, and the underscore character (_) when you're naming variables.

In Figure 8.5, the wizard is setting up a boolean question that has a yes or no answer and the variable name ConvictedOfCrime.

FIGURE 8.5

Naming a variable that holds information on a form.

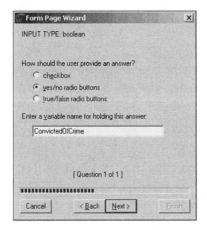

Choose from a List of Options

There are two input types in the Form Page Wizard that enable answers to be selected from a list of possible choices:

- one of several options—A single item can be picked from the list
- any of several options—An unlimited number of items can be picked (including none)

The prompt should identify what the list is being used to answer.

Each choice in a list must be a single line of text. Single-choice lists can be presented in three different ways on a Web page: a drop-down menu, radio buttons, or a list. All of these are shown on the portion of a Web page displayed in Figure 8.6.

FIGURE 8.6

Three ways a list of options can be presented.

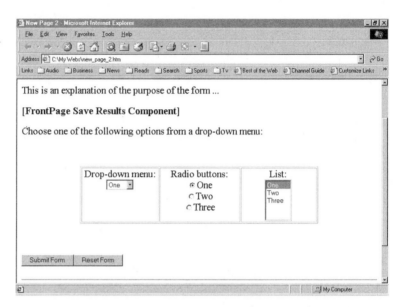

As shown, a drop-down menu shows only one possible answer at a time. If you click the arrow next to the answer, a menu of other answers will appear. Radio buttons and lists show several possible answers.

> To make a drop-down menu easier to understand, use the visible answer to provide explanatory text such as "Click to make your selection." This also prevents the visible answer from being picked more often than other answers simply because it is automatically displayed.

A multiple-choice list enables the user to select more than one answer from a list. Each possible answer is shown next to a check box. A single-choice list restricts the answer to a single item in the list. Both types of lists must have a named variable to store answers in.

Multiple-choice lists require a group of variables—one for each possible choice that can be selected. Instead of providing a name for each of these variables, you provide a *base name*. This will be combined with the text of each answer to form variable names.

Figure 8.7 shows the Form Page Wizard being used to create a multiple-choice list. The list is used to answer the question "Which of the following languages do you speak?" One of four answers can be selected: English, Spanish, German, or Esperanto.

FIGURE 8.7

Providing answers and a base variable name for a multiple-choice list.

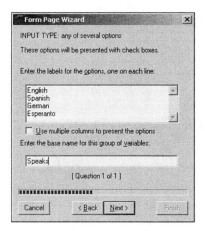

The base variable name is `Speaks`. The answers to this question will be saved in the variables `Speaks_English`, `Speaks_Spanish`, `Speaks_German`, and `Speaks_Esperanto`.

Ask Multiple Questions at Once

The remaining input types in the Form Page Wizard are used to ask several related questions at the same time. They include the following:

- `contact information`—Name, title, address, phone number, and other identification
- `account information`—Username and password
- `product information`—Product name, product version, and serial number
- `ordering information`—Products to order, billing information, and shipping address
- `personal information`—Name, age, physical characteristics, and related information

The Form Page Wizard automatically provides a prompt for each question in the group. If you provide your own prompt, it will be used to introduce the entire group rather than any specific questions.

These combined input types make it easy to add some of the most common questions to a form. You can customize these questions by removing any questions that you don't want to ask.

In Figure 8.8, the Form Page Wizard is being used to customize a group of questions after the `contact information` input type was selected. The figure shows all the customization options offered with the `contact information` input type. The Name and E-mail address questions are selected.

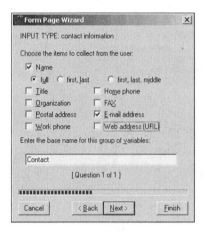

FIGURE 8.8

Selecting which contact information questions to use on a form.

For some of these input types, the variable names will be provided by the wizard. Otherwise, a base variable name must be provided for the group of questions. This will be used by the wizard to associate a variable name with each question.

Determine How the Form Will Be Presented

After you've finished adding questions to a form, you can choose how the questions are presented on a Web page. You can lay out the form as a series of paragraphs or as one of three different lists:

- A numbered list
- A bulleted list, in which each question is indented with a bullet character (like the list you're currently reading)
- A definition list

A definition list is a standard Web page element that's ideal for displaying a group of words and their definitions. The formatting varies depending on the browser being used. Generally, words are presented flush left, and definitions are indented below the word they define. The following text is presented in the style of a definition list:

```
Do
    A deer; a female deer
Ra
    A drop of golden sun
Mi
    The name I call myself
Fa
    A long, long way to run
```

On a form that's displayed as a definition list, questions are presented flush left and possible answers are indented.

8

Another presentation decision you must make is whether to use tables when laying out your form. Tables can be used to arrange elements on a page. If you decide to use a table, the Form Page Wizard places questions and answers into their own cells on the table, making the form appear more organized. The borders of this table are not visible when the form is created.

If you decide not to use a table, questions and answers are arranged more loosely as a series of paragraphs.

The main reason not to use tables is that a small percentage of the audience—from 1 to 2 percent, according to most estimates—is still using Web browsers that don't support them. Tables have been supported since version 1.1 of Netscape Navigator and the comparable version of Internet Explorer, so anyone who has downloaded and installed one of these browsers in the past five years can view tables.

A browser that doesn't support tables will display them in a manner that's confusing for the visitor.

Figure 8.9 shows a Web page that contains two versions of the same three-question form—a survey for owners of a company's bread-makers. The upper version of the form is formatted with a table, which lines up the questions and possible answers evenly in two columns. The lower version does not use a table.

FIGURE 8.9

Arranging a form with and without a table.

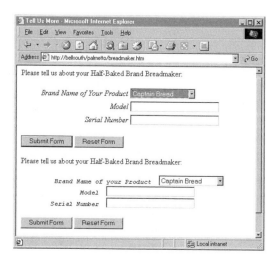

Save the Information Collected on a Form

The last step in creating a form with the Form Page Wizard is to decide how a user's answers will be saved. The following three options are available:

- `save results to a web page`

- save results to a text file
- use custom CGI script

To save a form's answers to a Web page or text file, you must be publishing your Web on a server that is enabled with FrontPage Server Extensions.

All answers submitted using the form are saved to the same page. A question is identified on this form using its variable name followed by a semicolon. The answer to that question is presented on the following line. Figure 8.10 shows two sets of form results saved to a Web page.

FIGURE 8.10

Viewing a form's results that have been saved to a Web page.

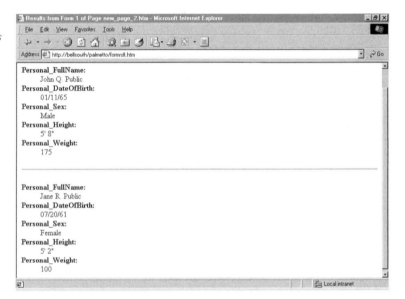

Displaying results as a Web page is useful when you want to view the answers in an easy-to-understand format.

If you're going to use form results with other software (such as Microsoft Access or another database program), they should be saved to a text file. This file can easily be imported into a database program. The first line of the file identifies each of the form's variables, and each subsequent line contain a set of results.

The following output contains the same form results shown in Figure 8.10, saved to a text file instead:

```
"Personal_FullName"     "Personal_DateOfBirth"     "Personal_Sex"
    "Personal_Height"    "Personal_Weight"
"John Q. Public"    "01/11/65"    "Male"     "5' 8"""     "175"
"Jane R. Public"    "07/20/61"    "Female"     "5' 2"""     "100"
```

This text file uses Tab characters to separate each field: "Personal FullName", "Personal DateOfBirth", "Personal Sex", "Personal Height", and "Personal Weight". A format like this is less readable to humans than HTML, but much more readable to database software.

When you save form results, you must name the file that will be used to store them. The Form Page Wizard will provide an .htm or .txt file extension for you, so all you'll need to choose is the name that precedes the extension. Results are saved in the same folder as the Web page that contains the form, unless you specify a different one along with the filename.

A FrontPage Web's _private subfolder is a useful place to save form results that shouldn't be viewed by the people who visit your site. To save results to this folder, precede the filename with the text "_private/". Also, make sure that access permissions for that folder have been established correctly.

The file that contains form results can be loaded within FrontPage 2002. If you'd like to delete all existing results, delete the file. A new file is created automatically when new results are submitted using the form.

The final option for saving form results is to use a custom *Common Gateway Interface (CGI)* script. CGI refers to the use of special programs—also called *scripts*—that are run in conjunction with Web pages. A Web server that supports FrontPage 2002 offers a lot of the same functionality as a CGI program. The main use of CGI on the World Wide Web is to handle the results of Web forms.

CGI programs require special access to the Web server that's hosting your Web. You'll need to know the name of the CGI program to run and its location on the Web site.

Workshop: Survey Visitors to Your Web

To test how familiar you've become with the Form Page Wizard, use it to create the form shown in Figure 8.11. This form is used to conduct a survey related to a popular theme park. Visitors are asked their name, e-mail address, number of visits to the park, favorite attraction, and favorite restaurant. The results are saved to a text file on the Web.

The user answers the first three questions by entering text into a box on the page, and answers the last two questions by choosing an option from a drop-down list of possible choices.

FIGURE **8.11**

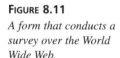

A form that conducts a survey over the World Wide Web.

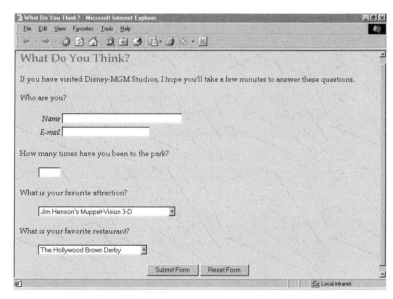

The favorite attraction and restaurant questions should each include several of the most popular places at the park. If you're not familiar with the theme park shown in Figure 8.11, replace it with one you're more familiar with or make up an imaginary one.

Save the form's results to a text file, giving it a name that describes its purpose.

When you're done, give the page a title and a descriptive headline, such as "What Do You Think?". You can also add a theme and some introductory text if you want to create a more presentable page. Then name it and save it to your Web.

A description of one possible solution follows.

Solution

There's more than one way to use the Form Page Wizard to create a form, so the steps you took may be different from those offered in this solution. The most important thing is to ask the same kinds of questions, collect the same kinds of answers, and save the results in the same manner.

The form shown in Figure 8.11 was created using the following steps in the Form Page Wizard:

- A question was added with the input type contact information and the prompt "Who are you?".

8

- Only two of the `contact information` questions were selected: Name and E-mail address.
- A question was added with the input type `number` and the prompt "How many times have you been to the park?".
- The question was given the variable name `Visits`.
- A question was added with the input type `one of many options` and the prompt "What is your favorite attraction?".
- Labels were provided for several attractions at the park, and the base variable name was set to `FavoriteAttraction`.
- A question was added with the input type `one of many options` and the prompt "What is your favorite restaurant?".
- Labels were provided for park restaurants, and the base variable name was set to `FavoriteRestaurant`.
- The wizard was told that no more questions would be added.
- The default presentation options were used: normal paragraphs and the use of tables to arrange questions and answers.
- Results were saved to a text file named `parksurvey.txt`, and the wizard created the form on a new page.

To see this form on the World Wide Web, visit the book's official Web site at `http://www.cadenhead.org/frontpage` and open the Hour 8 page.

Summary

By using the Form Page Wizard, you can easily add interactive features to your FrontPage 2002 Web. As you explored the wizard's capabilities and created your own form in this chapter, some ideas on how to use this Web page capability probably sprang to mind. Forms can be employed to offer user surveys, visitor feedback, polls, questionnaires, tests, and many other interactive features.

Elvis Presley, not having a satisfactory way to communicate with television programmers, shot one of the devices in his home. Forms give visitors to your Webs a satisfactory way to communicate with you that do not involve possible violations of federal, state, or local law.

You'll learn how to create forms during Hour 21, "Create a Form by Hand."

Q&A

Q **Using the Form Page Wizard, I created a form and chose not to lay it out using tables. Some parts of the form extend beyond the right edge of the browser instead of wrapping around to the next line. Why is this happening?**

A To line up forms without using tables, the Form Page Wizard formats the page using a technique that causes text to appear exactly as shown—ignoring the normal rules of Web page formatting such as wrapping text around the right margin. This technique is useful when you want to use spaces to line up text.

The disadvantage to this approach is that the text is shown exactly as it appears, even if it scrolls off the right edge of the browser window. To avoid this problem, create forms that don't use tables within the FrontPage editor rather than relying on the wizard.

Exercises

Challenge your knowledge of FrontPage 2002 and the Form Page Wizard with the following exercises:

- Create a form that surveys people's opinions about at least five controversial political issues, providing multiple-choice answers. Ask a question to determine the person's political party affiliation, and save the results in a form that a database program can handle.

- Add a feedback form to one of the Webs you have already created. Save the results to a Web page so you can easily review the answers that have been submitted.

For solutions to these exercises, visit the book's official Web site at http://www.cadenhead.org/frontpage/.

PART III

Using Graphics in FrontPage 2002

Hour

HOUR 9

Display Graphics on a Page

One of the easiest things to do in FrontPage 2002 is add a picture to a page. This is fortunate because images are an essential part of the World Wide Web experience.

During this hour, you'll become an image-conscious FrontPage 2002 user. You'll lay out large pictures with paragraphs of text, and you'll line up smaller pictures with text and other page elements.

To feed the World Wide Web's enormous appetite for imagery, you'll also explore the Microsoft Design Gallery Live, a Web archive that includes hundreds of icons, buttons, drawings, and photographs you can use on your own FrontPage Webs.

Add a Graphic to a Page

In FrontPage 2002, to add a graphic to a Web page, choose Insert, Picture, From File. The Picture dialog box is displayed (see Figure 9.1).

FIGURE 9.1

Inserting a picture on a Web page.

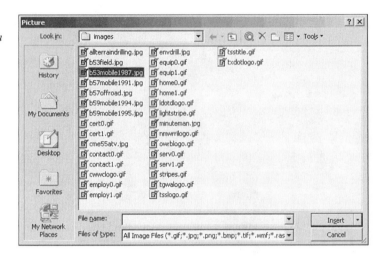

Use this dialog box to navigate to the folder that contains a graphic you want to add to a page, choose the graphic, and then click Insert. The file will be displayed as part of the page in the editing window, enabling you to see how it looks immediately.

Most pictures that are displayed on the World Wide Web are in the GIF or JPEG formats because they're supported as a built-in feature of all graphical Web browsers. A newer format, an improvement on GIF called *PNG*, is becoming the third-most popular choice for Web imagery.

One way to work with pictures is to import them into your Web before you add them to any pages:

1. Choose File, Import. The Import dialog box opens (see Figure 9.2).
2. Click the Add File button. The Add File to Import List dialog box is displayed.
3. Find the file you want to add, choose it, and then click the Open button. The file will be added to the list in the Import dialog box.

You can add more files by clicking Add File or by clicking OK to import the files you have added into your Web. When you import files, they are placed in the folder you most recently edited in the Web.

You also can add an image that isn't a part of your Web. It can be on any folder on your system or any address on the World Wide Web.

To import files from any Web address, click the From Web button in the Import dialog box. The Import Web Wizard will open, enabling you to choose a Web or Web page to import.

FIGURE 9.2

Importing pictures into a Web.

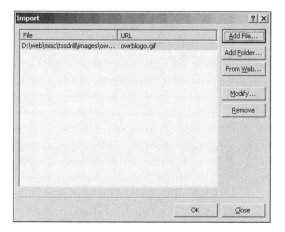

If you use pictures that are not part of your current Web, when you first save the page that contains the picture, the Save Embedded Files dialog box opens (see Figure 9.3).

FIGURE 9.3

Saving inserted pictures into a Web.

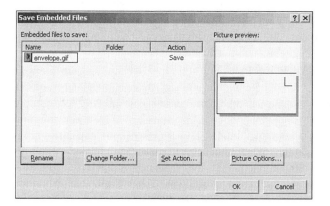

FrontPage makes copies of these pictures and saves them in the Web. Click Rename to give a picture a new name or Change Folder to choose the folder where it will be stored. Click OK to copy these pictures into the Web.

Another good reason to work with copies of common images is that FrontPage 2002 can make changes to images. As you see during Hour 10, "Create and Edit Graphics for Your Web," FrontPage can edit images directly to alter their quality and size. By keeping originals outside of any Webs, you prevent them from being modified.

Align a Picture on a Page

After you add a picture to a page, you can determine how it should be displayed in relation to everything else on the page.

To make changes to how a picture is displayed, select the picture in the editing window, right-click it, and then choose Picture Properties from the shortcut menu that appears. The Picture Properties dialog box opens (see Figure 9.4).

FIGURE 9.4

Changing how a picture is displayed.

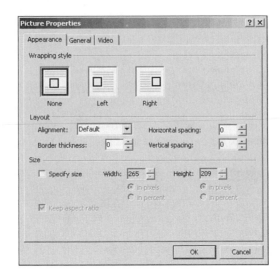

Click the Appearance tab to bring it to the front. This tab determines the display size of the picture, how it is arranged with other elements on a Web page, and whether it has a border.

On a Web page, large pictures are generally aligned in one of three ways:

- *Left alignment*—The picture appears to the left of the text and other page elements that follow (like the Left Wrapping Style in Figure 9.4).
- *Right alignment*—The picture appears to the right of the text and other page elements that follow (like the Right Wrapping Style in Figure 9.4).
- *Top alignment*—The picture appears above everything that follows.

The easiest of these three to lay out is the third option: placing the picture above the following part of the page. To do this, place the cursor to the right of a picture in the editing window and press Enter to begin a new paragraph or press Shift+Enter to insert a line break.

Default alignment arranges the picture between text and other page elements, which is shown as the None Wrapping Style in Figure 9.4. The bottom edge of the picture is lined up with the bottom edge of the text.

Figure 9.5 shows two Web pages that are identical in every way but one: the picture of a city square has been set to a different alignment.

FIGURE **9.5**

Viewing two alignments of the same picture.

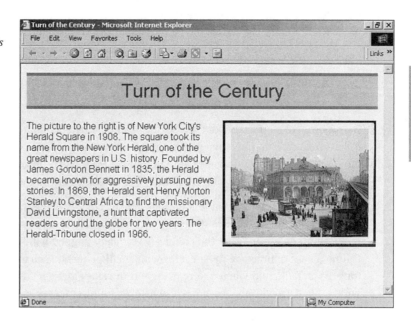

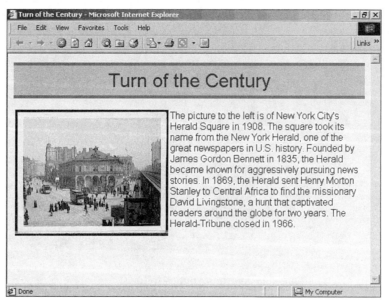

9

The pictures are set to either right or left alignment on the pages in Figure 9.5. This alignment controls the layout of the text that follows.

Left alignment causes the picture to appear to the left of the text that follows it on the page. Right alignment causes the picture to appear to the right.

On a Web page, text follows a picture if the picture was inserted in one of two places:

- A cursor position closer to the top of the page than the text
- A cursor position to the left of the text on the same line

If you become confused about the cursor position where a picture has been added, the easiest remedy is to move the picture using cut-and-paste. Press Ctrl+X to delete the picture and add it to the Windows Clipboard, place your cursor in front of the text that should follow the picture, and press Ctrl+V to paste it back to the page.

The remaining picture alignment options are selected by using the Alignment drop-down box in the Picture Properties dialog box. Options such as Top, Middle, Absolute Middle, and Bottom determine how the picture is vertically aligned with the page elements that follow. These options are most useful with small pictures, such as icons and menu buttons. By default, and when you're using left or right alignment, the top edge of a picture will be lined up with the top edge of whatever follows: text or another picture.

Figure 9.6 shows four "walking man" icons followed by lines of text. A box surrounds each icon to show exactly how big the picture is.

FIGURE 9.6

Aligning a picture vertically.

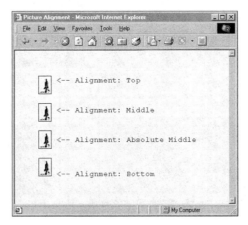

These alignments control layout as follows:

- Top alignment lines up the picture with the top of the following text.
- Bottom alignment lines up the bottom of the picture with the bottom of the text.

- Middle alignment lines up the middle of the picture with the bottom of the text.
- Absolute Middle alignment lines up the middle of the picture with the middle of the text.

You can use these and other vertical alignment options with text, images, or anything else that is narrow enough to be displayed on a page side-by-side with a picture.

If using these alignments to arrange text and pictures isn't sufficient, you can also place page elements within the cells of a table, as described during Hour 7, "Organize a Page with Lists and Tables."

Add Hyperlinks and Descriptions to a Picture

A common use for pictures on a Web page is to add hyperlinks to them. To do so, follow these steps:

1. Select the picture in the editing window. Small boxes appear at the corners and sides of the picture.
2. Right-click the picture.
3. Choose Hyperlink from the shortcut menu that appears. The Insert Hyperlink dialog box is displayed (see Figure 9.7).

FIGURE 9.7

Adding a hyperlink to a picture.

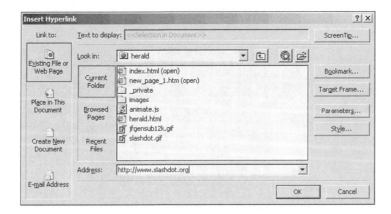

Hyperlinks are added in the same manner that they're associated with elements of a Web page. You can specify the URL of a site on the World Wide Web or pick a file that's on your own system.

If you are linking to a file on your system rather than an address on the World Wide Web, the linked file should be part of your Web.

Add Alternative Text

Providing a text description of each picture is important for making your Webs more usable. When a page is being downloaded, the text description is shown in the area that will be occupied by the picture. If the picture is a menu button or part of a link bar, this text enables people to use the picture's function before the picture is downloaded. If you're using a 28.8Kbps or slower Internet connection, you've probably done this many times to get to the page you wanted before the pictures finished loading at glacial speed.

Also, text descriptions are the only way a nonvisual Web browser can make any sense of hyperlinked images. If images are required to navigate your Web, each image should have text that describes its purpose.

Figure 9.8 shows how a Web page looks before the images have been loaded to replace the text descriptions. The text for Interests, Photo Album, and Favorites is shown next to icons with a square, circle, and triangle. These are all part of a link bar—FrontPage 2002 automatically creates descriptions for them—and they have active hyperlinks associated with them.

FIGURE 9.8

Viewing a Web page using descriptions in place of pictures.

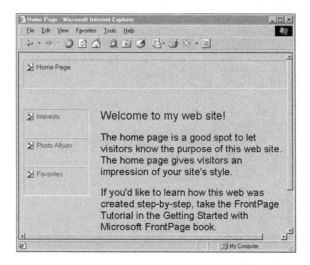

To add a description to a picture, select the picture and right-click it, and then choose Picture Properties from the shortcut menu that appears. The Picture Properties dialog box is displayed.

Click the General tab to bring it to the front. Enter a description of the graphic in the Text text box (see Figure 9.9) and click OK.

FIGURE 9.9

*Adding a description
to a picture.*

Text text box

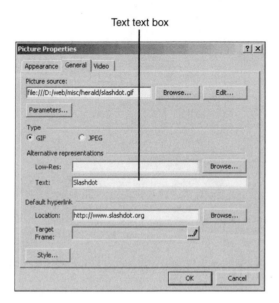

One of the ways to improve the usability of the Webs you design is to turn off pictures in your Web browser and try to use your site. Without descriptions for pictures, you might not be able to use the site at all.

To turn off picture display in Internet Explorer 5:

1. Choose Tools, Internet Options. The Internet Options dialog box opens (see Figure 9.10).
2. Click the Advanced tab to bring it to the front.
3. Scroll the Settings list until you find a Show Pictures check box.
4. Remove the check and click OK.

FIGURE 9.10.

Turning off picture display in Internet Explorer 5.

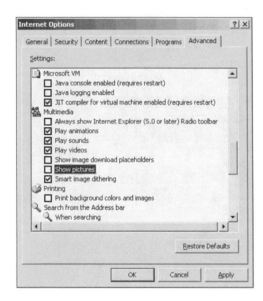

Pictures will not be displayed for all Web pages you load after that point, although some pages in your cache will still come up with graphics.

You can turn picture display back on by selecting the Show Pictures check box.

Choose Between GIF, JPEG, and PNG Graphics

Most images on the World Wide Web are in the Graphics Interchange Format (GIF) or Joint Photographic Experts Group (JPEG) format. A third format, Portable Network Graphics (PNG), has become more popular in recent years as a substitute for GIF.

JPEG files, which usually have the .jpg file extension, use a data-compression algorithm that shrinks the file size (and more importantly, the download time) at the expense of image quality. When you save a JPEG file, you must decide how to balance these two factors.

Because of the data compression, JPEG is usually the format chosen to display complex images with a large number of colors. JPEG files are often good for displaying scanned photographs that don't have large areas of solid colors, even when the file sizes of the images have been greatly compressed.

GIF files have the .gif file extension and are often the best choice for simpler images with fewer colors. You can't display more than 256 colors in a GIF picture, so if a photograph is to be displayed as a GIF, it must first be reduced so that no more than 256 different colors appear in the image.

Despite the reduction in colors, GIF pictures often look much better than JPEG files for photographs and other images. The problem with displaying a large, multicolor GIF file on the Web is that it takes much longer to download than a corresponding JPEG of the same image. For this reason, GIF files are normally used with small images that don't have a large number of colors, sometimes even eight or fewer.

GIF is much better than JPEG at handling images with large areas of a single color. Because of the way the JPEG data-compression algorithm saves file space, wavy lines will appear along the edges of any solid blocks of color, making the image appear more blurry.

The link bar buttons in each of FrontPage 2002's themes are GIF files. Many of them use solid colors and do not take up a lot of room on a page, so GIF is the better choice.

> The Reports view will keep track of the download time required for the pages on your Web. You can use this to see when a page might need some JPEGs instead of GIF files to speed things up.

A third format that's becoming more popular on the World Wide Web is *PNG*, which stands for *Portable Network Graphics*. PNG was introduced as an enhanced alternative to the GIF format.

> The PNG format was created in response to a 1994 announcement by CompuServe that it would begin charging royalties for some uses of the GIF format. Unisys claimed that the GIF format violated a file compression patent it owned, so PNG was created to be a legally secure public standard for image files.

PNG images have the .png filename extension. They're often used in the same way as GIF files, but PNG also can support thousands of colors and can be used as an alternative to the JPEG format.

Past versions of PNG were supported by Web browser plug-ins—programs that are downloaded and installed separately from a browser and that enhance its functionality. Versions 4.0 and later of Netscape Navigator and Microsoft Internet Explorer can display PNG files without a plug-in, as can the current Opera Web browser.

Add Clip Art to a Page

FrontPage 2002 includes clip art—images you can freely use on your own Webs. To find and add clip art to a page, choose Insert, Picture, Clip Art.

The first time you use FrontPage's clip art feature, you will be asked whether Microsoft Clip Organizer should search for graphics and multimedia files on your system and create a catalog of them. Setting up this catalog enables you to add graphics to your Web from the organizer, but it's a time-consuming task that will also catalog a lot of pictures and multimedia that would not be useful on a Web.

After you decide whether to use the Clip Organizer, the Insert Clip Art task pane will open alongside the editing window (see Figure 9.11).

Search text box

FIGURE 9.11

Finding clip art to insert on a page.

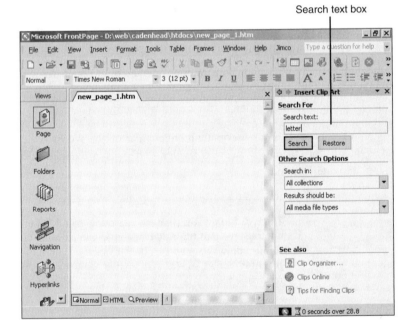

Clip art is arranged according to more than a dozen section headings. If you know what you're looking for, you can use the search feature to view only the clip art related to that topic.

Enter a topic in the Search text box and click Search. A thumbnail drawing of each matching picture is displayed alongside a button.

To add a clip art picture to your Web, click the picture in the Insert Clip Art task pane.

A copy of the picture will be added to the page. You can resize it and edit its properties just as you can with any other image in your Web.

When you save the page, the Save Embedded Files dialog box is displayed with a list of all clip art added to the page. Use this to select the format in which to save the graphic in your Web: GIF, JPEG, or PNG.

When you select a GIF file, you can configure the picture to be displayed in an interlaced pattern. *Interlacing* displays a picture as a series of increasingly focused images. If that definition is itself a little blurry, think of a set of binoculars that are completely out of focus when you first look into them. As you adjust the focus, the thing you're looking at changes from a blur of colors into an increasingly sharp image. Interlacing is similar to that; it displays an image as if you were bringing it into focus. On the other hand, a *non-interlaced* GIF displays the image in successive horizontal lines as it downloads them, so you'll see the top half of a picture in full before the bottom half arrives.

Clip art that's saved as a JPEG file must have a quality percentage indicated. The scale ranges from 1 (compressed as much as possible) to 100 (no compression at all). The default is 75 percent.

A JPEG file that is compressed loses quality every time it is compressed again. Whenever you create JPEG graphics, you should keep an original file that isn't compressed at all—as the FrontPage Clip Organizer does. This enables you to return to the original and compress it at a different quality.

One thing you'll want to do often with clip art is resize it. All the pictures on a Web page can be displayed at different sizes, whether it's larger, smaller, or even distorted so that the width is at a different scale than the height.

To resize a picture, first select the picture by clicking it in the editing window. Boxes, called *selection handles*, will appear at the corners of the picture and the middle of each side, as shown in Figure 9.12.

To change the size, place your mouse over one of the boxes for a moment. Your cursor will change into a left/right, up/down, or diagonal arrow. Drag the box to a new location to make the picture larger or smaller.

Selection handles

FIGURE 9.12
*Altering a picture's
display size.*

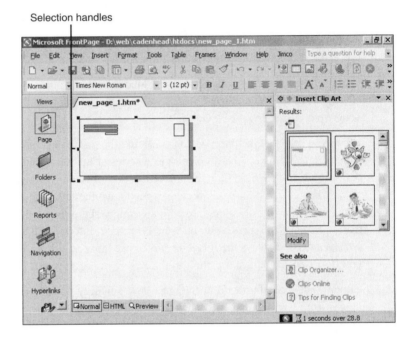

When you are resizing graphics in FrontPage 2002, you will have much better results when you make them smaller rather than making them larger. Enlarged graphics often end up with jagged edges, a boxy appearance, and other visual glitches.

You can change the picture's size in pixel increments or as a percentage of the original. This does not alter the actual picture, so an image displayed at 10 percent of its normal size still takes the same amount of time to download.

If you can't find suitable clip art that's included with FrontPage 2002, you can find more pictures, photographs, and movie files in Microsoft's online version of the gallery.

To view this giant library of clip art that's free for use in your FrontPage Webs, choose Insert, Picture, Clip Art, and then click the Clips Online hyperlink in the Insert Clip Art task pane.

Your Web browser will open at the Microsoft Design Gallery Live site, where you can browse through it by category or search for specific keywords. Clip art you select will be imported automatically into FrontPage 2002.

Workshop: Use Clip Art in a Business Report

This hour has introduced you to FrontPage 2002's gallery of clip art, so it's only fitting that the workshop uses it in the production of a company's annual report. Produce the first page of the annual report using the following:

- A large image to the left of the introductory text
- A smaller image that's placed somewhere to the right of a paragraph of text in the body

The images you choose aren't important, although searching for "business" and "money" is likely to yield more businesslike results in the Design Gallery Live than "whipped cream" or "Tyra Banks."

The text isn't important either. Although you're free to research a company and summarize its financial condition as of the most recent year, you're even freer to copy the same text over and over again into several different paragraphs.

Solution

Figure 9.13 shows one solution to this workshop. The page has two pictures: a large image of increasingly smaller men at increasingly smaller desks and an image of a compass.

FIGURE 9.13

The annual report of Quick Brown Fox, Inc.

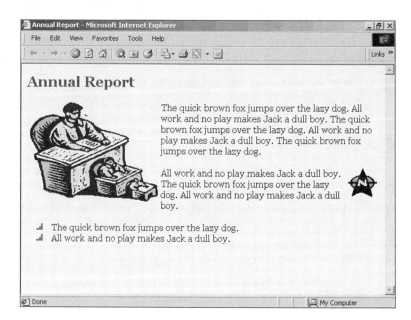

Because most clip art available in FrontPage 2002 is large, the Picture Properties dialog box was used to shrink each image to different degrees.

Each picture was added from clip art and edited by selecting the picture, right-clicking it, and choosing Picture Properties.

The Picture Properties dialog box also was used to set the desk men to the left and the compass to the right.

All the pictures were saved as GIF files. Download time could have been reduced by making the desk men image a JPEG file, but because it contains so many solid colors, it's a poor choice for the JPEG format. The image would have appeared much fuzzier at the edge of all solid areas.

Working with clip art in this way makes it easier to produce a page.

Summary

This hour enabled you to set your sights higher on your FrontPage Webs.

By looking into the subject of image handling, you've learned how to make pages and entire Webs more visually compelling. You saw how to add pictures, align them with other parts of a page, and change how they're displayed. You took a gander at the three most common formats for graphics files: GIF, JPEG, and PNG. Finally, you found a sight for sore eyes in the FrontPage 2002 Design Gallery Live, a collection of pictures you can easily add to your own pages.

During the next hour, you'll enhance the presentation of pictures on your Webs by editing them within FrontPage.

Q&A

Q Is there a limit to how much you can expand a graphic? I'd like to create a tiny, all-brown GIF and stretch it to cover a large part of a page.

A There's no reason you can't do that. One trick that Web designers do is to use small, one- or two-color GIFs as vertical or horizontal borders, stripes, and other parts of a page. They load almost as quickly as the text does.

Q Are there any restrictions to how I use pictures from the Design Gallery Live in my own Webs?

A At the time of this writing, Microsoft's license for Design Gallery Live states that you can use the pictures as part of your own FrontPage Webs, newsletters, brochures, postcards, and other printed materials. You cannot make them available as part of a library of clip art offered to others.

The licensing terms for Microsoft's clip art might have changed by the time you read this, so you should check the Design Gallery Live site for the most current guidelines.

Exercises

Challenge your knowledge of FrontPage 2002 pictures with the following exercises:

- Add a few images into FrontPage 2002 from Microsoft's World Wide Web version of the Design Gallery Live. Create a Web page that contains these images, which might need to be displayed at a smaller size to fit on a page.
- Experiment with different alignments for several different small pictures on the same line, such as arrows, icons, or symbols taken from clip art.

For solutions to these exercises, visit the book's official Web site at `http://www.cadenhead.org/frontpage/`.

9

Hour **10**

Create and Edit Graphics for Your Web

For most of the World Wide Web's development, images displayed on the Web have been created with drawing and editing software, and Web pages have been created in an entirely different manner, such as with Web editing software like FrontPage, Macromedia Dreamweaver, Claris Home Page, and others.

FrontPage 2002 blurs the line between the two types of software by offering image-editing features. Many tasks that used to require specialized graphics software, such as Adobe Photoshop, can now be done within FrontPage.

You can make several changes to an existing image file, including its size, contrast, and brightness. If the image is in the GIF format, you can make part of it transparent and add editable text to the image. You can also crop the image, keeping the parts you want while discarding the rest.

Although these are some of the simplest features of a professional graphics tool, when you combine them with the clip art that is available in FrontPage 2002 and with background pictures or colors, you can quickly improve the look of your own Webs.

Work with Graphics

Most of FrontPage 2002's image-manipulation features can be found on the Picture tool-bar, which shows up whenever you select a picture in Page view. (You also can make it appear by clicking View, Toolbars, Pictures.) This toolbar is shown in Figure 10.1. (you might see it as a docked toolbar along the bottom edge of the editing window).

FIGURE 10.1

The Picture toolbar.

Hover your mouse over each of the buttons to find out its purpose. These buttons are organized into several different groupings. One group contains four buttons with pairs of right triangles on them. These buttons are used to rotate or flip the picture. You can rotate a picture to the left and right, and flip it horizontally and vertically.

Another group of four buttons contains icons that look like either a half moon or the sun. These control the contrast and brightness of the picture—two things that any television owner should be familiar with (unless you have a much better TV than mine).

The black-and-white button turns a color image into a monochrome one, and the bevel button makes a photograph or other picture look like a 3-D button by giving it shadowed edges.

Because these buttons cause instantaneous changes to a picture, you might get the im-pression that they just change the way it's displayed. (During the last hour, you altered a picture's display size without actually changing the picture itself.) However, these but-tons do make permanent changes to a picture. You can undo these changes before the page or your Web has been saved, and then use the toolbar's Restore button to return the picture to its last saved version.

You also can use this toolbar to change the size of a picture permanently. If you have resized a picture's display area and you want to make this the actual size of the picture, click the Resize button.

Crop a Picture

As you're working with drawings, photographs, and other images in FrontPage 2002, you might decide that the shape of a picture doesn't fit with the layout of a page. You can reshape a picture either by changing its dimensions and clicking Resample or by cropping it. *Cropping* is a photography term for keeping a portion of an image and dis-carding the rest.

To crop a picture, select it in the editing window and click the Crop button on the Picture toolbar, which is identified in Figure 10.2. A thin border will appear that's similar to the one used for imagemap hotspots. In Figure 10.2, a cropping border appears on a drawing of a stereo boom box.

FIGURE 10.2

Cropping an area of a picture.

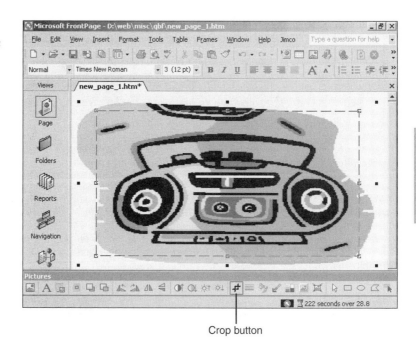

Crop button

When the picture is cropped, everything within the border will be saved and the rest will be deleted. In Figure 10.2, the cropping removes the edges of the background behind the boom box.

To crop a picture, drag the handles around the border until it displays the portion of the picture you want to keep, then click the Crop button again (or press the Enter key). The picture is cropped and redisplayed.

Add Text to a Picture

Using the picture-editing tools in FrontPage, you can manually add text to any picture that's in GIF format. This text appears on top of the picture, so you'll need one of the image-editing buttons on the Picture toolbar.

To add text to a picture, start by clicking the picture so that the Picture toolbar appears, and follow with the Text button—an icon on the Pictures toolbar with the letter A. A border appears on top of the picture, and you can begin entering text with your keyboard. You can do all of the following to format this text:

- Adjust the borders so that there's more room for the text
- Use all the text-editing buttons on the Standard and Formatting toolbars, including the font selection, font size, and bold/italics/underline buttons
- Click Format, Font to select a font, color, size, and special effects

If you try to add text to a picture that isn't in GIF format, FrontPage 2002 asks whether you want to convert the picture to a GIF file. This might not be feasible with some large pictures that are in JPG format because GIF files of comparable height and width take up much more disk space. However, there's no way in FrontPage to add text to JPG or PNG files.

Text that you add can be moved and resized at any time. It is combined with the background GIF when the Web is saved or published.

Figure 10.3 shows text being added to a drawing of a globe from the Microsoft Design Gallery Live, and the text button that was used to add it.

FIGURE 10.3

Adding text to a picture.

Text button

Make Part of a Graphic Transparent

Another special effect you can use only with GIF files is transparency. A transparent picture has one color that has been chosen as the invisible color. All parts of the picture that are this color will not be displayed, exposing the background behind the picture.

To add transparency to a picture, select it in Page view and click the Set Transparent Color button on the Pictures toolbar. FrontPage 2002 will ask whether the picture should be converted to GIF, if it isn't already in that format. After you click the Set Transparent Color button, the cursor will turn into an eraser-tipped pencil with a small arrow at one end. Place this arrow over the color that you want to make transparent and click once. This color will vanish as if it were deleted from the picture.

> To remove transparency, you can click Set Transparent Color and select the invisible area of the picture. You also can open the Picture Properties dialog box and uncheck the Transparency check box on the Appearance tab.

Making a color transparent doesn't actually change the picture's colors—it just uses a feature supported in the GIF format. If you remove all transparency later, you'll see that the original color has been retained.

Transparency is especially useful when you're working with graphical page backgrounds. For example, Figure 10.4 shows two images of cows over a striped background. The cow on the left has a white background that covers up the page's background. The cow on the right uses transparency to more closely blend in with its surroundings.

10

FIGURE 10.4

Working with transparent and nontransparent pictures.

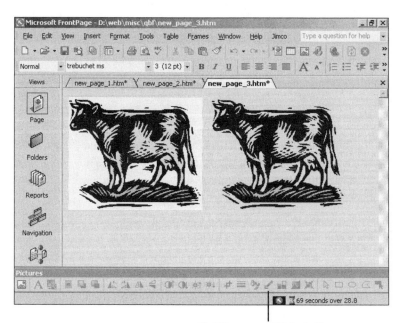

Set Transparent Color button

The Set Transparent Color button shown in Figure 10.4 can be used to set or change the current transparent color. If you try to use transparency with a graphic that isn't in the GIF format, FrontPage 2002 will convert it to GIF before enabling a transparent color to be selected.

Select a Background for Your Page

One of the ways you can dress up a Web page is to give it a background. The background can be either a solid color or a picture that's loaded from a graphics file.

To add or change a page's background, choose Format, Background. The Page Properties dialog box opens with the Background tab on top (see Figure 10.5).

FIGURE 10.5

Selecting a page background.

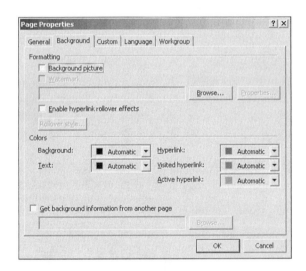

To use a background picture, select the Background Picture check box and click the Browse button. The Select Background Picture dialog box opens, enabling you to find and choose any file on your system. A background picture must be in the GIF, JPG, or PNG format.

You can use a Web address to specify the background picture, but this causes FrontPage 2002 to use a graphic that isn't part of your Web. If the graphic is removed from that URL, it will stop appearing on your pages. For that reason, it's better to make a copy of the image on your system—if you have permission to do so—and work directly with that copy.

If the contents of a Web page are larger than a background picture, which is often the case, the picture is displayed multiple times under the contents of a page. This is called *tiling* because each copy of the graphic is like an identical tile on a kitchen floor.

If you would like the background to be displayed once, select the Watermark check box in the Page Properties dialog box. The background won't scroll along with the rest of the page.

To choose a background color instead of a picture, deselect the Background Picture check box and click the Background drop-down box. The standard FrontPage color selection dialog box appears with 16 basic colors to choose from. If none of these fits what you're looking for, click the More Colors button and a more advanced color dialog box will appear, as shown in Figure 10.6.

FIGURE 10.6

Choosing a background color for a page.

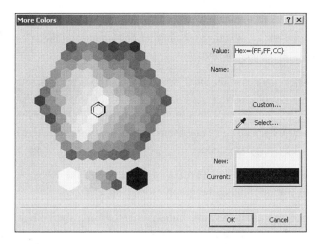

10

You can select one of the colors shown in the More Colors dialog box or enter a color's hexadecimal value in the Value box. You also can click the Custom button to open a third color selection dialog box with even more options.

> Knowledge of hexadecimal values is completely unnecessary to using FrontPage 2002 because you can pick colors in other ways. For the curious: Hexadecimal values are numbers on a base-16 system, which means there are 16 different single-digit numbers. They're often useful in computer programs because you can represent values up to 255 in only two digits. The first 20 hexadecimal numbers are 0, 1, 2, 3, 4, 5, 6, 7, 8, 9, A, B, C, D, E, F, 10, 11, 12, and 13. Microsoft could have impressed some people in the hexadecimal crowd by naming its software FrontPage 7D2.

The color you select is displayed underneath the contents of the page.

When a page has both a background color and a picture selected, the color will be replaced by the picture when the page is fully loaded. To cause only the color to display, deselect the Background Picture check box in the Page Properties dialog box.

If you want to designate a background for an entire Web, it's much easier to create a new theme with the desired background and apply that theme to the Web. The theme will also be available for use in other projects, unlike a background that is selected manually.

Workshop: Create Graphical Menu Buttons

Two features of FrontPage 2002 make it easy to turn graphics into buttons: beveling and adding editable text.

This hour's workshop is to create three graphical buttons for a Web. Each button should have the same shape, whether rectangular or square, and there should be enough room to place a text label on each one.

To find images for these buttons, search for clip art. If you're connected to the Internet, you can extend the search to include the Microsoft Design Gallery Live. Images selected from the online gallery will be stored in FrontPage 2002's version for permanent use. Pick three buttons with the same theme: animals, business, sports, the business of animal sports, or whatever you choose.

In addition to the Bevel and Text buttons, use any of the other elements on the Picture toolbar that can help make the graphics look appealing.

When you're done, put the three buttons together in a shared border for a new Web, and create pages that are linked to each button.

Solution

Figure 10.7 shows a Web page containing three buttons from the Microsoft Design Gallery Live online archive, which is updated monthly with new material.

As you've worked on your own buttons, you've probably learned one of the limitations of the bevel feature: It doesn't work well with pictures that are either too dark or too light.

By adjusting the contrast and brightness of a picture, you can make it more suitable for the bevel effect. In Figure 10.7, the top button needed to be brightened before the bevel effect could be applied.

After the pictures were resampled at their new size, a text label describing a page on the Web was added to each of them. The buttons were placed within a shared border to make them accessible throughout the site.

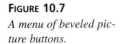

FIGURE 10.7

A menu of beveled picture buttons.

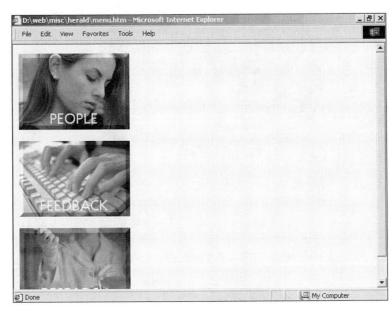

Summary

Now that you've beveled some buttons and cropped some clips, you've seen what FrontPage 2002's image-editing features can accomplish. Although the resizing, editing, and conversion features of FrontPage aren't on par with professional image-editing tools, they place some of the most common tasks within easy reach.

Making a transparent GIF, which wasn't even offered in most graphics software packages a few years ago, is immediately available from the Page view.

Applying a background picture or color to a page is another way to dress up a Web. By combining editing with the Design Gallery Live and the many graphics packaged with each theme, you can create a fully graphical Web without ever leaving FrontPage 2002.

Q&A

Q I've been working with a graphic for a while and the edges are starting to look jagged. What can I do about this?

A Any picture you edit within FrontPage 2002 is going to change each time you save or resample it. If you've altered the size several times, you'll lose some clarity each time as FrontPage tries to anti-alias the picture.

Anti-aliasing is a graphic design term for adjusting the edges of an image so that it blends in more smoothly with the background. FrontPage can't always anti-alias smoothly if pictures are repeatedly resized. If possible, revert to the original version of the picture and redo your edits to get better clarity.

Exercises

Challenge your knowledge of FrontPage 2002's image-editing features with the following exercises:

- Using the Design Gallery Live as source material, create buttons, a background picture, and other graphics that can be incorporated into your own modified theme.
- Paste a picture onto a Web page four separate times, and then crop each one so they combine to form a single copy of the picture. Try to line up the pieces with each other so that they look like a single picture.

For solutions to these exercises, visit the book's official Web site at http://www.cadenhead.org/frontpage/.

HOUR **11**

Add Links to a Graphic with Imagemaps

On your FrontPage 2002 Webs, a common use for a picture is to associate a hyperlink with it, enabling a Web to be navigated in a more visual manner than clicking on text.

Using a new type of Web element called an imagemap, you can add more than one hyperlink to a single picture.

Imagemaps enable you to associate specific portions of a picture with different hyperlinks. You can use them to create menus, maps, and other complex navigational features.

During this hour, you'll create and edit imagemaps using FrontPage 2002's built-in drawing tools.

Create an Imagemap

There are two kinds of imagemaps you can use on a Web page: client-side maps and server-side maps. A client-side map is handled by the Web browser, whereas a server-side map is handled by the browser and a Web server working together.

FrontPage 2002 supports client-side maps, which can be handled entirely by adding an imagemap to a Web page. Server-side maps require special access to the server that will deliver the page.

When you select a picture on a page in the FrontPage editing window, a Pictures toolbar is added to the FrontPage 2002 interface. Normally, this toolbar appears along the bottom edge, but as with all Microsoft Office toolbars, it's highly mobile. You can drag it to any edge of the interface or even off the interface entirely.

Figure 11.1 shows the Pictures toolbar as a separate window.

FIGURE 11.1

Editing pictures in FrontPage 2002.

The Rectangular Hotspot button shown in Figure 11.1 is one of three buttons that you can use to add a hyperlink to a region of a picture. The other two are the Circular Hotspot and Polygonal Hotspot buttons, which are next to the Rectangular Hotspot on the toolbar.

This group of buttons is used to create imagemaps, in which each special hyperlink is associated with only a portion of a picture instead of the whole thing.

Imagemaps are commonly used for the following purposes on a Web page:

- To add hyperlinks to an image that serves as a link bar
- To add hyperlinks that describe a specific part of an image
- To add hyperlinks that pinpoint specific regions of a graphic, such as a map

When you're associating an imagemap with a picture, you designate specific regions of the picture that will be associated with hyperlinks. These regions—also called *hotspots*—are created using the hotspot buttons on the Pictures toolbar.

Rectangular and elliptical hotspots are defined by dragging your mouse over part of the picture:

- Click a hotspot button on the Pictures toolbar—either Rectangular Hotspot or Circular Hotspot.
- Click a spot on the picture and hold down your mouse.
- Drag your mouse to another spot and release it.

As you drag your mouse around the picture, FrontPage will draw an outline of the area the hotspot will occupy. When the hotspot takes up the desired part of the picture, release the mouse. The Insert Hyperlink dialog box opens so that you can associate a Web address with it. The hotspot can link to anything a hyperlink can—a file in your Web, a file on your system, or a URL address on the World Wide Web.

FrontPage 2002 draws a hotspot as a thick border that overlays a picture in the editing window. Figure 11.2 shows a hotspot over the word News on a picture.

FIGURE 11.2

Defining a hotspot on a picture.

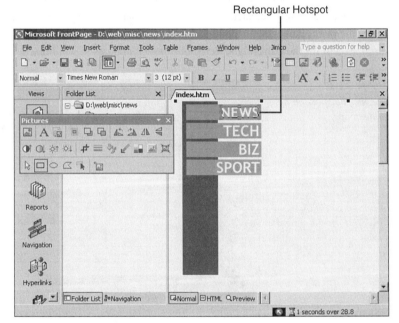

Rectangular Hotspot

11

To define a polygon-shaped hotspot, select a picture, click the Polygonal Hotspot button and then click once on the picture at each intersection of the polygon. When you finally define the last intersection, finish the hotspot with a double-click. The Insert Hyperlink dialog box opens, which you can use to associate a hyperlink with this hotspot.

After you associate a link with a hotspot, you can change it by double-clicking it.

Some imagemaps will have a default hyperlink that is used if a visitor clicks the picture in an area that doesn't have a hotspot. To set a default hyperlink, right-click the picture and choose the Picture Properties dialog box.

> If two hotspots overlap each other, only the most recently created hotspot
> will be used in the overlapping area. A hotspot on an imagemap is limited
> to a single hyperlink.

The currently selected hotspot can be deleted by clicking the hotspot and pressing the
Delete key.

In a picture with several different hotspots, you might have trouble determining which hotspot is currently selected. The Pictures toolbar has a Highlight Hotspots button that makes
the picture invisible, leaving the hotspots behind. All hotspots show up as black outlines
except for the currently selected one, which appears in solid black, as shown in Figure 11.3.

FIGURE 11.3

Viewing hotspots on an imagemap.

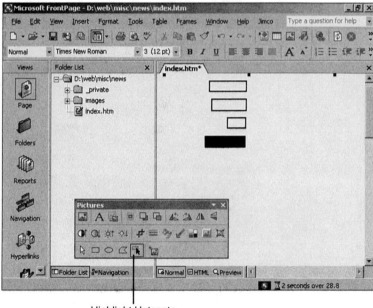

Highlight Hotspots

The Highlight Hotspots view can be used to select different hotspots for editing or deletion.

Workshop: Use Imagemaps to Describe a Picture

This is one of the shorter hours in the book, so it's a good opportunity to tackle a more
challenging project.

Imagemaps can be an informational tool in addition to a navigational one. For this hour's workshop, you will add a map of an area to a Web page and place an imagemap on top of it. Each link in the imagemap will be associated with a city's official Web site.

To find a map you can use, the book's official Web site at http://www.cadenhead.org/ frontpage includes one on the Hour 11 page.

Solution

By combining frames and imagemaps, you can make a lot of information available on your Webs in an easy-to-use format.

To add a map to a Web page and associate cities on the map with their official home pages, do the following:

1. Open FrontPage and create a new Web page.

2. Import a picture of a map into your Web.

3. Add the map to a page.

4. Select the picture. If the Pictures toolbar does not appear, choose View, Toolbars, Pictures.

5. Click the Rectangular Hotspot button.

6. Click a spot on the map near a city name and drag your mouse until the whole city name is covered with a hotspot outline, and then release the mouse. The Insert Hyperlink dialog box opens.

7. Enter the Web address of the city in the Address text box.

By adding hotspots for each of the cities on your map, you create a visual way to find local information.

If you can't find the official Web page for each city, try the Google search engine at http://www.google.com. Because of the way that Google ranks search results, a city's official site is likely to be one of the first things that comes up when you search for its name.

Figure 11.4 shows a Web page that displays information about points on a map.

The finished product can be viewed on the book's World Wide Web (http://www. cadenhead.org/frontpage) on the Hour 11 page.

11

FIGURE **11.4**

An interactive map Web page.

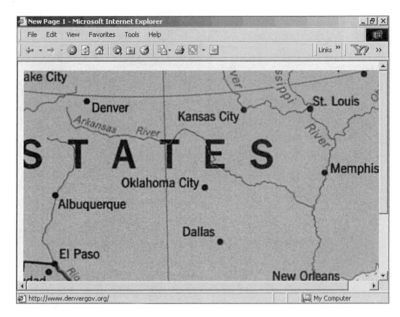

Summary

During this hour you turned a picture on a FrontPage 2002 Web into an imagemap, dividing the picture into different regions that contain different hyperlinks.

Imagemaps are useful for site navigation and other visual ways to request information on a Web page. You create them in FrontPage 2002 using buttons on the Pictures toolbar, which appears when you select an image for editing.

Q&A

Q I've seen imagemaps that display the cursor's position on the browser's status line. How is this done?

A Those imagemaps rely on an older form of Web imagemaps that was handled by the Web server. The imagemaps you created during this hour are called *client-side* maps because the Web browser that displays the map does all the work of identifying hotspots with hyperlinks.

The other type of imagemap is the *server-side* map. The Web server that sends the page to a browser must receive mouse clicks on the image and must know what to do with them. Client-side maps are much easier to create and maintain because they don't require special access to a Web server.

Exercises

Challenge your knowledge of FrontPage 2002 imagemaps with the following exercises:

- Explore the images folders of some past FrontPage Webs you have created. When you find one that contains an image used for a link bar, copy that image to a new folder and use it to manually create a navigation bar using an imagemap.

- If you have a photo of yourself that's in electronic form, create a Web page in which your various body parts are all hotspots (hubba hubba!). The hyperlinks you associate with these body parts are up to you, but remember that there might be children visiting your page.

For solutions to these exercises, visit the book's official Web site at http://www.cadenhead.org/frontpage/.

11

HOUR 12

Animate a Web Page

When you're viewing pages on the World Wide Web, few things grab your attention better than animated graphics. It can be difficult for static text and still pictures to compete with the moving graphics on banner ads and other trickery, such as spinning logos and dancing hamsters.

FrontPage 2002 makes it easy to add special effects to your own Webs.

During this hour, you'll learn how to create animation effects, such as transitions that appear when a new page is loaded and buttons that change when a mouse passes over them. You'll use Dynamic HTML to make text and pictures on your pages swoop down from above, hop into position one piece at a time, and bounce elastically into place. You'll also learn how to place animated graphics on your pages.

The material should be fairly…well…moving.

Add Animation and Other Special Effects to a Page

You might not realize it, but you've already learned how to work with one type of animation in FrontPage 2002. Adding an animated GIF file to a page is no different than adding any other picture.

Animated GIFs are the primary form of animation on the Web. Almost all nonstatic banner ads are in this format, as are many of the moving images you see on personal pages, such as spinning envelopes and other small graphics.

These GIF files are created by software that combines several GIF pictures into a single file. This file also contains information that determines the order in which to display these pictures, how much time to pause between each picture, and how often to cycle through all the pictures.

The final product is treated like a GIF within FrontPage 2002 and has the same filename extension: .gif. You can import this graphic, add it to pages, and resize its display area.

One thing you can't do within FrontPage is edit your animated GIF. You can't add beveling, adjust its contrast, or use any of the other image-editing features you learned about during Hour 10, "Create and Edit Graphics for Your Web." This is because any changes to the GIF will remove its animation and reduce it to a single picture. FrontPage prevents this from happening by graying out everything on the Picture toolbar that would damage the animated GIF.

Create a Transition Effect Between Pages

One of the easiest special effects you can add to a page in FrontPage 2002 is a *page transition*. This displays something out of the ordinary when you either load a page in your browser or leave it to load another page.

In movies, transition effects have been a staple of adventure serials such as the original *Star Wars* trilogy and *Raiders of the Lost Ark*. To move from one scene to another, filmmakers use transitions such as the wipe, which replaces a new scene for the old one as if it were wiped on with a rag.

Figure 12.1 shows a Web page in mid-transition. Two Web pages are visible: a Turn of the Century title page and a page from the exhibit it's announcing. This is called a *circle transition* because the old page is shown in a shrinking circle until it disappears.

FIGURE 12.1

Transitioning between two Web pages with the Circle effect.

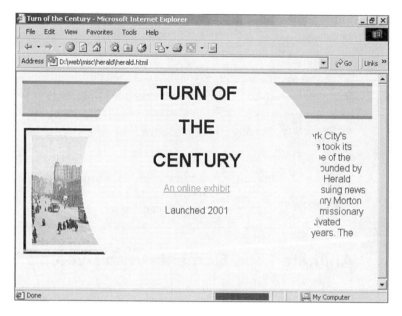

To add or remove transitions from a page, choose Format, Page Transition. The Page Transition dialog box opens (see Figure 12.2).

FIGURE 12.2

Choosing a Web page transition.

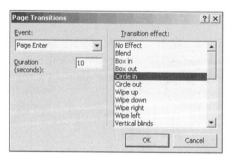

12

You can associate transitions with four different events:

- When the page first loads
- When the page is exited
- When the Web first loads
- When the Web is exited

There are 25 different page transitions you can use, each with a name that describes the special effect such as Wipe, Blend, Circle, and Checkerboard.

Some transitions are associated with a direction. For example, Wipe Right, which wipes the new page onscreen from left to right. The Random transition loads one of the other transitions at random each time the event occurs.

When you select a transition, you also can select its duration, measured in seconds. This determines how long it will take to display the effect. You can choose longer transitions, such as a 10-second or 20-second effect, but keep in mind that this slows down people who are using your Web. They might not want to wait that long between page loads.

> The easiest way to see all the transitions is to apply a Random page transition to the loading and exiting of a test page, preview the test page in a browser, and reload it repeatedly.

Animate Page Elements with Dynamic HTML

FrontPage 2002 offers another group of special effects that you apply to specific elements of a page instead of the entire thing. These effects can be associated with text, hyperlinks, and images, animating them upon such events as loading a page, clicking a link, or hovering a mouse over text or a picture.

Dynamic HTML, an extension of HTML also called DHTML, offers additional support for animation and interactivity.

> FrontPage supports Microsoft's version of Dynamic HTML, which is different than a competing implementation in Netscape Navigator. You'll have to test the FrontPage-created effects thoroughly in Netscape Navigator to make sure that they work.

To animate a picture, text, or another element on a Web page, select it and click Format, Dynamic HTML Effects. The DHTML Effects toolbar is displayed (see Figure 12.3).

FIGURE 12.3
Setting up a special effect.

You can use the menus on this toolbar to pick a special effect that will be used on the selected item. Choose an event in the On drop-down list. The other lists on the Dynamic Effects toolbar will change, depending on the kinds of special effects that are available for that event.

Many Dynamic HTML effects can be applied to text. You can cause it to move into its correct place onscreen in a variety of different ways:

- *Elastic*—The text moves from offscreen to a little bit beyond the destination, and then bounces back to the correct place.
- *Drop in by word*—The text drops into place one word at a time.
- *Fly in*—Words fly in from several different directions.
- *Hop and Wave*—Words move into place one at a time in a leisurely circular motion.
- *Wipe*—Words are drawn in from the left or top edge of the page in a wiping motion.

These effects (and others) are set to occur when an event takes place. One of these events is the loading of the page that contains the text. For hyperlinks and pictures, you can also trigger an effect based on mouse actions. You can animate a text hyperlink when it's clicked or double-clicked, and cause a picture to react when the mouse hovers above it.

Figure 12.4 shows the Dynamic HTML toolbar being used to associate the Fly in effect with a picture when the page is loaded. The direction of the flying text is also chosen— this effect can display text and other Web page elements moving in 12 different ways.

Figure 12.4

Setting up a Dynamic HTML effect.

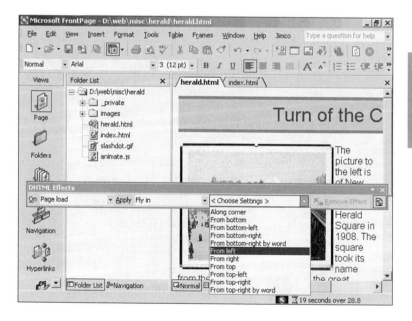

12

Create a Mouseover Picture

One of the most popular Dynamic HTML effects on the World Wide Web is the *mouseover picture*. The name comes from the way a picture changes when the mouse pointer is moved over it.

If you select the Active Graphics option when you apply a FrontPage 2002 theme, all graphical link bars function as mouseover pictures. The buttons on the bars change appearance when a mouse is in position to click them.

Before you can create this effect on your own using Dynamic HTML, you need two pictures: the original image and the changed version that will appear when a mouse is over it. The changed version can be a modified copy of the original or a different image entirely.

The easiest way to incorporate these pictures into your Web is to import them first. The original version of the picture should be added to the page in the same way any other picture is added:

1. Choose Insert, Picture, From File. The Picture dialog box opens.
2. Use the dialog box to find the picture on your system.
3. Click Insert.

The second picture is specified as a Dynamic HTML effect:

1. Click the original picture.
2. Choose Format, Dynamic HTML Effects. The DHTML Effects toolbar is displayed.
3. On the toolbar, select the Mouse over event, the Swap Picture effect, and in the Choose Settings drop-down box, select Choose Picture (see Figure 12.5). The Picture dialog box opens.

Use the Picture dialog box to find and select the changed version of the picture or another picture you want to swap.

The swapped picture should be the same size as the original. If it isn't, FrontPage 2002 will resize the picture's display area so that it fits the space available to it.

The Swap Picture effect also can be associated with a mouse-click, which enables you to create a three-image sequence of pictures: original, mouseover, and click.

Preview the page in FrontPage 2002 or a browser to see the effect.

FIGURE **12.5**

Adding a mouseover effect to a picture.

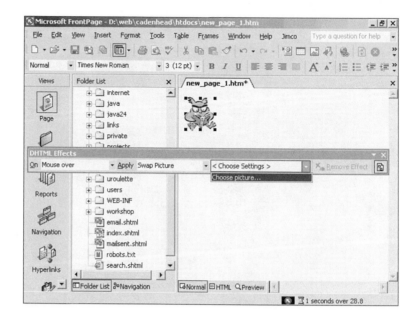

FIGURE **12.5**

Adding a mouseover effect to a picture.

Paint a Format Around a Page

Using Dynamic HTML can be a tedious process when you're applying the same effect to several different elements of a page, such as a row of navigational buttons. FrontPage 2002 has a feature that makes it much easier to copy one page element's formatting to any other: the Format Painter.

Figure 12.6 shows the Format Painter button on the Standard toolbar.

Format Painter stores the fonts, colors, special effects, and other formatting associated with a page element. To use it, select the item that has the formatting you want to duplicate and then click Format Painter. The button will be highlighted to show that it can be used for painting. Select the item that should receive the stored formatting information.

When you click the Format Painter button once, there's only enough "format paint" for a single item, so you'll have to click the button once between every copying operation.

To create an unlimited supply of "format paint," select the item that has the desired formatting, and then double-click the Format Painter button. Every item you select from that point on will use that formatting until you click the Format Painter button again.

12

Format Painter button

FIGURE 12.6

*The Format Painter
button.*

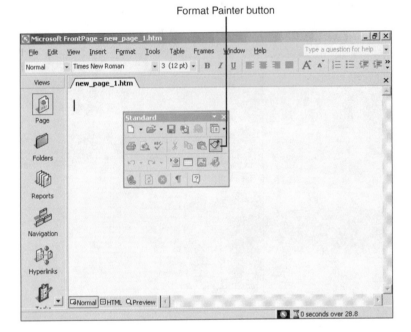

Workshop: Create an Animated E-Book

Dynamic HTML might not yet be an accepted standard like HTML, but there's a good
reason not to wait for Microsoft, Netscape, and the World Wide Web Consortium to
reach common ground: DHTML is fun to putter around with. After hours of working on
Web pages that stay exactly where you leave them, moving animated pictures and text
around ought to be an entertaining change of pace.

This hour's workshop is to do exactly that, using text from the first chapter of a public
domain novel available on the Internet.

Create an empty Web and add 5–10 new pages to it, giving each page a numbered filename (such as page1.htm, page2.htm, page3.htm, and so on).

Using a source for public domain online books such as the Project Gutenberg Web site
(http://promo.net/pg/), copy the text of a book's first chapter onto the empty pages of
your Web. Put hyperlinks at the bottom of each page so that you can read the pages of
the chapter.

When you're done with this task, create transition effects that are triggered when each
page is entered, and then preview the first page in a Web browser.

Solution

Figure 12.7 shows a sample solution created using the first chapter of *Moby Dick* by Herman Melville.

FIGURE 12.7

Creating a FrontPage Web with Dynamic HTML effects.

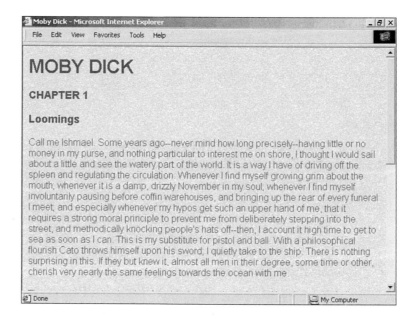

This Web can be viewed on the book's Web site at `http://www.cadenhead.org/frontpage/`—open the Hour 12 page. Each page uses the Elastic effect when the page is loaded, bouncing text in from the left.

Dynamic HTML effects are one of the more entertaining features of FrontPage 2002, offering you a chance to surprise visitors to your Webs who might not have encountered these kinds of effects before. By experimenting with the effects it offers, you should get a better idea of which ones might be suitable for your own projects.

You also should get a much better idea of how many special effects are too many.

Summary

Now that you've gone through all the motions, you shouldn't have any doubt that your FrontPage 2002 Webs can compete visually with other animated offerings on the World Wide Web.

You can use several different kinds of animation on your Webs: animated GIF pictures, page-to-page transition effects, and Dynamic HTML tricks such as elastic text, zooming pictures, and mouseover graphics.

This hour's workshop showed you many, if not all, of the animation effects that are possible in FrontPage. These effects are much livelier in person than can be conveyed in the pages of a book. No one has invented Dynamic Print yet, so the text of this chapter will remain the same. (Just imagine this paragraph flying in from the shadows of the binding and hopping into place, doing the two-dimensional version of the hokey-pokey dance...)

Q&A

Q FrontPage 2002 won't let me use Format, Dynamic HTML Effects or any other features like it—the Dynamic Effects toolbar is all grayed out and inactive. What's causing this?

A You should check whether Dynamic HTML has been deselected as a feature your Web can use. FrontPage 2002 enables developers to target a Web to a specific audience by specifying some features they can't use. Because Dynamic HTML won't work on older versions of Netscape Navigator and Microsoft Internet Explorer, you can disable it from being used on a specific project.

To check this and similar options, click Tools, Page Options to open the Page Options dialog box and then click the Compatibility tab to bring it to the front. If the Dynamic HTML check box is not selected, FrontPage 2002 prevents you from using its features in your Web.

Exercises

Challenge your knowledge of FrontPage 2002 animation with the following exercises:

- Place the same picture (from the Clip Art Gallery or another source) on a Web page three times. Use FrontPage 2002's image-editing features to create three slightly different versions of the picture, and use them for normal, mouseover, and click effects.

- Copy an animated banner ad from this book's Web site at `http://www.cadenhead.org/frontpage/`—the Hour 12 page has several ads from some of the World Wide Web's best-designed sites. Incorporate the ad into one of the Webs you have already created to see how it works as a part of the Web's design.

For solutions to these exercises, visit the book's official Web site at `http://www.cadenhead.org/frontpage/`.

PART IV

Publishing and Maintaining Your FrontPage 2002 Web Page

Hour

HOUR 13

Make Your Web Compatible with Multiple Browsers

A word that's often used in conjunction with the World Wide Web is "standards." There are standards in place for most of the languages and protocols used to exchange information on the Web: HTML, FTP, ActiveX, CSS...the list grows every month. The Internet thrives because of open standards such as TCP/IP for communication, SMTP for sending mail, and NNTP for Usenet messaging.

Unfortunately, if you're a Web designer who's trying to make a page look the same on all browsers, the only standard that you can count on is chaos.

During this hour, you'll learn how to create a FrontPage Web that's targeted to a specific audience and designed with your Web hosting provider in mind.

Handle Differences Between Web Browsers

Trying to make a Web page work in all leading Web browsers is a challenge. The audience is split between Microsoft Internet Explorer and Netscape Navigator, and each browser has non-standard Web features that make it challenging to create a Web that works on both browsers.

FrontPage 2002 makes it easy to add many of these non-standard features to your Webs. Fortunately, it also makes it easier to sort through the chaos and decide which features to use and which to avoid.

The World Wide Web Consortium has been entrusted with creating a standard version of HTML, the language used to create Web pages. You can visit the group's site at http://www.w3.org to learn about the current version of the standard and proposed improvements for the next version. The consortium also develops other standards that affect Web development.

Since Netscape launched its first browser in 1994, the consortium's standards have often been at odds with the companies that are most involved in following them: the browser developers at Netscape and Microsoft. The fierce competition between the two has prompted both companies to introduce their own enhancements to HTML, Web page scripting, and Cascading Style Sheets.

Many of these new features are appreciated by Web users. Adding images to a page was once a non-standard enhancement, and many designers have been calling for new solutions such as Cascading Style Sheets to be fully adopted. However, it has been common practice at both companies to introduce new features in the browsers without waiting for them to become standards.

One of the simplest examples of this involves blinking text. For an early version of its browser, Netscape added a way to make text on a Web page blink on and off like a "VACANCY" sign outside a motel. It's a simple, eye-catching effect that calls attention to a word, sentence, or more.

Making your text blink is easy in FrontPage 2002. Select the text in the editing window, choose Format, Font, then check the Blink option, shown in Figure 13.1.

Try this in one of your own FrontPage Webs. You're likely to find that the Blink tag has been disabled and can't be selected in the Font dialog box. By default, FrontPage 2002 is set to create Webs that work in both Navigator and Internet Explorer, and Navigator is still the only browser to support blinking text.

FIGURE **13.1**

Making text blink.

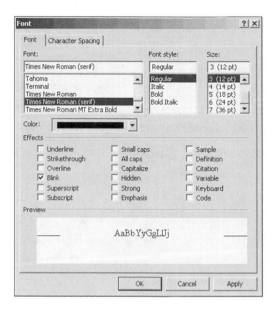

 It's likely that Navigator will always be the only browser to support blinking text. The World Wide Web Consortium, faced with widespread sentiment that blinking text should be banned by the United Nations, has kept it out of the standard for HTML.

"To blink or not to blink" is only one of the questions you must ask when you design a FrontPage Web. The software includes more than a dozen different features that are affected by differences between the popular Web browsers.

Select an Audience for Your Web

One of the goals of FrontPage 2002 is to shield you from many of the complexities of Web design. At this point you might not be too familiar with technology such as HTML, Dynamic HTML, and JavaScript because FrontPage uses these things behind the scenes as you work on a Web. You can focus on the effects and presentation that you want on your page, not the techniques used to make it happen.

The easiest way to keep it like this is by answering four questions before you start a FrontPage Web:

- Which Web browsers will be used by my target audience?
- Which versions of those browsers will the audience use?

13

- Which Web server will my Web be published on?
- Does my Web server have FrontPage Server Extensions?

Although there isn't a definitive source for Web usage statistics, a look at several different surveys provides a pretty good picture of what people are using to browse the World Wide Web.

As of this writing, it appears that the Web audience is composed of the following users:

- 70% of all Web surfers use Microsoft Internet Explorer 4.0 or 5.0
- 85% of those Internet Explorer users have upgraded to version 5.0
- 20% use Netscape Navigator 4.0 or 5.0
- 80% of those Navigator users have not upgraded to 5.0 yet
- 10% use older versions of these two browsers, Opera, Lynx, or other programs

These statistics are based on the stats for the author's own Web sites, which currently receive around 7.3 million visits a year.

Although Navigator and Internet Explorer have the browsing audience largely to themselves, a third browser is developing a following: Microsoft's WebTV, the consumer device that displays Web pages on a television.

Most Webs are developed for Navigator and Internet Explorer users with version 4.0 or later. This means that Web designers can take advantage of the newest features in these browsers. Some designers have taken the more conservative approach of aiming at version 3.0 or later of these two browsers.

You can also choose to design a Web for a specific browser, such as Navigator, Internet Explorer, or even WebTV. This enables you to use specific features, such as the oft-maligned blinking text, that aren't available in any other browser.

Another thing you can determine when you're selecting a browser's target audience is whether you'll be relying on FrontPage 2002 Server Extensions. Several of the features of a FrontPage Web rely on these extensions, including some of the feedback submission options and discussion Webs.

The Web server you use to host a Web affects browser compatibility to a much lesser degree because few features offered in FrontPage 2002 rely on a specific Web server.

Use Technology on a Web

After you've chosen the audience for your Web, you can configure FrontPage 2002 to reflect this decision. To set your Web's target compatibility, choose Tools, Page Options, and click the Compatibility tab, shown in Figure 13.2.

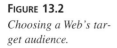

FIGURE 13.2

Choosing a Web's target audience.

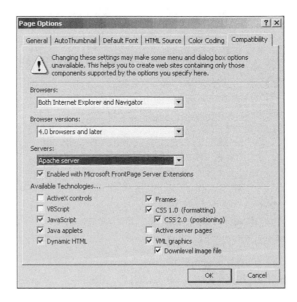

The choices you make in the Compatibility tab don't change existing features of a Web. They simply disable some features in FrontPage 2002 because your target audience won't be able to use them.

For example, page transition effects rely on Dynamic HTML, which is not supported in version 3.0 of either popular browser. If you want to include the folks who are still happy with Navigator 3.0 in your target audience, FrontPage 2002 won't allow you to add page transitions unless you change the selected audience in the Compatibility tab.

You can change the Compatibility settings as often as you want during the development of a Web. However, you might end up with features on your Web that aren't suited to your intended audience.

The Compatibility tab shown in Figure 13.2 has a set of check boxes that represent different kinds of technology that can be applied to a Web. Some of them are covered in other hours of this book, such as frames, Dynamic HTML, and Cascading Style Sheets. You might not be as familiar with the following:

- *ActiveX controls*—Programs that run as part of a Web page using a programming standard developed by Microsoft

- *VBScript*—A scripting language developed by Microsoft that enables some interaction between a user and a Web page

13

- *JavaScript*—Netscape's Web scripting language, which preceded VBScript and is still the most commonly used and widely supported in browsers
- *Java applets*—Interactive programs, written with the Java programming language, that run as part of Web pages
- *Active Server Pages*—Web pages that contain programs that are run by Microsoft Internet Information Server as they are loaded

The check boxes will be selected or deselected depending on the browser, browser version, and server you select.

If you're writing a Web only for Microsoft Internet Explorer version 4.0 and later, all the Technologies check boxes will be selected. As you might expect, FrontPage 2002 works best when you're aiming directly for the most recent versions of Internet Explorer. Every one of these technologies works in Microsoft's most current browser.

If you're writing for both popular browsers, or only for Navigator 4.0, ActiveX controls and VBScript technologies will be deselected while everything else is selected.

Losing the use of VBScript doesn't make much impact on a Web. JavaScript is so similar that you can achieve almost all the same effects with it.

ActiveX was developed by Microsoft and has never been adopted by Netscape's browsers. Without ActiveX controls, you can't add an ActiveX Web component to your FrontPage Web.

Writing strictly for Internet Explorer 3.0 or later makes two of the technologies unusable: Dynamic HTML and CSS 2.0, which stands for Cascading Style Sheets 2.0. You'll learn more about style sheets during Hour 24, "Format Your Web Through Cascading Style Sheets."

Writing for both browsers at version 3.0 excludes an additional technology: CSS 1.0.

Without Dynamic HTML, you can't use any of the following on your Web:

- Page transitions
- Hyperlink rollover effects on a page's background
- Collapsible outlines

Writing only for WebTV restricts you from using any of the technologies shown in Figure 13.2 except for Active Server Pages, which will be usable if your Web is hosted by Microsoft Internet Information Server.

This might change as WebTV adopts more of Internet Explorer's functionality in its new versions. WebTV's browser isn't as sophisticated as either Navigator or Internet Explorer, so you're limited to the basics of Web page design and cannot have any frame-based pages.

Several Web elements can be used in FrontPage 2002 only if your target audience is limited to Internet Explorer users:

- The Marquee and Video components
- Background pictures that are displayed under a table instead of an entire Web page
- Borders around table cells, background colors for specific cells, and background pictures for cells

Restrict Specific Technology on a Web

The check boxes on the Compatibility tab enable you to override the selections that were determined when you picked a browser audience. If you do this, you might spend time on features that aren't really usable by your audience. For example, if you enable ActiveX controls for a Web, you'll be able to add things such as Office XP components. However, if you're targeting an audience that includes Navigator users, they won't be able to see or use that Office component.

You might find it handy to disable a technology simply because you don't want to use it anywhere. For example, some Web developers choose not to place any Java applets on their pages. Although these programs can be a compelling way to present interactive content on a Web page, Java can reduce the speed with which a page loads. A Web browser must load an applet into a special environment called a *virtual machine* before it can begin running.

If you disable Java technology on a Web, none of the following FrontPage features can be used:

- Java applets
- The Banner Ad manager component
- The Hover Button component

FrontPage 2002 themes use JavaScript to create mouseover graphics on link bars, so if this scripting language is disabled, you can't select the Active Graphics option when applying a theme. The graphics on link bars will not change when a mouse hovers over them.

13

Deal with Server Compatibility Issues

The last compatibility-related factor is the one you have the least control over: the Web server that's hosting your site.

If your Web is hosted on Microsoft Internet Information Server, you can use Active Server Pages no matter which browser or browser version you're targeting. On the other hand, an Apache server running on Linux or another operating system doesn't support Active Server Pages.

Use Browser-Specific Features

As you start to deal with the issue of browser compatibility, you're more likely to restrict yourself than to expand the possibilities of your FrontPage 2002 Webs. This is because, like most people, you probably want to reach both Navigator and Internet Explorer users as your primary audience.

Using FrontPage 2002, there are two routes you can take to use browser-specific features on a Web aimed at everyone.

The longer route: Duplicate some of the pages in your Web and create two navigational structures, one for Navigator users and one for Internet Explorer users. Visitors can click hyperlinks on one of the Web's main pages to select the Web that matches their browser, and each one can have different compatibility options.

The shorter route: Put browser-specific features on separate pages and provide hyperlinks to those pages for people with the right browser.

For example, if you have a page that uses an ActiveX control, you could provide a link to it indicating that it requires Internet Explorer. This prevents visitors from wasting time loading a page that they can't use.

These two techniques expand the amount of work you have to do, especially if there are a lot of duplicated pages.

Given the present statistics on browser usage, anything that's limited to one of the popular browsers will be unusable by at least 20% of the Web's audience. This might not be a problem in some cases—a corporate intranet Web could be limited to the Web browser that's installed on all desktop machines.

 This book's official Web at http://www.cadenhead.org/frontpage is another example of a site that can count on a big audience that's using a specific browser, so there are plenty of FrontPage-specific features on it.

Workshop: Install Additional Browsers

The easiest way to sort through the chaos of multiple browsers is to test a Web thoroughly with each of them.

This hour's workshop is the quickest to describe and takes the longest to accomplish: download your target audience's Web browsers.

The most popular Web browsers are available from the following Web sites:

- Microsoft Internet Explorer—http://www.microsoft.com/ie
- Netscape Navigator—http://home.netscape.com
- Opera—http://www.opera.com

Solution

On my Web sites, the primary audience I am targeting at present are people using Internet Explorer 5.0 and Netscape Navigator 4.0.

By limiting the features on my sites to those supported in both browsers, I present Web pages that are usable for at least 90% of the people who are visiting. Most people in the remaining 10% can view the site, although the presentation isn't as nice because I make use of Cascading Style Sheets, a feature you'll learn about in Hour 24.

After deciding what versions of Internet Explorer and Navigator you are targeting, install each browser if you haven't already. Internet Explorer is probably already set up because the FrontPage 2002 installation wizard offers to install it along with FrontPage.

Download and install the current version of Navigator, if you haven't already. The quickest way to find it is by visiting the Web address ftp://ftp.netscape.com. You also can visit http://home.netscape.com, although you'll have to dig around the site a little bit longer to find the browsers page.

The most up-to-date version of Internet Explorer is available from http://www.microsoft.com/ie.

When multiple browsers are installed on your system, open a Web in FrontPage 2002 and test them out: choose File, Preview in Browser to open the Preview in Browser dialog box (see Figure 13.3). Choose a browser and click Preview.

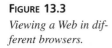

FIGURE 13.3

Viewing a Web in different browsers.

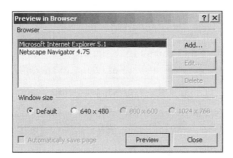

13

For most Web projects, the Opera browser isn't used by enough people to justify testing your Web in that browser. However, there's another reason to load your Webs in Opera: It implements more of the HTML and CSS Web standards than any other popular browser.

Because Opera follows standards in ways that Navigator and Internet Explorer do not, you can use it to find errors that would not be evident in other browsers. This is especially true when you're using HTML to edit pages.

Summary

Over the past few years, there have been numerous articles in business and computer magazines about the "browser war" between Netscape and Microsoft. After sorting through the material in this hour, you might believe that the first casualty of this war is your sanity.

At present, there are three HTML standards being used on the World Wide Web in any significant numbers: Microsoft's standard, Netscape's standard, and the real standard determined by the World Wide Web Consortium. As you can tell, it's standard operating procedure in the Web browser business to create non-standard additions to HTML.

FrontPage 2002 makes it simpler to do two things on your Webs:

- Stick with the features that different browsers share with each other.
- Avoid using features that your audience can't use anyway.

By determining your Web's audience before you develop the Web, you can concentrate on the features offered in FrontPage 2002 rather than thinking about the technology that makes them possible.

Q&A

Q What's the point of having an HTML standard if neither Netscape nor Microsoft follows it?

A The idealist's answer is that these companies can be persuaded to begin complying with the standard. If enough developers insist on following the HTML standard and Web users support sites that adhere to it, the browser developers will start following the standardization process instead of trying to stay ahead of it.

The pessimist's answer is that the browser companies are using these new features to gain a competitive edge over each other, and HTML's standard will always be underutilized until one of the browsers takes over the market.

Frustrated Web developers who want to stop spending so much time dealing with incompatibilities have been lobbying both companies to standardize. One such effort is the Web Standards Project at http://www.webstandards.org.

Exercises

Challenge your knowledge of FrontPage 2002 browser compatibility with the following exercises:

- Configure FrontPage 2002 for a WebTV audience on an Apache server. Create a personal Web and see which elements you can use in FrontPage's most restrictive configuration.
- If you've installed both Internet Explorer and Navigator, add a page to a Web that includes page transitions and Dynamic HTML animation. Test it in both browsers to see whether it's fully supported in each.

For solutions to these exercises, visit the book's official Web site at http://www.cadenhead.org/frontpage/.

13

HOUR 14

Publish Your Web

All the Webs you have created so far were viewed locally on your own system. After 13 hours of dress rehearsal, you might be wondering when this production is ever going to open to the public.

It's showtime.

During this hour, you'll learn how to publish a FrontPage 2002 Web on the World Wide Web. The same techniques can be used to put it onto a corporate intranet. You'll be able to publish Webs and partial updates to a server and save Webs directly to a server.

The curtain opens on a lonely FrontPage Web, eager to see—and be seen by—the world…

Choose a Server to Host Your Web

Before you can publish your Web with FrontPage 2002, you must have a place to publish it. Unless your company has its own Web servers, you must set up an account with a Web hosting service.

There are thousands of companies that offer Web hosting, all competing for your business in several different ways:

- Price—Some hosts are free if they can put banner ads on each page of your Web. Others generally range in price from $9 to $49 per month.

- Disk storage—Hosts offer from 5MB to 100MB of storage space for all the pages and files in your Web.

- Bandwidth—Hosts often put restrictions on how often pages and files in your Web are requested, limiting it to a set amount such as 3 gigabytes per month. Going over this can result in an additional charge per-gigabyte or a total shutdown of the Web until the next billing period.

- Operating system—Some hosts specialize in hosting on servers that use a specific operating system such as Windows 2000, Linux, or Apple Macintosh.

- Features—Hosts offer different features based on the technology they have implemented on their servers.

The features offered by a Web hosting service are extremely varied. They can include Common Gateway Interface (CGI) scripting, Java servlets, PHP, and MySQL database access.

For FrontPage 2002 users, the most important features to look for in a Web host are support for FrontPage 2002 Server Extensions and Active Server Pages.

FrontPage Server Extensions are programs that run on a Web server to extend the capabilities of a FrontPage Web. Extensions are available for several popular Web servers, including Microsoft Internet Information Server and the Apache server.

You make use of extensions in a FrontPage Web by using components. You have already used one during Hour 8, "Add a Form to a FrontPage Web." The program that sends form data through e-mail is a component.

FrontPage components that require server extensions include the following:

- Form handler—Collects information from a form on a Web page and sends it using e-mail

- Hit counter—Counts the number of times a page is loaded

- Web Search—Searches a Web for specific text and returns a results page

- Photo Gallery—Displays a group of photos on a page, automatically creating small "thumbnail" versions of each image

To add components to a Web page, choose Insert, Web Component. The Insert Web Component dialog box displays a list of more than 30 components that can be implemented on a Web that uses FrontPage Server Extensions. Many of these components are covered during Hours 17–20.

Another important feature offered by Web hosts is domain name service. One of the best ways to promote your Web and make it look professional is to give it a short, memorable Web address.

Many hosting services will let you pick out a domain name for your site—an Internet address that begins with a descriptive word or phrase and ends with .com, .net, .org, or another designation.

If you can find a domain name you like or you already own one, it can be used as the address of your Web. The cost ranges from $15 to $45, although some companies offer free domain registration as a benefit to paid subscribers.

Microsoft offers a Web Presence Providers directory that you can use to find a hosting service that supports FrontPage server extensions. To use it:

1. Connect to the Internet.
2. Open any Web in FrontPage.
3. Choose File, Publish Web. The Publish Destination dialog box is displayed (see Figure 14.1).
4. Choose the Click here to learn more hyperlink. The Web Presence Provider site will be opened in your browser.

FIGURE 14.1

Finding a Web hosting service.

You can search the directory by region or by criteria such as price and operating system. When you find one you like, you can go directly to that site to learn more and sign up for an account.

14

If you want to start publishing FrontPage Webs before choosing to pay for a hosting service, two popular free Web hosting services, Yahoo! GeoCities and Tripod, support FrontPage 2002 Server Extensions at no cost.

After you have set up an account with a hosting service, you are ready to publish a Web.

Publish Your Web to a Server

FrontPage 2002 can publish Webs to three different places:

- A hard drive on your system or local area network
- A Web server on your system, such as the Microsoft Personal Web Server
- A Web hosting service

By saving your Web on your hard drive, you have published it on your system. Using a Web browser, you can view pages in the Web, test hyperlinks, and try out features supported by FrontPage 2002 as long as they do not require FrontPage Server Extensions or other server-based technology.

Publishing to a Web Host

The only difference between publishing on your system and the World Wide Web is how you specify the destination. In both cases, you're copying files from one location to another.

Publishing on your system requires the name of a folder. Publishing to the World Wide Web requires the address of the machine that will host the Web and the folder where it can be stored.

Before you can publish a FrontPage Web to another machine on the Internet, you need a username and password that grant you permission to store files on that machine. You also might need the name of the folder where the Web can be stored, depending on how the Web hosting service is configured.

The location where you can store your Web is indicated by a Web address. Here are some fictitious examples:

- `http://www.fp2k.com/yourusername`
- `ftp://ftp.fp2k.com/users/yourusername`

Both of these examples specify a machine name (www.fp2k.com and ftp.fp2k.com) followed by a folder name (/yourusername and /users/yourusername). The folder name tells the Web hosting machine where the files should be stored when they're published by FrontPage 2002. In many cases, it also can be used as a Web address to view the site in a Web browser.

The first example has an address preceded by http://, which means that it is a Web address. HTTP stands for Hypertext Transfer Protocol, the main way that Web browsers and servers communicate with each other.

The second address is preceded by ftp://, which identifies it as an FTP server. FTP, File Transfer Protocol, is a way for two machines connected to the Internet to exchange files.

Web hosts that support FrontPage Server extensions often use HTTP addresses as the location where a customer's Web should be published. Other hosts usually use FTP addresses instead.

The Web host you have chosen will specify an HTTP or FTP address to use as the location for your Web.

Publish Your Web

To publish one of the FrontPage Webs you have created, open the Web and choose File, Publish Web.

If you have never published the Web before, the Publish Destination dialog box opens (see Figure 14.2).

FIGURE 14.2

Publishing a Web.

In the Enter publish destination text box, you can specify a folder on your system or network, HTTP address, or FTP address.

To try out publishing for the first time by publishing something on your system, click the Browse button. The New Publish Location dialog box opens (see Figure 14.3).

14

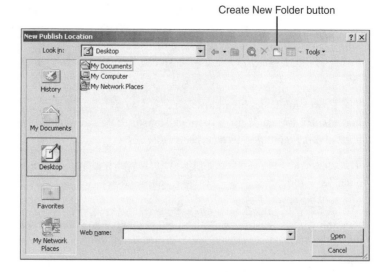

FIGURE 14.3

Choosing a location for your Web.

The New Publish Location dialog box includes a column of icons that resembles the Views bar. Click the Desktop icon to explore your system's drives and file folders and find a place where your new Web can be published.

To publish something on a Web server, enter the HTTP or FTP address provided by your hosting service in the Enter publish destination text box in the Publish Destination dialog box.

> If you are using Yahoo! GeoCities to try out FrontPage's publishing features, enter http://fp.geocities.com in the Enter publish destination field. Before any files are published, you will be asked for your Yahoo! username and password.

When you decide on a location for your Web, click the Create New Folder button shown in Figure 14.3. The New Folder dialog box opens. Use this dialog box to give your new folder a name. Because the folder will be used to store the files associated with your Web, choose a short name that describes the Web.

After creating and naming the folder, choose it and click Open. The folder's location and name are displayed in the Publish Destination dialog box.

Click OK to begin publishing the Web. The Publish Web dialog box is displayed, listing the files in your Web and the files currently in the folder where the Web is being published (see Figure 14.4).

FIGURE 14.4

Preparing to publish a Web.

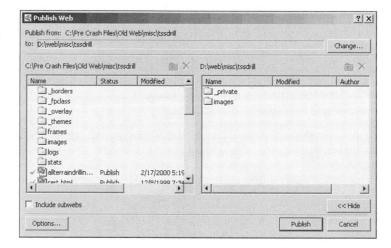

You can use the Publish Web dialog box to customize how the Web will be published. By default, FrontPage will publish everything in the Web that has changed since it was last published to that location.

If you are publishing to a server on the Web or a local network folder that limits access, a dialog box will appear asking for your username and password (see Figure 14.5).

FIGURE 14.5

Logging in to your Web hosting account.

FrontPage begins publishing by comparing the Web with any files that are currently at the location. If a page is the same in both places, it is not published.

FrontPage also reports any files that are found at the publishing location but not in the Web, asking whether you want to delete them.

Unless you know that it's okay to delete a file, you shouldn't let FrontPage delete it. Many Web hosting services put files in your folder that support some of their features. If the files are deleted, the features might no longer work correctly (or at all).

14

The Publish button begins the transfer of files. You must be connected to the Internet before you can publish to a server that's on the World Wide Web.

Barring any login problems, FrontPage will then begin copying files from your system to the Web server. This process can take five minutes or more, depending on the speed of your Internet connection and the number of files in your Web. (Publishing to a folder on your system is much quicker, of course.)

A successful transfer ends with a dialog box stating that your Web has been published (see Figure 14.6).

FIGURE **14.6**

Publishing your Web.

After you have published a Web for the first time, it will be set up to use the same publishing location until you choose a different one.

Publishing Specific Parts of a Web

One thing you learn quickly about FrontPage publishing is how slow it is. The process of comparing the contents of your Web with the contents of the publishing location is a time-consuming one, especially if you are connecting to the Internet using a 28.8 dialup line.

You can skip this step by choosing specific pages or files to publish. In the Folders list or Folders view, select what you want to publish, right-click, and choose Publish Selected Files from the shortcut menu that appears.

This technique saves time at the cost of accuracy in your Web. You might make a change to a page and forget to publish it (or FrontPage might encounter an error while publishing that prevents it from transferring all files).

You should publish the entire Web whenever possible so that FrontPage has a chance to make sure everything is fully up-to-date.

Solve Any Publishing Problems

When you're learning how to publish a Web, there are several different problems that can stymie the process. You might begin to suspect that there's no happy dialog box and that Web publishing is a myth, like the 40-hour work week, the Wizard of Oz, and tax refunds.

The following suggestions might help you bring up this wonderful dialog box, and none of them involve clicking your ruby slippers together while wishing you could return to Kansas.

 Wearing ruby slippers can't hurt, but be warned that I cornered the market on them in a Men's 14 when I was preparing this book.

Try the following when good Web transfers go bad:

- Double-check your username and password to make sure that they're correct.
- If you're specifying a Web address and folder name, such as `http://www.fp2k.com/~yourusername/`, load this address in your Web browser. In most cases, a test page or file listing should appear because Web hosting services often create the folder before you ever publish to it.
- If you're specifying a folder name, try taking it out and specifying only the machine name, as in `http://www.fp2k.com`. Some Web hosting services will find the right folder for your username automatically.

These examples cover the most commonplace problems that might occur as you're publishing a Web. In some instances, you might encounter problems because the hosting service doesn't offer FrontPage 2002 Server Extensions, although this normally doesn't prevent pages and files from being transferred to the Web server.

Most Web hosts provide rudimentary documentation on publishing Webs using their hosts. At the very least, they can provide the HTTP or FTP address you should use when publishing, your username, and your password.

Workshop: Take Your Web Online

During the first 13 hours of this book, you've had the chance to create several different Webs. This hour's workshop is to publish one of these Webs to a World Wide Web server and load your site in a browser.

If you don't have a hosting service yet, you can sign up with either of the following free home page providers:

- GeoCities at `http://www.geocities.com`
- Tripod at `http://www.tripod.com`

14

These services give you a username, a password, and an address where your Web can be loaded with a browser. They also provide additional information on how to publish FrontPage 2002 Webs to their servers, including the address you should use when publishing your site.

All you need to sign up for either service is a valid e-mail address.

These services are suitable for publishing a FrontPage Web, but they might not have implemented FrontPage 2002 Server Extensions at the time you try this workshop. As the book was written, Yahoo! GeoCities supported FrontPage 2002 and Tripod supported FrontPage 2000, the previous version of the software. You can publish to these services even if they don't support FrontPage fully, but you won't be able to make use of components that require server extensions.

Solution

When you go through the Yahoo! GeoCities sign-up process, the address of your Web will be `http://fp.geocities.com/` followed by your Yahoo! username.

With your username and password, you can publish a Web. The destination to which you should publish is simply `http://fp.geocities.com`, with no folder specified. After you log in with your username and password, Yahoo! GeoCities will publish your Web to the folder associated with your account.

One quirk of publishing on GeoCities is that the service allows only approved filename extensions. If you try to publish a file with an unapproved file extension, you'll get an error message and the Web won't be fully published.

This shouldn't affect any of the files contained in the Webs you have created up to this point.

What it will affect are which files you may import into a Web. The most notable example of a forbidden extension is `.exe`. For security reasons, GeoCities does not allow executable programs to be stored on its Web servers as part of a site.

One place a GeoCities user could run into trouble is Hour 19, "Add a Database to Your Web." When you create a database in FrontPage, one option is to save it to a file with an extension of `.csv` (such as `phonebook.csv`). GeoCities won't allow the Web to be published until you change the file extension from `.csv` to something else that is permitted (such as `.txt`).

Summary

The curtain closes on your FrontPage Web, which has fulfilled its lifelong dream of being published, met a nice girl, and saved the town's building-and-loan from being closed by mean old Mr. Potter. The production should be viewed as a success if you've published a FrontPage 2002 Web to a server.

During this hour, you learned how to publish a Web to a folder on your system and a folder on a machine that could be anywhere else in the world. There are thousands of Web hosting providers you can use as the home for your FrontPage Webs.

Publishing a Web in FrontPage 2002 is a task that's easy after you've done it successfully, quickly becoming as simple as saving files from one folder to another.

Getting to that point can be a challenge sometimes, depending on how FrontPage 2002 and your Web hosting provider work in conjunction with each other.

Q&A

Q If a Web hosting provider doesn't offer FrontPage 2002 Server Extensions, should I use them?

A The answer depends on two things: whether your Web is reliant on server-specific features, and whether you can live without some FrontPage 2002 maintenance features.

You'll learn about Web maintenance during the next hour. To see whether a Web is reliant on the extensions, publish it to the hosting provider and try all of its features. Some of them, such as forms, can be rewritten to use an alternative. Others, such as threaded discussions, require the extensions and can't be replaced easily.

Q My Web hosting service puts a bunch of files in the folder where I publish my Web. Is there a way to make FrontPage stop asking me if I want to delete them?

A One way to solve the problem is to make copies of those files in your Web. Use the Import Web Wizard or FTP software to create a second copy of your Web on your system, including the files your hosting service put there for you.

After making the copy, open your original Web and import your hosting service's files into it. When that's done, select the files in the Folder list or Folders view, right-click, and then choose Don't Publish from the shortcut menu that appears. From that point on, FrontPage 2002 will stop asking whether you want to delete the files when you publish the Web.

14

Exercises

Challenge your knowledge of FrontPage 2002 publishing with the following exercises:

- Use the Click here to learn more link in the Publish Destination dialog box to see the list of FrontPage 2002–equipped hosting services. The directory is organized by area, so you might find that your own Internet provider (or one near you) is on the list.
- Publish a Web that contains pages that should not be published. View the site after it has been published to make sure that FrontPage has not included the page.

For solutions to these exercises, visit the book's official Web site at http://www.cadenhead.org/frontpage/.

HOUR **15**

Keep Your Web Up-to-Date

Creating a useful, functional Web with FrontPage 2002 is only part of the challenge. Unless your Web is something you intend to publish once and never update, you still have a lot of work to do.

Most Webs require regular maintenance, much like a car, spouse, friend, or Chia Pet.

Web pages must be edited to keep them accurate. Hyperlinks must be checked to make sure that they still lead to real Web addresses. Tasks must be assigned to the folks who actually do all this work—or in some cases, to a single, overworked person.

FrontPage offers features to make these site-management chores easier. During this hour, you'll learn how to automatically verify hyperlinks and how to break a Web project down into the tasks that must be accomplished.

Keep Hyperlinks Current

Hyperlinks are the backbone of the World Wide Web, creating instant association between millions of Web pages and other files. During a typical session using the Web, you might circle the globe to chase down information, using hyperlinks to surf through seven different sites in seven different countries.

If your FrontPage 2002 Web contains numerous links to other places on the World Wide Web, one of your continuing maintenance tasks will be to keep these links current. FrontPage makes this task easier by automatically verifying links for you.

When FrontPage verifies a link, it tries to load the Web page, image, or other file associated with the link. If it is not successful, FrontPage reports it as a broken hyperlink.

Link verification is a feature of the Reports view in FrontPage. Open a Web and click the Reports icon in the Views bar. A summary of your Web will open in place of the editing window, as shown in Figure 15.1.

FIGURE 15.1

Viewing reports about a Web.

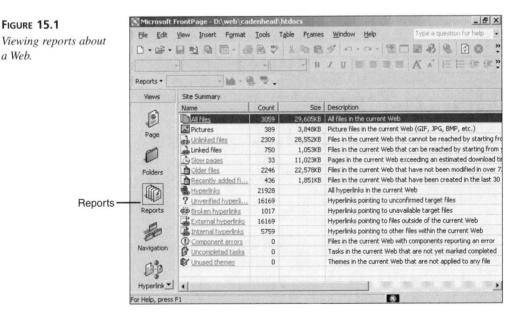

In the Reports view, you can list hyperlinks by the following criteria:

- All hyperlinks
- Unverified hyperlinks
- Broken hyperlinks

15

- External hyperlinks
- Internal hyperlinks

Several reports have hyperlinks associated with their names. Click one of these links to see a more detailed report.

Before you check any of the hyperlinks in a Web, choose Tools, Recalculate Hyperlinks, which causes FrontPage 2002 to look for all the hyperlinks in your Web. If you don't do this, FrontPage might not include all hyperlinks in the reports about your Web.

As you are viewing the list of hyperlinks in each report, you can verify any hyperlink: Right-click the link and select Verify Hyperlink from the shortcut menu that appears. If the link is to a World Wide Web address rather than a page or file on your own system, you must be connected to the Internet before you can verify the link.

To verify all links in a report, press Ctrl+A to select all the links, and then right-click and choose Verify Hyperlink.

FrontPage 2002 will attempt to connect to the Web address associated with each hyperlink, so the verification process can take quite a while if a large number of links are being verified. "OK" will be reported for every address that contains a page or file. Otherwise, "Broken" will be reported. This status will remain as long as the Web is open—when you close it, all hyperlinks are switched back to "Unverified" status.

Some broken links might be the result of a temporary problem connecting to the Web address, so you shouldn't automatically remove broken links that turn up in these reports.

FrontPage 2002, like the previous version of the software, appears to have trouble checking hyperlinks on some Web sites, including popular sites such as ESPN.Com and Disney.Com. Links to those sites are reported as broken when they work correctly—another reason to check a link yourself before deleting it.

In general, a Web server must respond with a "Page not found" error or be offline entirely for a hyperlink to be reported as broken. Some Web hosts send an alternative page if a hyperlink isn't working, which FrontPage will report as an "OK" link.

To edit a hyperlink from the Reports view, right-click the link and select Edit Hyperlink. The Edit Hyperlink dialog box will open (see Figure 15.2).

FIGURE 15.2

Editing a hyperlink.

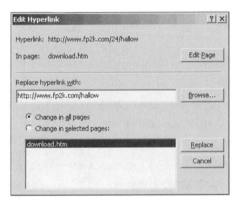

If you know the correct address for the hyperlink, enter it in the Replace hyperlink with text box. If the link is going to a file included in your Web, click the Browse button to open the Edit Hyperlink dialog box to find and choose the file. You can make the change in selected pages or the entire Web. Click the Replace button to replace the broken link with your corrected link.

If you want to work with the page that contains the broken link, click the Edit Page button. The page will open in the editing window.

> FrontPage 2002 makes it easy to keep the links to pages within a Web current. If you rename a page, a dialog box will ask whether this new name should be reflected in all pages of the Web that link to it.

Rate Your Web's Content with RSAC

To address concerns about objectionable content on the World Wide Web, the Recreational Software Advisory Council (RSAC) and the Internet Content Rating Association have established a voluntary ratings system that judges the level of sex, nudity, language, and violence on a Web.

The RSAC rating for a Web is determined by the person or group who published it, and uses the Platform for Internet Content Specification (PICS) guidelines for rating content that were established by the World Wide Web Consortium (W3C), the group that shepherds the development of Web publishing technology such as Hypertext Markup Language (HTML).

The system is entirely voluntary, so your FrontPage Webs don't have to be rated by RSAC or any other organization before you can publish them.

Some Web browsers can be configured to lock out all Web sites that don't have a rating from RSAC or another group.

The purpose of RSAC ratings is to provide information for consumers who want to filter what appears on their browsers, such as parents, corporations, and libraries. If you publish a Web that contains offensive language, you can use an RSAC rating to provide a warning about this content.

You can rate a site or Web page manually by visiting http://www.icra.org/. The RSAC ratings add-in makes the process easier by turning it into a FrontPage wizard, which asks a series of four questions. Your answers are used by RSAC's system to assign a numerical rating from 0 (either nonoffensive or mildly so) to 4 (Katie, bar the door) in four categories: sex, language, nudity, and violence.

The wizard creates the HTML coding needed to establish the RSAC rating for your Web and adds it to the rated page or an entire Web. It also prepares an e-mail that will be sent to the RSAC about the newly rated Web.

As you might expect, the subject of content ratings is a controversial one on the World Wide Web, so the RSAC ratings add-in might not be a wizard you call on for your own Webs.

To see how these ratings systems affect a Web browser, you can activate content restrictions in Internet Explorer 5:

1. Choose Tools, Internet Options. The Internet Options dialog box is displayed.
2. Click the Content tab to bring it to the front (see Figure 15.3).
3. Click the Enable button to open the Content Advisor.

The Content Advisor in Internet Explorer uses the same numerical ratings for sex, violence, nudity, and violence (see Figure 15.4).

If a user requests a site with content that participates in RSAC's rating system has higher ratings than you allow, it will not be loaded.

FIGURE 15.3

Enabling content re-strictions in Internet Explorer.

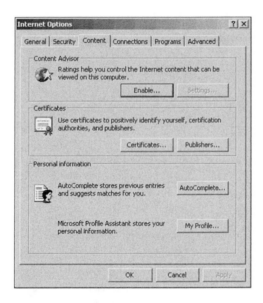

FIGURE 15.4

Filtering a browser by using RSAC ratings.

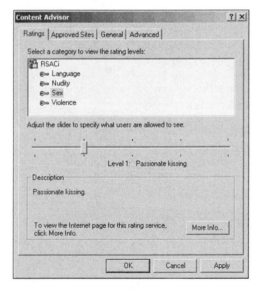

Sites that do not participate in the RSAC ratings system cannot be viewed if the Content Advisor has been enabled in Internet Explorer 5.

More information about the development of these systems is available from the ICRA Web site and from the World Wide Web Consortium at http://www.w3.org.

Establish a To-Do List of Tasks

Publishing a Web can be a complex process, especially if it involves a large number of pages, a large number of people working together, or both. FrontPage 2002 includes a task management system to better organize the work that's involved in developing and maintaining a Web.

A task in FrontPage 2002 is any job that needs to be done to a Web. It's given a one-line title, with room for a longer description if needed. It can be assigned to a specific person or groups of people, if you're collaborating with your colleagues on a project, and given a priority of Low, Medium, or High.

To see the tasks that have been assigned in a Web, click the Tasks icon in the Views bar (see Figure 15.5).

FIGURE 15.5

Viewing a Web's current tasks.

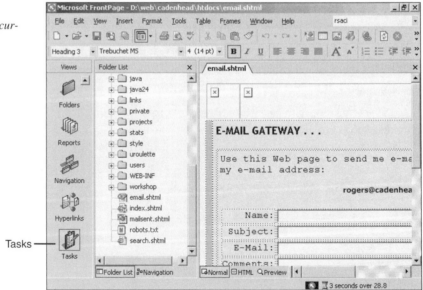

Tasks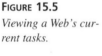

Tasks can be sorted by their priority in the Tasks view. So if your boss leaves on a week-long business trip, you can downshift tasks to low priority and take your own unplanned sabbatical.

One way to structure tasks is to associate them with specific files contained in a Web. To add a new task this way, open Folders view, choose the file, and then choose Edit, Tasks, Add Task. The New Task dialog box opens (see Figure 15.6).

FIGURE **15.6**

Describing a new task.

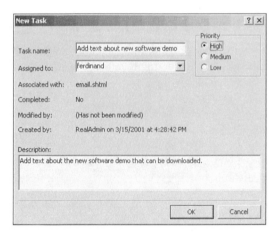

When you add a new task, it shows up in the Tasks view with a description of its status: Not Started, In Progress, or Completed.

After you associate a task with a file, you can begin working on it from Tasks view: Click the task and choose Start Task from the shortcut menu that appears. If the file is a Web page, it will be opened in the editing window.

When you close the page, FrontPage will display a dialog box asking whether the task has been completed. The task's status will be listed as In Progress or Completed, depending on your answer.

If you try to start a task associated with a file that is not a Web page, FrontPage 2002 will open the software identified as its editor.

 If there's no editor configured for a task's file type, an error message will be displayed. To configure editors, click Tools, Options and click the Configure Editors tab.

You can also indicate that a task has been completed in another way: Open Task view, right-click the task, and then choose Mark Complete from the shortcut menu (see Figure 15.7).

FIGURE **15.7**

Completing a task.

Workshop: Verify Your Favorite Links

15

Although task management is useful no matter how many people work with you on a FrontPage Web, it's most needed on collaborative projects.

FrontPage 2002's hyperlink verifier is useful even if your Web publishing endeavors are a one-person production.

This hour's workshop is to create a Web containing hyperlinks to at least 25 of the sites you visit.

You might already be using your Web browser's bookmark feature to keep track of your favorite links. Placing these links on a Web gives you much more control over how they are organized and displayed.

When you're done, verify all of the Web's hyperlinks. You can either delete the ones that don't work or leave them in to check again later (in case the problem is temporary).

Solution

One of the new features introduced in FrontPage 2002 is the ability to cut-and-paste text from a Web page and keep all the formatting intact.

Using this feature, you can easily compile a list of links by grabbing them from a Web site that you like.

It comes in handy for this workshop. Here's one way to create a list of favorite politically oriented sites and verify the links:

1. Open Internet Explorer 5 and visit one of the political links sites such as the Drudge Report at `http://www.drudgereport.com` or BuzzFlash at `http://www.buzzflash.com`.

2. Highlight a list of links from the page and press Ctrl+C to copy them to the Clipboard.

3. In FrontPage, open a Web or create a new one.

4. Create a new page and place your cursor on the page in the editing window.

5. Press Ctrl+V to paste the list of links on the page. A Clipboard icon appears next to the list.

6. Click this icon and choose Keep Source Formatting from the menu that appears.

After you've designed a personal portal and placed all your favorite hyperlinks on it, switch to Reports view and choose Tools, Recalculate Hyperlinks.

In Reports view, click the Unverified Hyperlinks report to see all links you haven't checked in the current Web.

Press Ctrl+A to select all the links, and then right-click and choose Verify Hyperlink from the shortcut menu.

Summary

FrontPage 2002's task- and hyperlink-management features make it easier to publish your Webs on an ongoing basis.

You can use the software to keep your hyperlinks current, break down your work into manageable tasks, and assign tasks to specific people or groups, making it easier for different parts of the Web to be handled by the appropriate people.

Using these maintenance features in FrontPage makes more time for upkeep of your car, spouse, friends, and all the animals in the Chia Pet kingdom.

Q&A

Q Where does FrontPage 2002 get the names that appear when tasks are created, such as my own?

A FrontPage 2002 looks at the name that was used when you logged on to your system during bootup. If you're the only person who uses the computer, you might have configured Windows to log on automatically.

The name you assign to a task doesn't have to be a valid user of the system. However, everyone who shares your system to use FrontPage 2002 should have his or her own username and login. This way, they'll show up under that name in the Tasks view so that you can monitor each other's progress at any time.

Q If FrontPage falsely reports broken links so often when it verifies them, what's the feature good for?

A The best reason to use FrontPage to verify links is that it finds a lot of typos and other obvious errors, such as leaving `http://` off the beginning of a Web address.

The hyperlink reports also show instances where you have linked to a local file on your computer, which won't work when the Web is published. These links are prefixed with `file://` in front of them. By looking for them in Reports view, you can remove a nettlesome error that's difficult to find when working on pages in the editing window.

Exercises

Challenge your knowledge of FrontPage 2002 maintenance with the following exercises:

- Go task-happy on the next Web you create, assigning tasks to everything you must do prior to actually tackling any of the work. Start every part of the project in the Tasks view, creating a new task if you've overlooked something that must be done.

- Assign the pages and pictures on a Web to different categories based on how frequently they require updates. View the categories report to see how this could be used to manage the frequency of required tasks.

For solutions to these exercises, visit the book's official Web site at http://www.cadenhead.org/frontpage/.

15

HOUR **16**

Track Visitors to Your FrontPage Web

One of the most significant improvements to FrontPage 2002 is easy to completely overlook. The Reports view has a new report: Usage data.

If you host on a Web server equipped with FrontPage Server Extensions, you can find out more about how your Web is being used:

- The number of times your site is visited each day
- The number of times each page is requested
- The terms used to find your site in popular search engines
- The pages on other sites that contain links to your Web
- The Web browsers used by your visitors

By analyzing these reports, you can often find ways to make a FrontPage Web more useful to its audience and more prominent in search engines.

Learn More About a Web's Audience

The introduction to this hour contained all the *sensible* reasons to use FrontPage 2002's site usage reports.

There's also another reason: Tracking the visits to your Webs in obsessive detail is one of the most entertaining things about publishing on the World Wide Web.

As a Web publisher, you have the ability to continuously receive information on how popular your work is and what people are saying about it. It's like being a network TV executive with an unlimited budget to spend on overnight Nielsen rating reports and focus groups.

You can learn a lot about the people visiting your Web and the ways they get there by checking out a few simple reports.

The data used by FrontPage 2002 to create usage reports is stored on the Web server that hosts your Web. This data requires a server that is equipped with FrontPage Server Extensions, an enhancement that's available for Microsoft Internet Information Server, the Apache Web server, and other Web hosting software.

For this reason, you won't see any evidence of usage data in FrontPage if you open a Web stored on your computer or on a Web server that doesn't have FrontPage extensions.

If your Web hosting service doesn't offer extensions, it might offer its own usage reports, created with a program such as WebTrends, MkStats, or Analog. The reports from those programs are a lot different than the ones described this hour, but they are produced using the same kind of usage data.

To see the usage data for a Web you have published, choose File, Open Web. Enter your Web's address in the Web Name field, and then click Open.

If you are connected to the Internet, FrontPage 2002 will open the Web for editing directly on the Web server. You also will have access to some features of the Web that are not available when you open a copy that is stored on your computer.

To see one of these server-only features, click the Reports icon in the Views bar. The Site Summary report will be displayed with a new report in the list: Usage data (see Figure 16.1).

Usage data hyperlink

FIGURE **16.1**

*Viewing reports for a
Web.*

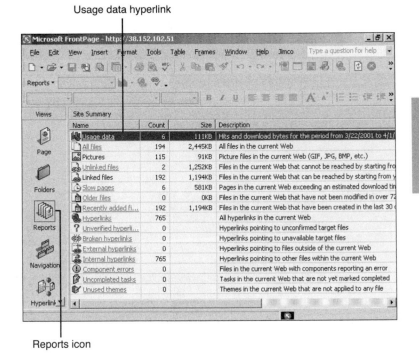

Reports icon

Click the Usage data hyperlink to open the Usage Summary, a collection of reports
related to how people are accessing your Web.

Reports are organized into the following subjects:

- *Page hits*—The number of times each page is requested
- *Users*—The number of people visiting your Web
- *Operating systems*—The number of visits received from people on Windows,
  Macintosh, Linux, and other systems
- *Browsers*—The software used to request pages and navigate your Web
- *Referring domains and URLs*—The Web pages that contain links used to visit your
  Web
- *Search strings*—The text used in search engines to find your Web

A few of the reports in the Usage Summary contain a single line of information, such
as the number of pictures in the Web. Most reports can be viewed in detail: click the
report's hyperlink in the Usage Summary (see Figure 16.2).

FIGURE 16.2

Learning about visitors to your Web.

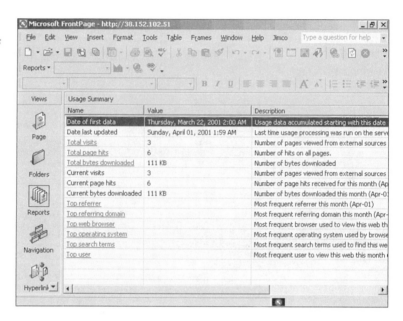

Logging Information on a Web Server

To produce reports like the ones available in FrontPage 2002, a Web server must keep track of how it is used.

Servers accomplish this by producing data files called *logs*. Typically, a server can generate four kinds of log files:

- access_log—A list of requests for Web pages and other files the server was asked to transmit

- agent_log—A list of Web browser identification tags that were sent along with each request

- referer_log—A list of Web addresses that contain hyperlinks requesting pages from the server

- error_log—A list of errors generated by the server as it is used

The log files kept by your Web hosting service might be different—some servers don't keep Web browser or referral information, and others combine all these logs into a single file.

FrontPage uses these logs behind the scenes to prepare usage reports, so you don't have to work with them directly. Looking them over is a good way to see what you can learn from a server, so an introduction to each log file is worthwhile.

Access Logs

Listing 16.1 contains 20 lines from an access_log file produced by Apache Web server.

LISTING 16.1 An Example of a Server's access_log

```
128.252.112.7 - - [01/Apr/2001:00:04:21 -0800] "GET / HTTP/1.1" 200 14081
128.252.112.7 - - [01/Apr/2001:00:04:21 -0800] "GET /images/amazonclock.gif
➡HTTP/1.1" 304 -
128.252.112.7 - - [01/Apr/2001:00:04:21 -0800] "GET /images/retort.gif
➡HTTP/1.1" 304 -
128.252.112.7 - - [01/Apr/2001:00:04:21 -0800] "GET /images/gray.gif HTTP/1.1"
➡304 -
128.252.112.7 - - [01/Apr/2001:00:04:21 -0800] "GET /images/amazon.gif
➡HTTP/1.1" 304 -
rb01.proxy.aol.com - - [01/Apr/2001:00:05:36 -0800] "GET / HTTP/1.1" 200 14081
rb01.proxy.aol.com - - [01/Apr/2001:00:05:37 -0800]
➡"GET /images/amazonclock.gif HTTP/1.1" 200 9867
rb01.proxy.aol.com - - [01/Apr/2001:00:05:42 -0800] "GET /images/retort.gif
➡HTTP/1.1" 200 11897
198.76.187.254 - - [01/Apr/2001:00:05:48 -0800] "GET /favicon.ico HTTP/1.1"
➡304 -
rb01.proxy.aol.com - - [01/Apr/2001:00:05:49 -0800] "GET /images/gray.gif
➡HTTP/1.1" 200 56
rb01.proxy.aol.com - - [01/Apr/2001:00:05:50 -0800] "GET /images/amazon.gif
➡HTTP/1.1" 200 1338
216.136.153.219 - - [01/Apr/2001:00:06:41 -0800] "GET / HTTP/1.1" 200 14081
216.136.153.219 - - [01/Apr/2001:00:06:41 -0800] "GET /images/amazonclock.gif
➡HTTP/1.1" 200 9867
216.136.153.219 - - [01/Apr/2001:00:06:41 -0800] "GET /images/retort.gif
➡HTTP/1.1" 200 11897
216.136.153.219 - - [01/Apr/2001:00:06:42 -0800] "GET /images/gray.gif
➡HTTP/1.1" 200 56
216.136.153.219 - - [01/Apr/2001:00:06:42 -0800] "GET /images/amazon.gif
➡HTTP/1.1" 200 1338
208.23.188.210 - - [01/Apr/2001:00:06:57 -0800] "GET / HTTP/1.1" 200 14081
208.23.188.210 - - [01/Apr/2001:00:06:58 -0800] "GET /images/amazonclock.gif
➡HTTP/1.1" 200 9867
208.23.188.210 - - [01/Apr/2001:00:07:00 -0800] "GET /images/retort.gif
➡HTTP/1.1" 200 11897
208.23.188.210 - - [01/Apr/2001:00:07:03 -0800] "GET /images/gray.gif
➡HTTP/1.1" 200 56
```

16

Each line in the access log contains the following information, in order from left to right:

- The Internet address that requested the file
- The date and time of the request
- The file that was requested
- The HTTP protocol used to make the request

- A status code
- The amount of data transferred, in bytes

Each request from the server is logged separately, whether it is looking for a page, graphics displayed on a page, or a request for a listing of files in a folder. If a Web page contains three graphics, four items will show up in the log—one for the page and three for the graphics.

The Internet address requesting a file can be represented as a number (such as 128.252.112.7) or a machine name (such as rb01.proxy.aol.com). This address could represent any number of things, such as a home computer with a 24-hour-a-day Internet connection, an Internet service provider machine used by different dial-up users, a proxy at a corporate office that takes employee requests for Web files, or a cache that stores pages for faster retrieval.

The address of the requested file is relative to the folder that contains your Web's home page. In Listing 16.1, the request for /images/gray.gif file is seeking a graphics file called gray.gif in the images subfolder of the Web.

Agent Logs

Listing 16.2 contains 20 lines from an agent_log produced by the same server.

LISTING 16.2   An Example of a Server's agent_log

```
Mozilla/4.0 (compatible; MSIE 5.01; Windows NT 5.0)
Mozilla/4.0 (compatible; MSIE 5.5; Windows 98; PeoplePC 1.0; HP)
MSProxy/2.0
Mozilla/4.61 (Macintosh; I; PPC)
Mozilla/4.61 (Macintosh; I; PPC)
Mozilla/4.0 (compatible; MSIE 5.01; Windows NT 5.0)
Mozilla/4.0 (compatible; MSIE 5.0; Windows 98; DigExt)
Mozilla/4.0 (compatible; MSIE 5.0; Windows 98; DigExt)
Mozilla/4.0 (compatible; MSIE 5.5; Windows 98; Win 9x 4.90)
Mozilla/4.0 (compatible; MSIE 5.5; Windows 98; Win 9x 4.90)
Mozilla/4.0 (compatible; MSIE 5.01; Windows 98)
Mozilla/4.0 (compatible; MSIE 5.01; Windows 98)
Mozilla/3.01 (compatible;)
Mozilla/4.75 [en] (X11; U; Linux 2.2.14-4.0 i686)
Mozilla/4.76 (Windows 98; U) Opera 5.02  [en]
None-of-your-business!
Mozilla/4.0 (compatible; MSIE 4.01; Windows NT)
Mozilla/4.0 (compatible; MSIE 5.5; Windows 98; Win 9x 4.90)
Mozilla/4.0 (compatible; MSIE 5.01; Windows 98)
Mozilla/4.0 (compatible; MSIE 5.01; Windows 98)
```

Each line in the agent log only contains one item: the identification text sent by a program as it requested a file from the server. The program, which is usually a browser, is also known as a *user agent*.

Most lines in an agent log refer to browsers, and by far the most common is Microsoft Internet Explorer. Listing 16.2 contains several references to Microsoft Internet Explorer, which uses the acronym "MSIE," along with a version number such as 4.01, 5.01, and 5.5.

There's also a line that contains the word "Opera," which indicates that the Opera browser was used.

Netscape Navigator generally shows up as the text "Mozilla" followed by a slash, a version number, and additional information.

16

As you can see in Listing 16.2, Internet Explorer also identifies itself as Mozilla. This is a throwback to the early years of the Web's popularity, when Navigator was used by more than 80 percent of all Web surfers and Internet Explorer was just being introduced. Microsoft was trying to achieve full compatibility with Navigator in page presentation, so it identified itself as "Mozilla" and "compatible."

One line you might have been surprised by in Listing 16.2 is "None-of-your-business!", which doesn't sound at all like a Web browser. The text used to identify a browser or Web-retrieval program is at the discretion of the visitor to your Web.

A small number of people consider agent logging to be an invasion of their privacy, so they use a program that changes their user agent text to prevent their browser from being identified. "None-of-your-business!" is actually one of the tamer things I've seen in the server logs of my own Webs over the years.

Referral Logs

Listing 16.3 contains 20 lines from a server's `referer_log`.

LISTING 16.3 An Example of a Server's `referer_log`

```
http://www.cadenhead.org/ -> /images/amazonclock.gif
http://www.cadenhead.org/ -> /images/retort.gif
http://www.cadenhead.org/ -> /images/amazonclock.gif
http://www.cadenhead.org/ -> /images/gray.gif
http://www.cadenhead.org/flash.shtml -> /images/amazonclock.gif
http://www.cadenhead.org/flash.shtml -> /images/lilretort.gif
http://google.yahoo.com/bin/query?p=screensaver&hc=0&hs=0 -> /flash.shtml
[unknown origin] -> /index.shtml
```

LISTING 16.3   Continued

```
http://search.msn.com/results.asp?RS=CHECKED&FORM=WEBTV&v=1&cfg=WEBTV
➥&q=yellow+journalism -> /index.shtml
http://www.cadenhead.org/ -> /images/gray.gif
http://www.google.com/search?q=preshrunk+stalinist -> /tshirt.shtml
http://www.google.fr/search?q=zapruder+movie&hl=fr&meta= ->
➥/1998/07/073198.shtml
http://www.cadenhead.org/ -> /images/amazonclock.gif
http://www.cadenhead.org/ -> /images/retort.gif
http://www.cadenhead.org/ -> /images/gray.gif
http://www.cadenhead.org/ -> /images/amazon.gif
http://www.cadenhead.org/ -> /images/retort.gif
http://www2.shore.net/~dkennedy/ -> /index.shtml
http://www.cadenhead.org/ -> /images/gray.gif
http://www.cadenhead.org/ -> /images/gray.gif
http://www.cadenhead.org/ -> /images/amazon.gif
```

Each line in a referral log contains two items, from left to right:

- The page containing the link to the file
- The file that was requested

The bulk of a `referer_log` file consists of referrals from your own Web because the pages of your Web contain links to each other and links to graphics displayed on each page. (The filename is sometimes spelled correctly as `referrer_log`.)

Most Web usage reports can be configured to ignore these kinds of referrals, focusing on the ones that come from other Web sites.

The most useful information in a referral log is links to search engines, which often contain the text used in the search that led someone to your Web.

In Listing 16.3, there are several of these from Google, a search engine that is rapidly becoming the most popular on the World Wide Web. The following searches brought people to the Web: screensaver, yellow journalism, Zapruder movie, and preshrunk Stalinist.

In regard to "preshrunk Stalinist," referral logs are often filled with such bizarre, off-color, or vulgar search terms that Web publishers compile lists of the oddest ones on their sites. There's even a Web site devoted to these called Disturbing Search Requests at `http://searchrequests.weblogs.com/`. (Note: the content of the site, like your own referral log, is likely to contain things that you might consider to be objectionable.)

If your Web analysis software can recognize these links in a referral log, as FrontPage 2002 does, a report can be compiled of the most popular search terms used to find your Web.

Error Logs

Listing 16.4 contains 10 lines from the last of the log files kept routinely by a server: error_log.

LISTING 16.4 An Example of a Server's error_log

```
[Sun Apr  1 01:01:52 2001] [error] [client 38.144.151.137] File does not
➡exist: /usr/local/etc/httpd/cadenhead.org/htdocs/1900/10/110700.shtml
[Sun Apr  1 03:18:07 2001] [error] [client 216.37.223.71] File does not
➡exist: /usr/local/etc/httpd/cadenhead.org/htdocs/exec/obidos/acn-redirect-to-
➡partner/ref=acn_au_bs/107-7111780-0119714
[Sun Apr  1 06:02:24 2001] [info] [client 198.77.58.123] (32)Broken pipe:
➡client stopped connection before rwrite completed
[Sun Apr  1 06:02:24 2001] [info] [client 198.77.58.123] (32)Broken pipe:
➡client stopped connection before rwrite completed
[Sun Apr  1 07:21:49 2001] [info] [client 207.173.146.56] (32)Broken pipe:
➡client stopped connection before send body completed
[Sun Apr  1 07:52:30 2001] [info] [client 63.44.198.51] (32)Broken pipe:
➡client stopped connection before send body completed
[Sun Apr  1 12:16:32 2001] [error] [client 205.188.208.137] File does not
➡exist: /usr/local/etc/httpd/cadenhead.org/htdocs/1900/10/110700.shtml
[Sun Apr  1 14:41:30 2001] [error] [client 64.81.100.27] File does not exist:
➡/usr/local/etc/httpd/cadenhead.org/htdocs/1900/10/110700.shtml
[Sun Apr  1 14:55:41 2001] [info] [client 24.24.104.252] (32)Broken pipe:
➡client stopped connection before send body completed
[Sun Apr  1 15:35:11 2001] [info] [client 63.44.103.48] (32)Broken pipe:
➡client stopped connection before send body completed
[Sun Apr  1 17:56:53 2001] [error] [client 63.251.248.45] File does not
➡exist: /usr/local/etc/httpd/cadenhead.org/htdocs/1900/10/110700.shtml
```

Each item in this log file contains the following information, from left to right:

- The date and time it took place
- A status term indicating whether it was an error or some other kind of unusual event
- The Internet address that requested the file involved in the error
- A message describing the error

The most common errors in the log are "File does not exist" messages and interrupted connections between the Web server and the machine requesting a file.

FrontPage 2002 does not currently include error log analysis in its usage data reports. Consult your Web hosting service to see whether it offers its own reports—these usually include a summary of the error messages that appear most frequently in your logs.

Viewing Web Usage Reports

Before you can make use of FrontPage 2002's Web usage reports, you must publish your Web on a server equipped with FrontPage Server Extensions and wait until your host has processed the server logs.

To view a usage report:

1. Connect to the Internet.
2. Choose File, Open Web. The Open Web dialog box is displayed.
3. Enter your Web's address in the Web name text box and click Open. A dialog box opens, asking you to log in with your username and password.
4. Click the Reports icon in the Views bar. Your Web's Site Summary report is displayed.
5. Click the Usage data hyperlink.
6. Click the hyperlink of the usage report you want to view.

The Browsers report is displayed (see Figure 16.3).

FIGURE 16.3

Viewing the Browsers report.

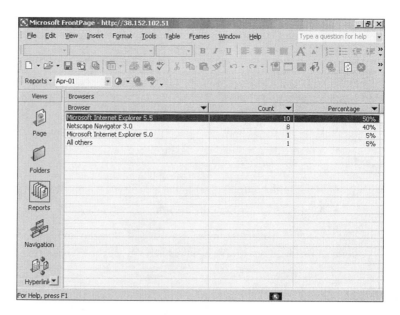

The Usage Summary lists a few statistics about your Web and offers hyperlinks to reports that are more detailed:

- Total visits
- Total page hits
- Total bytes downloaded
- Top referrer
- Top referring domain
- Top Web browser
- Top operating system
- Top search terms
- Top user

The visit and page hit reports are two attempts to determine how popular your Web is. A *hit* is a request to the Web server for a file contained in your Web. If someone requests a page containing 13 graphics files, 14 hits will be counted. The visit count disregards requests for image files contained on a page, ignoring requests for graphics files presented as part of a page.

The other reports use other data stored in server logs, tracking pages that refer to files in your Web, browsers used to visit it, and operating systems that can be determined from the browser identification.

The top user report counts only users who are logged in to your Web when they request files. If your Web does not require a username and password, you won't see any users in this report.

As you are viewing each of the reports, you might be unclear on how to return to the Usage Summary: Choose Reports, Usage, Usage Summary, as shown in Figure 16.4.

One of the most important reports for many FrontPage publishers is the Total Bytes Downloaded report—a "traffic report" that approximates how much demand your Web puts on the server that hosts it.

Many Web hosting services put a cap on the amount of data users can request from a Web in any month. A typical limit is 3 gigabytes (3 million bytes).

When you reach this limit, some hosting services shut off your Web and stop responding to requests for your files until the next month.

FIGURE 16.4

Returning to the Usage Summary report.

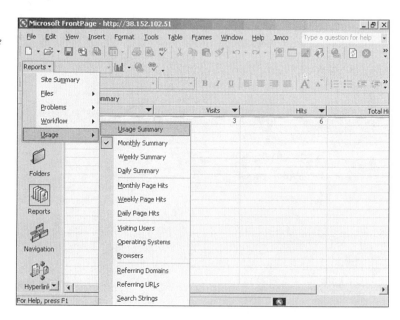

Others charge an additional fee based on how much extra traffic you attract. Occasionally, the Internet press reports about the problems that can result from policies like this—some Web publishers don't realize there is a problem until an extra charge of $100 or more is made to the credit card used to pay for hosting.

Unless you are publishing a large Web with an audience numbering in hundreds of people each day, you are unlikely to reach a host's traffic limit. On a 1,000-page Web that I publish, my files were requested 589,000 times in March 2001 and still amounted to only 3.2 gigabytes of data.

Workshop: Create a Link-Swapping Page

Because so many publishers keep close track of their referral reports, hyperlinks are often treated like a unit of value on the World Wide Web.

As one of your Webs becomes popular, publishers of the sites you link to will often take note of how many people you are sending their way. They might write an e-mail suggesting a link to something else they publish or let you know they have published a link to your site on their Web.

Many Web publishers routinely exchange hyperlinks, usually on an informal basis rather than trying to work out some kind of promotional arrangement. Even if you're not expecting a link back in return, publishing links to other Webs is a good way to let your visitors know some other sites they might be interested in.

For this hour's workshop, put the log-analysis skills you have acquired to use and find the sites that are linking to your Web most often.

After gathering data, return the favor by adding a page to your Web linking to these sites and publish your Web.

Solution

Figure 16.5 shows a Web page that contains a list of links to the publisher's favorite Webs.

16

FIGURE **16.5**

Publishing Webs that link to your own Web.

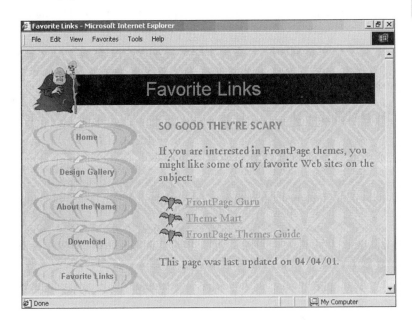

This workshop is well-suited to a personal Web, especially if you are using it to discuss a subject that others are covering on their own sites.

Some publishers put a list of their favorite links on the main page of their Web, usually in a column along the left or right side of the page.

When related Webs link to each other on the World Wide Web, it often results in a form of community building. As publishers exchange links and promote each other's work, a network arises of people who are publishing in areas of shared interest.

The Web search engine Google takes these kinds of relationships into account as it ranks sites in its database. When deciding which sites to list highest in search results, Google takes the number of pages linking to a site in consideration.

To see a self-organizing community that has arisen out of hundreds of publishers swapping links to each other, visit one of the popular Weblog sites.

Weblogs—sites that present links to other sites of interest on a timely basis—have become a highly popular form of Web communication.

Because of all the shared links, you can learn about Weblogs simply by visiting a few of the popular ones:

- Pop Culture Junk Mail, an entertainment-themed Weblog published by *Minneapolis Star-Tribune* online editor Gael Fashingbauer Cooper at `http://www.popculturejunkmail.com/`.
- CamWorld, a programming and interface design Weblog published by Web software developer Cameron Barrett at `http://www.camworld.com/`.
- Queso Daily News, a personal Weblog by Jason Levine, a pediatrics resident at a New York City hospital at `http://q.queso.com/`.

Summary

As you are publishing your first Webs with FrontPage 2002, the software's Usage data report might not seem useful or particularly important.

By the time your Webs show up in search engines and attract a following, you might be consulting your usage reports on a regular basis.

Checking these reports enables you to learn which parts of your Web are most popular, what people are saying about your Web on other sites, and how your Web is being found by people using Yahoo!, AltaVista, Google, and other search engines and directories.

During the next hour, you learn how to make the pages of your Web show up more prominently in search engines, a task that greatly benefits from the use of the FrontPage Top search terms report.

Q&A

Q When I use the Top Referrers report, some of the pages that show up don't contain any links to my Web, and the content of those pages makes me doubt they ever did. What causes this to happen?

A The most likely cause is a Web browser that transmits inaccurate referral information to your Web server. A browser is supposed to log a referral only when someone uses a hyperlink to reach your Web. If a user visits your Web by typing its address in the browser's Address bar, no referral should be reported.

Some Web browsers transmit this information anyway, revealing the last page someone visited before they came to your Web. As a result, you'll see some odd things in the Top Referrers report from time to time, such as the main page of popular sites like Yahoo!, CNN.com, and Hotmail.

A good rule of thumb is to ignore any referral that shows up fewer than five times in a month.

Q My server's logs don't look anything like the ones listed in this hour. Why are they different?

A Each Web server saves log files differently. The ones displayed in this hour are generated by the Apache server using Common Log Format (CLF), the most popular format for logging Web server activities.

Microsoft Internet Information Server, which is frequently used by companies that offer FrontPage hosting, keeps logs in its own format. The same information is contained in these logs—file requests, referrals, user agents, and errors—so you can view the same kinds of usage information that are available for Apache.

Exercises

Challenge your knowledge of the FrontPage 2002 graphical user interface with the following exercises:

- Use the Google search engine (`http://www.google.com`) to find sites that contain links to a specific Web. Enter the text "link:" followed by the address of the Web, as in `link:teevee.org` or `link:tvbarn.com`.

- Use the Top Search Terms report to pick a few of the most popular terms used to find your Web. During the next hour, you can use this information to make your Web easier to find in search engines such as AltaVista (`http://www.altavista.com`) and HotBot (`http://www.hotbot.com`).

For solutions to these exercises, visit the book's official Web site at `http://www.cadenhead.org/frontpage/`.

PART V

Enhancing a FrontPage 2002 Web

Hour

HOUR 17

Add a Personal Search Engine to Your Web

FrontPage 2002 has several different features that make your Webs easier to use. If your Web has been organized in Navigation view and makes use of link bars, most visitors should be able to quickly find what they're looking for.

For the times when a user can't find something, a search engine can look through all pages in a Web for specific text. FrontPage 2002 offers a personal search engine that functions like AltaVista and Google, two popular Web sites that scour millions of Web pages for specific text, hyperlinks, and other content.

The search form component is a text search engine that requires a Web server equipped with FrontPage Server Extensions.

During this hour, you'll learn how to add a search form component to your FrontPage Web page and keep it up to date. You'll also learn how to make your Web pages turn up more often when people are searching the entire World Wide Web.

Make Your Web Searchable

FrontPage 2002's search form component requires FrontPage Server Extensions, so you'll need a Web hosting service that supports them in order to use this feature.

The easiest way to add a search engine to your Web is with the Search Page template, one of the standard documents you can choose when creating a Web page. This template adds a search page containing the following:

- A search form component with Start Search and Reset buttons
- Text describing how searches are conducted

Figure 17.1 shows how the search form looks on a Web page.

FIGURE 17.1

Searching a FrontPage Web.

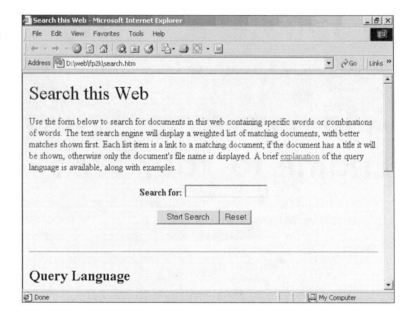

If you change the text provided on the Search Page template, you should keep or rewrite the documentation that explains how to conduct a search. Every search engine on the World Wide Web has its own rules for how to find things, so visitors to your FrontPage Web will need some guidance on how to compose a search query.

To add a search engine to a FrontPage Web:

1. Click File, New, Page or Web. The New Page or Web task pane opens next to the FrontPage editing window.

2. Click the Page Templates hyperlink. The Page Templates dialog box is displayed.

3. Choose the Search Page template icon and click OK (see Figure 17.2).

FIGURE **17.2**

Choosing the Search Page template.

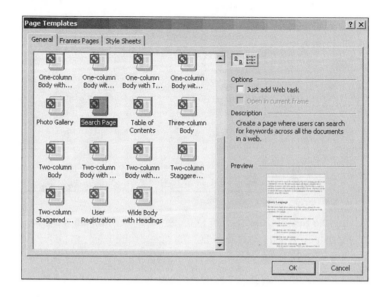

A new page opens in the editing window that contains a search form component and text that explains how to use it.

Although this component looks like any other Web form, you can't add or remove buttons, move buttons around, or do anything else that's possible when you're working with forms.

Instead, to edit the search form component, double-click inside the form in the editing window. The Search Form Properties dialog box opens.

This dialog box contains a Search Form Properties tab and a Search Results tab. In the Search Form Properties tab, you can change each of the following:

• The text of the label and buttons

• The width of the search text box

• The text on the two buttons

The Search Results tab, which is shown in Figure 17.3, is used to format the list of pages that contain the text you're looking for.

FIGURE 17.3

Changing how search results are reported.

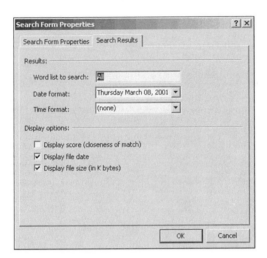

Using the Search Results tab, you can pick the information that is displayed about each page that comes up in a search—the size of the page, the date and time it was last updated, and the page's score.

The score represents how often the search term shows up on the page. The higher the number, the better—the search form component ranks results based on this number.

When a FrontPage 2002 Web contains a search component, a special file is created that contains a text index of the words used on each page in your Web. With the exception of 300 common words such as "a," "an," and "the," this index contains all words that appear on the Web.

After a search is requested, the search form component creates a results page.

When setting up a search component, you can limit a search to a specific folder of your Web. Enter the folder name in the Word list to search text box shown in Figure 17.3. For example, if you have a Web folder called oops that contains the text of several class-action lawsuit settlements made by your company, put oops in the Word list to search text box. The search form component will look through only that folder. Use All instead of a folder name when you want an entire Web to be searched.

If you're publishing a large Web, you can offer several targeted searches by placing more than one search form component on the same page.

FrontPage 2002 automatically creates the searchable text index for your Web and each folder in it. Every uncommon new word that shows up on a page will show up in the index.

One thing FrontPage doesn't take care of is the removal of words as they are removed from pages in your Web. For example, if you edit a class-action settlement page on your company's Web to remove all references to the words "willful negligence," those words will remain in the index. Anyone searching for "willful negligence" will receive a link to the page even though the words are no longer contained on it.

To fix this, rebuild the search text index: Connect to the Internet and choose Tools, Recalculate Hyperlinks.

When FrontPage recalculates hyperlinks, it re-creates the index while simultaneously looking at all hyperlinks on your Web to see whether they're still valid. This process can take five minutes or longer, depending on how many hyperlinks on your pages link to sites on the World Wide Web.

Figure 17.4 shows how the results of a search are displayed on a Web page.

17

FIGURE 17.4

Viewing the results of a Web search.

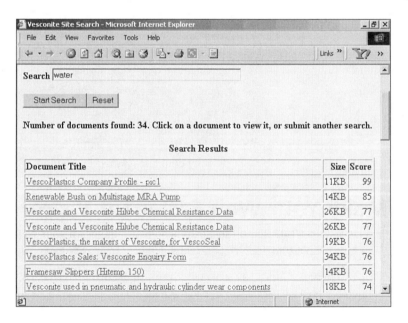

Search results are displayed on a page that's very similar to the search page. It will have the same theme, graphics, and layout, a search form component, and a table of results.

After you modify a search form component, be sure to choose Tools, Recalculate Hyperlinks to rebuild the word index that's used during searches.

Another way to add search capabilities to a FrontPage Web is to add a search form component to an existing Web page:

1. Click Insert, Web Component. The Insert Web Component dialog box is displayed.

2. Choose Web Search in the Component type list. A list is displayed in the Choose type of search box (see Figure 17.5).

3. Choose Current Web and click Finish. The Search Form Properties dialog box is displayed.

4. Configure how the search will be conducted and click OK. A search box is added to the page.

FIGURE 17.5

Adding a Web search to an existing page.

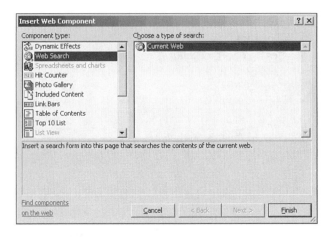

A search form component added in this manner will be exactly like the one on the Search Page template. Edit it by double-clicking the component.

Make Your Web Easier for Visitors to Find

FrontPage 2002 doesn't just help people find things on your Web. It also offers a way to help people find your Web in search engines such as Google, AltaVista, and HotBot.

In a previous hour, you gave descriptive titles to your Web pages by right-clicking an empty area on the page and choosing Page Properties from a shortcut menu. A good title helps your page in two ways:

- Some search engines can look for specific text in titles. To see an example, visit AltaVista's Advanced Search page at http://www.altavista.com/r?L05 and enter the text title "FrontPage 2002" in the Boolean query box. AltaVista will respond with a list of pages containing those words as part of their titles.

- Some search engines rank words in a title higher than words on the page, causing a good title to give your page a higher score on a results page.

Another thing you can do to help your Web get noticed in a search engine is to add keywords to each page.

Keywords are a list of words and phrases hidden on a Web page that describe the contents of the page. You can list as many keywords as desired for each page in a list separated by commas.

The following text is an example of keywords for a Web page:

```
class action, lawsuit, litigation, sued, sue, defendant, defense,
us, settlement, settled, settle, payment, paid, multi-million,
million, money, moolah, lawyer, law, legalese, plaintiff,
litigant, consumer, customer, apologized, apology, sorry,
contrition, contrite, public relations, public, PR, Anna
Kournikova
```

Although this might read like beatnik poetry, it's a list of several dozen words and phrases that a person might use when looking for the page in a search engine. All of these keywords have something to do with a company's multimillion-dollar class-action settlement and its feelings of genuine contrition.

Actually, the last keyword on the list has nothing to do with settlements or contrition. There's no requirement that page keywords must accurately describe a page's content. Someone searching the World Wide Web for "Anna Kournikova"—as if anyone would want to do such a thing—could find this sample page even if the tennis player is never mentioned in its text.

Support for keywords varies in the popular search engines. They're fully supported by AltaVista, HotBot, and Inktomi, but are not used by Yahoo!, Google, or Lycos.

> You can find a comprehensive guide to the things that search engines support from Search Engine Watch at http://www.searchenginewatch.com. This site also offers tips for making your Webs appear more prominently in each of the search engines and site directories.

To add keywords to a page or edit the current keywords, right-click an empty area of the page and click Page Properties from the shortcut menu. The Page Properties dialog box appears.

Choose the Custom tab to bring it to the front. Two different Add buttons are shown—one for system variables and one for user variables (see Figure 17.6).

FIGURE 17.6

Editing a page's hidden variables.

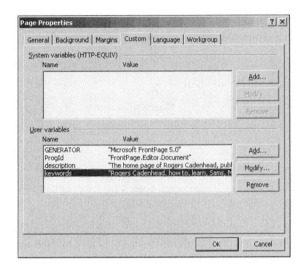

A *variable* is a storage place for information in a computer program or document. Each variable has a name and a value. For keywords, the name is "keywords" and the value is the list of keywords separated by commas.

To add keywords to a page, click the Add button next to the User variables box. The User Meta Variable dialog box is displayed (see Figure 17.7).

FIGURE 17.7

Adding keywords to a page.

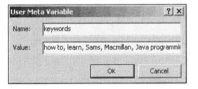

Enter the text keywords in the Name field and a list of keywords in the Value field, and then click OK. Your keywords will be added to the HTML of the page—click the HTML button below the editing window to see them.

Workshop: Make a Web Search-Friendly

Keywords on a Web page are so useful that they are occasionally the cause of legal disputes on the World Wide Web. The publisher of *Playboy* magazine sent cease-and-desist letters to numerous World Wide Web sites that used the word "playboy" in their keywords.

Your workshop for this hour is to add keywords to an existing FrontPage Web—preferably one that you plan to publish at some point. Start with a set of keywords that will appear on all pages, and add some to each page that are specific to that page.

If you're adding keywords to a site that was created with the Personal Web template, your main keywords could be about the person who the Web is about. On the page that lists the person's favorite links, these main keywords could be used along with a few extras, such as the names of the sites that are offered as links on the page.

Solution

The AltaVista search engine will take recommendations for new pages that should be added to its database. After you've published a Web page that includes keywords on a page, submit that page to AltaVista by visiting `http://www.altavista.com/cgi-bin/query?pg=addurl`.

Normally, you add a Web page to AltaVista by submitting its main page URL to the search engine. The page shows up in AltaVista searches within 1–2 weeks. AltaVista will eventually add the entire site to its database by visiting the links on the Web's main page, but this can take several months.

To more quickly test the keyword feature, add a page to AltaVista that contains keywords, even if it isn't the main page of your Web. Within a few days, you'll be able to search AltaVista for that keyword and see your page in the results.

> If all your keywords are common words and phrases, you might have trouble finding your Web page among all the other pages containing the same search terms. You might want to use your own name or some other uncommon text as one keyword. That way, you can find the page by that keyword.

Summary

Any FrontPage Web of more than a dozen pages can benefit from a search engine. Even if you create a well-designed site, some visitors will be unable to find what they want and will look for a Search button on your Web's link bar.

During this hour, you learned how to create a search engine that's specific to your Web. This is one of the features that makes it worthwhile to seek out a hosting service that offers FrontPage Server Extensions.

You also learned how to make your Web more prominent in the search engines that cover the entire World Wide Web by using keywords. They're a time-consuming aspect of Web design, but they result in more hits from people who are randomly wandering the Web for specific information.

Q&A

Q Is there a way to change the text that appears when my page shows up in a search engine?

A Another user variable you can set up for a Web page is its description. Right-click a page, choose Page Properties and click the Custom tab to bring it to the front. Add a user variable named `description` with a value of 100 words or less explaining what's on the page in sentence form (rather than a bunch of keywords that identify its topics).

Some Web publishers use a page's main heading and the first few sentences that appear on it for the description. If you use `description`, it's important to make a different one for each page of your Web. Some search engines will conclude that pages with the same title and the same summary are duplicates of each other, and will only list one of them in its database.

Exercises

Challenge your knowledge of FrontPage 2002's search capabilities with the following exercises:

- Add a search page to a FrontPage Web, even if you aren't necessarily planning to use a host that offers server extensions. Preview the page in a browser to see how FrontPage 2002 handles components in any server that isn't equipped with the extensions.

- Add the keyword `frontpage24hours` to the main page of all Webs that you publish using FrontPage 2002 and this book. This will make it easy for readers to find each other's work in search engines. (If it catches on, we'll develop a secret handshake and award gold watches to each other in 25 years.)

For solutions to these exercises, visit the book's official Web site at `http://www.cadenhead.org/frontpage/`.

Hour **18**

Enable Discussions on Your Web

Keeping a Web from getting stale is a challenge. After you've published it, adding new content that keeps visitors coming back takes continued effort.

Sometimes the best solution is to let your visitors do the work.

Thousands of successful sites on the World Wide Web offer discussion forums where visitors can read and write public messages to each other. Some sites offer nothing *but* this service.

If you're using a Web server that has FrontPage Server Extensions, you can add a discussion forum to a Web and create new all-discussion Webs. During this hour, you'll learn how these Webs are created and maintained.

Create a Discussion Web

Discussions are implemented on a FrontPage 2002 Web through the Discussion Web Wizard, one of the templates you can choose when creating a new Web.

A discussion can be added to an existing Web or created as its own Web.

To create a new discussion, choose File, New, or Page Web. The New Page or Web task pane opens alongside the editing window.

In the task pane, click the Web Site Templates hyperlink. The Web Site Templates dialog box appears (see Figure 18.1).

FIGURE 18.1

Creating a new discussion Web.

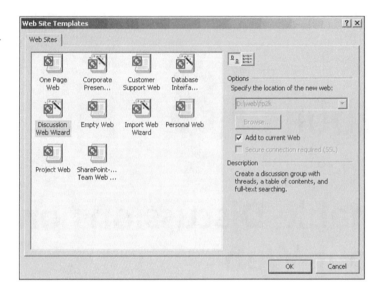

Choose the Discussion Web Wizard dialog box. If you want to add the discussion to the Web you're editing in FrontPage, select the Add to current Web check box. If you are creating a discussion as its own Web, you must choose a location for it on your system or a Web server.

After you have filled out this dialog box, click OK to load the Discussion Web Wizard.

FrontPage 2002's discussion forum enables visitors to read articles and post their own replies. These replies will become available immediately on the Web.

Articles can be threaded so that each article and all its replies are grouped together. This makes it easier for participants to read about the subjects they're interested in. A non-threaded discussion lists all articles based on the date and time they were written.

Choose the Discussion Features

The Discussion Web Wizard asks a series of questions about how you want the discussion forum to be structured. One of the first things you must decide is which features to offer, as shown in Figure 18.2.

FIGURE 18.2

Picking your discussion Web's features.

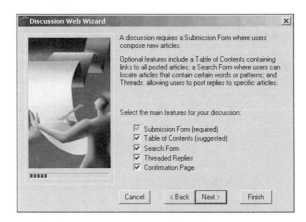

A discussion forum must have a submission form so that visitors can post articles. You can also include the following features:

- *Table of Contents*—Links to all articles that have been written.
- *Search Form*—A search form component for finding articles that contain specified text.
- *Threaded Replies*—Articles that are grouped together.
- *Confirmation Page*—A page indicating that an article has been posted.

Most of these features are standard for discussion forums on the World Wide Web. The search form component, which was discussed during the previous hour, requires FrontPage Server Extensions.

Name the Discussion Web

After you choose the features your discussion will include, you must decide what to call your discussion forum and where its messages should be stored. The name will appear atop most pages and articles on that Web, so it should be reasonably short. For example, "Everybody Loves Uncle Stan" is better than "A discussion area for all people hoping to get into Uncle Stan's will."

The folder name will determine where articles are placed in the Web. With the exception of the _private *folder,* all folder names that begin with an underscore character ("_") are normally hidden when you work on a Web in FrontPage 2002. The folder exists in your Web but is not listed when you display the Folders view or click View, Folder List.

Hidden folders also aren't indexed for searching by search form components you add to a Web. If you begin your discussion Web's folder name with an underscore, you'll need a search form as part of the discussion Web or it can't be searched.

> If you'd like to see the hidden folders, choose Tools, Web Settings, click the Advanced tab, and then check the box next to Show hidden files and folders. You'll see all folders you created that begin with the "_" character, along with several other hidden folders created by FrontPage 2002 to manage your Web.

Figure 18.3 shows the dialog box for selecting a discussion title and folder name.

FIGURE 18.3

Naming and storing a discussion Web.

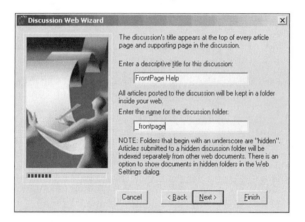

Choose How Postings Are Made

Next, the wizard asks which text boxes should appear on the discussion's submission form. You can select one of the following:

- Article subject and comments
- Article subject, category, and comments
- Article subject, product, and comments

You can make your FrontPage discussion open to all people who visit your Web, or only to those who have a valid username and password. The second option takes more time up-front because you'll be receiving requests to set up accounts.

> Requiring a username and password also will reduce the amount of participation in your Web's discussion forum—many Web-based discussion sites don't require any user registration before someone can post an article.

Making your discussion open to all participants requires more maintenance as the Web is being used. You'll have to remove articles that aren't consistent with your editorial goals for the Web, and there might be articles that contain illegal or objectionable material. For example, the publisher of the Everybody Loves Uncle Stan forum might want to delete all articles that discuss specific details about Uncle Stan's finances and his current state of health. Bad news about the former and good news about the latter could lead to fewer people being nice to Stan.

List Contents and Search Results

If you've added a table of contents to the discussion Web, you can configure it in two ways using the wizard:

- The order in which articles are listed
- The table's place in the Web

Articles can be listed in oldest-to-newest or newest-to-oldest order. The latter makes it easier to see what the most recent articles are, but participants are more likely to skip older articles.

The table of contents can be placed as the main page of a Web. If you choose this option, it will be given the name `index.htm`. So, you shouldn't do this if the discussion was added to an existing Web.

Although a discussion Web's articles are posted in their own folder, the pages that are used to post and read articles are stored in the main folder of a Web. When you're using the Discussion Web Wizard, it's easy to accidentally overwrite a Web's main page as you're adding a discussion Web to it.

If you elected to offer a searchable discussion Web, you can use the wizard to configure the search results page. The search can list results in four configurations:

- Article subject
- Article subject and file size
- Article subject, file size, and date
- Article subject, file size, date, and search score

The last configuration displays a score that indicates how often the searched-for text appears in the article.

Complete the Discussion Web

The last question asked by the inquisitive Discussion Web Wizard is how you want to display its articles. This dialog box is shown in Figure 18.4.

FIGURE 18.4

Choosing how to display articles.

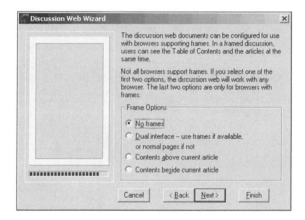

You can present the discussion using frames, no frames, or a combination that supports both.

Frames divide a browser window into smaller sections that each hold their own Web page. You learn how to create your own frames during Hour 22, "Divide a Page into Separate Frames."

In a discussion Web, the no-frames option places the list of discussion articles and the actual articles themselves on separate pages. Participants must jump back and forth between these pages as they read and write articles.

The two frames-only options show the list of articles in one section of the Web browser and an article in another section.

Using frames for a discussion Web makes it easier to read articles at the expense of some browser room. The area devoted to each article will be half as large as it would be on a no-frames Web, forcing readers to scroll more often. A frame-based FrontPage discussion Web is shown in Figure 18.5.

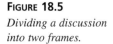

FIGURE **18.5**

*Dividing a discussion
into two frames.*

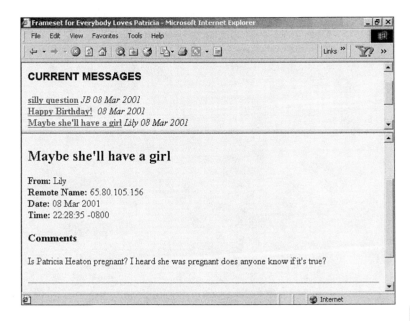

A frames-only Web can't be viewed on older browsers, text-only browsers such as Lynx or WebTV. The third way to present a discussion is to use frames but offer a no-frames alternative.

The dual interface option offers the no-frames discussion Web to people whose browsers don't support them, and one of the frames options to everyone else.

After you decide whether to use frames, click Finish in the Discussion Web Wizard dialog box to create your new discussion. Pages will be added to your current Web or to a new Web for reading, posting, and listing messages.

These pages will be named according to the title of the discussion Web and the purpose of the page. For example, if you're creating a Web called `frontpage` that supports searching, a table of contents, and message confirmation, the following pages would be added:

- `frontpage_cfrm`—The confirmation page, sent after an article is submitted
- `frontpage_frm`—The main frame of a frame-based discussion Web
- `frontpage_post`—The page where articles are posted
- `frontpage_srch`—The page for searching articles
- `frontpage_tocf`—The table of contents page, listing all articles

Figure 18.6 shows what a new discussion Web looks like in FrontPage 2002.

18

FIGURE 18.6

Editing a discussion Web.

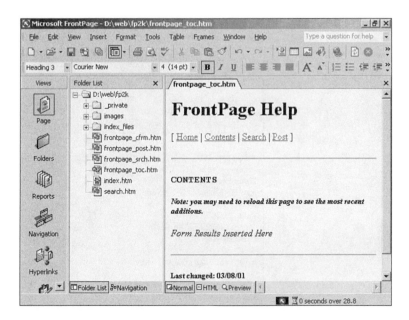

You can edit the text on each of the discussion Web's pages, adding graphics, using themes, and aligning the FrontPage components for posting, listing, and searching discussion messages.

A discussion Web can be created and edited on your computer, but you can't post or read messages until it has been published on a Web server that supports FrontPage Server Extensions. The only way to test it on your computer is to install a Web server on it that is equipped with extensions.

Maintaining Your Discussion Web

Your work is not over when a discussion Web has been published and tested. After users start posting messages to your discussion, you might want to monitor messages and delete any that contain inappropriate content (depending, of course, on your own definition of what's appropriate).

To review messages posted in your discussion, open your Web on the server that hosts it. Messages are stored as individual pages in the folder named after your Web. If you named the discussion lakers, messages will be in a lakers folder. If the name is _security, messages will be in a folder called _security.

As you might recall from earlier in the hour, if a folder name begins with an underscore ("_") character, it will normally be hidden by FrontPage 2002. The only exception to this rule is _private, a folder included with every new FrontPage Web, which is never hidden.

To view hidden folders, choose Tools, Web Settings, click the Advanced tab to bring it to the front, and then check the Show hidden files and folders box (see Figure 18.7).

FIGURE 18.7

Displaying hidden files and folders in a Web.

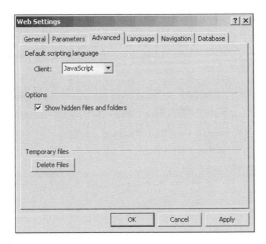

After your discussion Web's message folder is visible, you can open each message page for editing. To delete a message, right-click the message in the Folders list, and then choose Delete from the pop-up menu that appears.

> FrontPage discussions do not have a feature that automatically deletes old messages after a specific period of time. The only way to remove old messages is to do it yourself.

18

Workshop: Create a Discussion Web

This hour's workshop is to create and publish a no-frames Web with the Discussion Web Wizard.

Visitors to your discussion Web will be using the interface you choose on a frequent basis. Choosing a good one will go a long way toward establishing your Web as a popular destination on the World Wide Web.

Another way to improve the usability of a discussion Web is to offer plenty of guidance on its submission page, search page, and main page.

Solution

To create a new discussion Web:

1. Click File, New, Page or Web. The New Page or Web task bar opens alongside the FrontPage editing window.

2. Click the Web Site Templates hyperlink. The Web Site Templates dialog box is displayed.

3. Choose the Discussion Web Wizard icon and a location for your new Web on your computer, and then click OK. The Discussion Web Wizard will open.

4. Use the wizard to name your Web, choose a folder that will contain messages, and other options.

5. When the wizard asks how the Web should be presented, choose the no-frames option and click Next.

6. Click Finish to create your new discussion Web.

At this point, you have a discussion that can be published and used, but it is not very attractive. The text that describes how to use the discussion is also a dry read.

Before publishing your discussion, use themes and other features of FrontPage to make it more appealing. Rewrite the text that explains how to use the Web.

Figure 18.8 shows a FrontPage discussion Web that uses a theme, navigation buttons, and a table with its own background color.

FIGURE 18.8

A discussion Web for new FrontPage users.

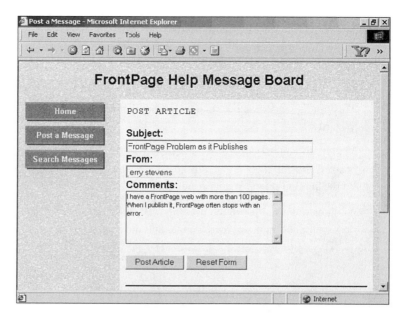

Summary

During this hour, you learned how to make it possible for users to create their own content on your FrontPage Web.

The Discussion Web Wizard makes it easy to create a place for messages to be read, posted, and searched. The real work on your part comes afterward, when visitors start using the discussion. Inviting discussion is an effective way to attract visitors to a Web, but it often requires maintenance work to delete inappropriate content and keep the list of messages from getting too large.

Discussions on World Wide Web sites tend to build their own momentum—the more people participate, the more likely it is that other people will find the place.

Hosting an area for Web-based discussion will give you a close look at the World Wide Web's ability to foster community. As you manage the discussions that take place and the inevitable controversies that will occur in any forum where ideas are freely debated, you might find yourself with a new job title: community leader.

Q&A

Q Whenever I try to publish my discussion Web, I get an error message stating that FrontPage Server Extensions are not installed. Do I need these on my computer?

A To use a discussion Web, you must be on a Web server that is equipped with FrontPage Server Extensions. If you are receiving that error, it normally means that your server does not currently support extensions.

Some Web hosting services have a different procedure for publishing FrontPage content than they do other Web documents. For example, GeoCities uses `http://fp.geocities.com` for FrontPage and `http://www.geocities.com` for other content.

Exercises

Challenge your knowledge of FrontPage 2002 discussion Webs with the following exercises:

- On a server equipped with FrontPage Server Extensions, create a discussion Web that's used to offer news updates about a Web.

- Add a product discussion forum to one of the company support Webs you created during a previous hour. Make this a nonthreaded Web with a search page for finding text in articles.

For solutions to these exercises, visit the book's official Web site at `http://www.cadenhead.org/frontpage/`.

HOUR 19

Add a Database to Your Web

FrontPage 2002 is part of Microsoft Office, the family of products that includes Word, Access, and Excel. During this hour, you'll get a strong idea of how close-knit this family has become.

FrontPage lets you interact directly with a database from a Web page. *Databases* are files that are used to store related information together in an organized manner. Each item in a database is called a *record*. Some uses for databases include customer orders, address books, inventory, and the like. You can read records from a database, save records to a database, and even create a new database. All these features are coordinated with Microsoft Access, the database program in the Office XP suite.

You'll create an Access database, populate it with records, and display those records on a Web page. All these tasks can be conducted entirely within FrontPage 2002, so you can use these features even if you don't own Access 2002.

Work Directly with Database Files

FrontPage 2002 is closely integrated with the other programs in the Microsoft Office XP productivity suite. You can easily exchange data between these programs and use some Office XP features within FrontPage.

Your FrontPage Webs can interact directly with database files created in Microsoft Access and Microsoft Excel. There are several different ways you can make them interact:

- Create a new Access database to hold the information collected on a Web form
- Display the contents of an Access or Excel database as a Web page
- Search an Access or Excel database from a FrontPage Web

You can create these database connections on any FrontPage Web. To publish a Web that uses database features, you need FrontPage Server Extensions and a hosting service that can support *Active Server Pages (ASP)*.

Active Server Pages is a scripting language created by Microsoft that complements JavaScript and VBScript, two scripting languages supported by FrontPage. An Active Server Page contains scripts that are run by a Web server as the page is loaded, producing output that can change dynamically. Most e-commerce sites use some kind of server technology like this to present products, offer discounts, and take orders.

Because database support in FrontPage requires Active Server Pages, you can use this feature only on a hosting service that uses Microsoft Internet Information Server (IIS) or another Web server that supports ASP in addition to FrontPage Server Extensions.

Create a New Access Database

When you collect information from a form on a Web page, you have several ways to store that data. You can send it to an e-mail address, save it as a Web page, or save it as a text file, as you've seen during previous hours.

You also can save the information to a database. To see how this works, add a form to a FrontPage Web using the Form Page Wizard, as you did in Hour 8, "Communicate on Your Web with Forms."

You can use the wizard to create forms that collect different kinds of information: product requests, contact information, and so on. To develop a database that can be used as an address book, create a form that collects contact information such as a person's name, address, phone number, e-mail address, and fax number.

When you create a form with the Form Page Wizard, the wizard does not ask whether you want to save the form's information to a database. You can save a form to a Web page, text file, or call a custom CGI script. Pick any of these alternatives and create the form—you will immediately be able to change this after the form is created.

After the wizard has created the form page, save it to a Web using a name that describes the kind of information it will collect. The filename must have the .asp file extension so that the Web server will know that the page uses Active Server Pages scripting. For example, if you are using the form to collect contact information, you could call the page address.asp.

After saving the page, right-click an empty area within the form and choose Form Properties from the shortcut menu that appears. The Form Properties dialog box opens (see Figure 19.1).

FIGURE 19.1

Saving form data to a database.

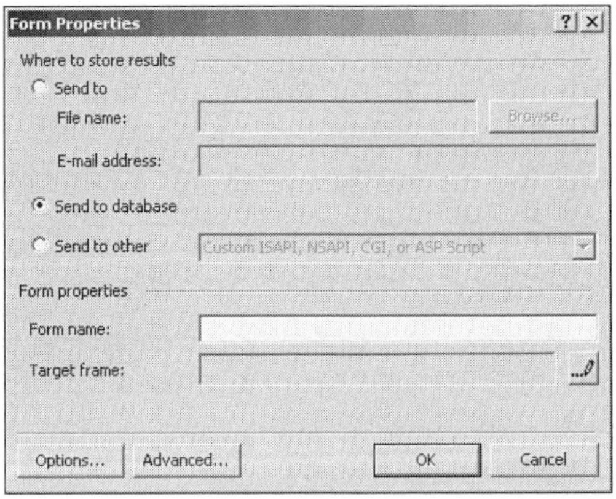

Select the Send to database option and click OK. Because this form has never been associated with a database, FrontPage displays a warning that the form will not work properly because the settings are invalid. Click Yes to change the settings immediately. The Options for Saving Results to Database dialog box is displayed (see Figure 19.2).

19

FIGURE 19.2

Choosing a database connection.

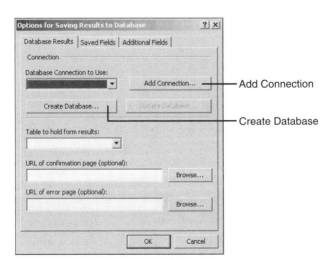

This dialog box enables you to select the database that will store the form's information.

There are two ways you can associate a form with a database:

- If you have already created an Access database or Excel spreadsheet that will contain the form data and imported the database into your Web, click Add Connection to associate the form with that database.
- If you have not created a database, click Create Database.

Using an existing database will be covered later this hour. Click Create Database to use your form as the basis for a new Access database.

The new database will hold the information that's collected from the form. FrontPage will use what's on the form to determine how the Access database should be structured, giving it the same name as the page, but with an .mdb file extension. If you named the page address.asp, the database will be named address.mdb.

The new Access database will be saved in a folder called fpdb.

After you publish the Web, you can use the form to add records to the new database. This database file can be loaded with Microsoft Access 2002, or you can use another feature of FrontPage 2002 to display records on your FrontPage Web.

Display Database Records on a Web

FrontPage 2002, with the assistance of server extensions, can display database records on a Web page from any Access or Excel database on your Web.

Add the database file to your Web: Choose File, Import to open the Import dialog box. Click Add File, and then find the database file and click OK. If the database is in a format that FrontPage 2002 recognizes, the Add Database Connection dialog box opens, as shown in Figure 19.3.

FIGURE 19.3

Creating a connection for a new database.

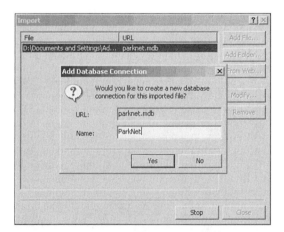

Every database is accessed from a FrontPage Web through a connection. You refer to this connection instead of the database filename when you access its records. When you created a new Access database from a form page, a default name was given to that connection. That name is displayed in the URL field of the Add Database Connection dialog box.

Give the database a name that describes its contents in the Name field, and then click Yes. Store the database in the `fpdb` folder of your Web.

After you've imported a database and created a connection for it, you're ready to start using that data on your Web. Create a new page in your Web that will be used to display records from the database. With the page open for editing, choose Insert, Database, Results. The Database Results Wizard will open (see Figure 19.4).

FIGURE 19.4

Displaying the contents of a database.

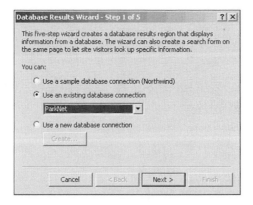

The Database Results Wizard asks a series of questions about the database you want to use, the parts of the database to display, and how they should appear on your page.

The first step is to choose the database connection associated with the database. The following database connections can be used:

- A connection to a sample database
- An existing connection that has already been added to a page on the current Web
- A new connection

Normally, you should have an existing connection to work with, either because you imported the database or you created it from a form page. Choose the connection of the database you just imported into the Web using the name you gave it.

The next questions the wizard will ask concern how the database will be displayed:

- Which database table to display records from
- Which fields in the database to display

- Which records to display (all records or a selection of records)
- How many records to display on a page

A table in a database is a grouping of records containing the same type of information. A movie database could have a table for movies and another table for actors and actresses, for example. Table 19.1 illustrates a database structure that contains two tables: Actors and TV Shows.

TABLE 19.1   A Television Database

ACTORS TABLE

ALISON LA PLACA RECORD

TOM (1994)

JOHN LARROQUETTE SHOW (1993)

JACKIE THOMAS SHOW (1992)

STAT (1992)

DENNIS BOUTSIKARIS RECORD

MISERY LOVES COMPANY (1995)

JACKIE THOMAS SHOW (1992)

STAT (1992)

TV SHOWS TABLE

JOHN LARROQUETTE SHOW (1992) RECORD

JOHN LARROQUETTE

ALISON LA PLACA

GIGI RICE

OPEN ALL NIGHT (1981) RECORD

GEORGE DZUNZDA

SUSAN TYRELL

SAM WHIPPLE

PINK LADY AND JEFF (1980) RECORD

KEIKO MASUDA

MITSUYO NEMOTO

JEFF ALTMAN

If you know Structured Query Language (SQL), you can use it to determine which records should be displayed. With the aforementioned movie database, you might want to limit the display to movies released during the current year.

Figure 19.5 shows the dialog box you use to determine the fields that will be displayed
for each record.

FIGURE 19.5

*Choosing which data-
base fields to display.*

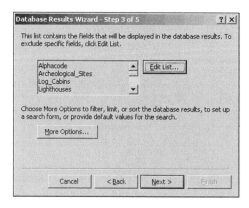

The next step in using the Database Results Wizard is to choose how the records will be
displayed on a Web page. You can structure the information in several different ways,
including paragraphs, lists, and tables. You also can limit each results page to a few
records rather than displaying all records on a single page.

After you decide how results will be displayed, the Database Results Wizard creates a
placeholder on a Web page for these results, as shown in Figure 19.6.

FIGURE 19.6

*Editing a Web page
containing database
results.*

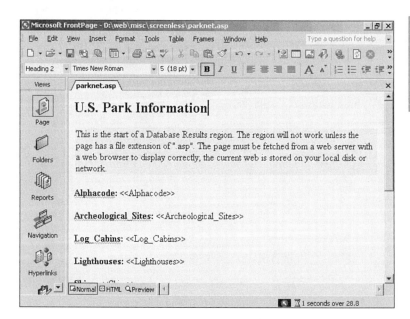

19

In the editing window, database results will show up as highlighted text and a record placeholder, as shown in Figure 19.6. The text explains how to view the records from the database. The placeholder contains a combination of text and database column values. Each column value represents a field in the database and is surrounded by << and >> characters, such as <<AlphaCode>> in Figure 19.6.

> You can make changes to how database results are displayed at any time. Click the highlighted text to open the Database Results Wizard again. All the answers you provided when creating the database will be used unless you change them as you work with the wizard.

You can move the text of the placeholder around, and delete database column values. If you change your mind after deleting a column value, you can add it back to the page by following these steps:

1. Place your cursor somewhere within the area that database results are displayed on the page.

2. Choose Insert, Database, Column Value. The Database Column Value dialog box appears.

3. Choose the value to display.

A database results page is displayed in a Web browser in Figure 19.7. On the page, four column values appear to the left of text: AlphaCode, ParkName, Primary_Designation, and CasualDesignation. Each value is listed on its own line with a line break separating the lines. There's also a blank line at the end of each record.

The way you format the placeholder while editing the page determines how each database record is displayed.

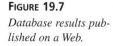

FIGURE 19.7

Database results published on a Web.

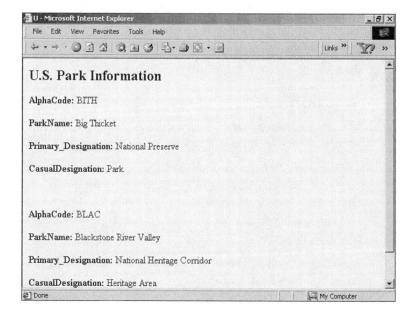

Workshop: Create an Access-Driven Web

An unusual aspect of FrontPage 2002's support for Microsoft Access 2002 is that you never need the latter software. You can create an Access database, query the database for specific records, and display those records entirely within FrontPage.

This hour's workshop is to create an Access-driven FrontPage Web without ever running Microsoft Access 2002. The purpose of the Web is twofold:

- To add records to a database
- To display those records with one of the fields sorted in alphabetical order

The database should be created specifically for this Web. Use the database to store something with at least four different fields, such as the following:

- Celebrity birthdays and birthplaces, along with their name and profession
- Your favorite Web sites, with the title, the address, and a short description of each
- Dallas Cowboys players, their positions, crimes they have been convicted of committing, and the length of their sentences

If possible, one of the fields in the database should have a small number of possible answers. For example, you might have a category for a Web site's database such as News, Sports, Personal, Tech, or Other.

19

After you've created the database, develop another page for displaying all of its records. You can choose any of the layout formats, but see whether you can figure out how to make the Database Results Wizard arrange records alphabetically according to one of the fields.

Solution

The first step in creating an Access database from within FrontPage 2002 is to develop an input form. This form will be used to add new records to the database.

The birthdays database has four fields: Name, DateOfBirth, BirthPlace, and Profession. Each of these uses a text box on the form, except for Profession, which uses a drop-down box. This drop-down box limits the choice of professions, so the database will have a Profession value equal to only one of the listed options. In this example, those options are Actor, Politician, and Musician.

Arranging records alphabetically is done in the Database Results Wizard as you're choosing which fields to display.

Open the wizard by clicking the highlighted text on the page above the database result placeholder. Click the Next button until you are on Step 3 of the Database Results Wizard (see Figure 19.8).

FIGURE **19.8**

Changing how records are displayed on a page.

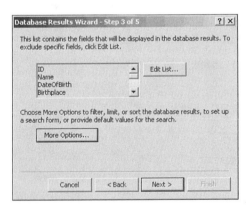

During this step, you can tell the wizard to sort database results, filter out unwanted database records, and set up a search form. Click the More Options button to open the More Options dialog box, and then click the Ordering button. The Ordering dialog box is displayed (see Figure 19.9).

FIGURE 19.9

Changing the arrangement of records on a page.

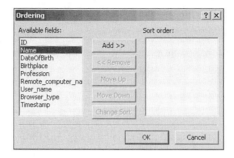

Use this dialog box to pick a field that will be used to determine the sort order of the records. Double-click the name of the field in the Available fields box. The field name will be moved to the Sort Order box. Click OK to make this change, and then click Next on each subsequent step of the Database Results Wizard. Click Finish to exit the wizard.

When the page is displayed on a Web server that supports FrontPage extensions, database records are arranged according to the new sort order.

Summary

If your Web hosting service supports Active Server Pages and FrontPage Server Extensions, you can create, edit, and display the contents of an Access database from your FrontPage Webs.

Working directly with a database often makes more sense than offering its contents as text on Web pages. Manually editing text is a time-consuming task, especially if the database is updated frequently. Displaying database results on a Web page offers immediate access to that data.

During the next hour, you'll see how FrontPage works with another member of the Office XP family: Microsoft Excel.

Q&A

Q Is there a way to rename a database connection? The default new_page_1 isn't very descriptive of what the connection is used for.

A You can't change the name, but it's relatively easy to create a new database connection to replace it.

When a new Access database is created from a form page, FrontPage 2002 uses the filename of the page to name the connection. Because the filename of a new page

19

is called something like new_page_1.htm when you create it, the connection ends up with a name like new_page_1.

To prevent this from happening, give the page a better name before you use it to create a new database.

Exercises

Challenge your knowledge of FrontPage 2002 database connections with the following exercises:

- Create a database of products with the name, price, category, and a short description of each. Use this database to offer a Web with different pages that display the records in each category.
- If you have Microsoft Access 2002, use it to open one of the databases that FrontPage 2002 developed during this hour. Add records from within Access, and check to see that they're displayed on the Web with all the other records.

For solutions to these exercises, visit the book's official Web site at http://www.cadenhead.org/frontpage/.

Hour **20**

Use FrontPage Components

Looking at the World Wide Web today, it's hard to believe that it began as an all-text medium. Before graphics were added to the Web by an enterprising student programming his own browser, the only difference between the Web and a book was the presence of hyperlinks.

Today, the World Wide Web is composed of a dazzling assortment of media: text, pictures, sound files, movies, Java programs, Flash animations, streaming audio, PDF files, vector graphics, and many other offerings that are delivered in conjunction with Web pages.

New ways to present information and engage an audience are introduced constantly on the Web as publishers and programmers continue to experiment.

During this hour, you will learn how to use Web components, a feature of FrontPage 2002 that makes it possible to add many of these unusual elements to your Web.

Adding Components to a Web

FrontPage 2002 includes more than 40 components you can incorporate into your Webs. Some of them, such as the Web search and hover buttons, have been described in previous hours of the book.

The other components include each of the following:

- Dynamic effects such as marquees and rotating banner ads
- Excel spreadsheets
- Hit counters
- Photo galleries, which create their own thumbnail images
- Page banners
- Pages and pictures that are displayed only at specified times
- Link bars
- A table of contents for a Web
- Usage reports—stats from your server logs that can be shared with visitors
- Microsoft bCentral components—free services for businesses putting themselves on the Web, including counters, banner ads, and affiliate links
- Links to Expedia.com maps
- MSN search boxes and stock quotes
- MSNBC headlines and weather reports
- Java applets and ActiveX controls
- Browser plug-ins

To add a component to a page, choose Insert, Web Component to open the dialog box shown in Figure 20.1.

Choose a category in the Component type list, a component in the Choose a usage list box, and then click Finish.

If the Web component does not require anything else to set up, it will appear on the page in the editing window.

FIGURE 20.1

Adding a component to a Web.

FIGURE 20.1

Adding a component to a Web.

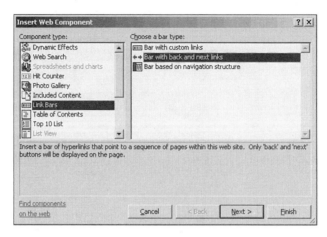

Otherwise, a dialog box will open where you can configure the component. Figure 20.2 shows the Hit Counter Properties dialog box, which is used to choose the appearance and starting number of a page counter.

FIGURE 20.2

Setting up a FrontPage page counter.

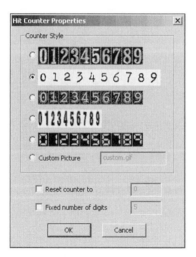

20

Headlines and Weather from MSNBC

Some of the new components offer headlines and weather reports from MSNBC, a television and Internet news service founded by Microsoft and NBC.

You can add headlines in five topic areas to any page of your Web: business, living and travel, news, sports, and technology. There also is an MSNBC weather component that can be set up to present a city's current forecast and temperature.

In Figure 20.3, a Web page containing several of the components is displayed.

FIGURE 20.3

*Viewing current
MSNBC headlines and
weather on a page.*

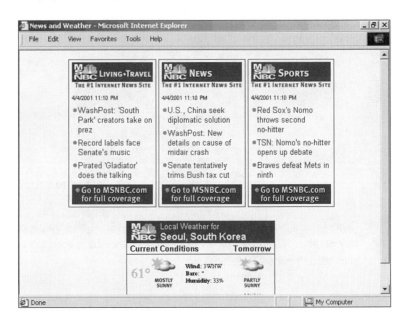

These headlines are offered as pictures stored on MSNBC's Web server, so you can use them on any of your Webs. The pictures are updated automatically by MSNBC to keep the headlines current.

To add a headline graphic to the page you are currently editing:

1. Connect to the Internet.
2. Choose Insert, Web Component.
3. In the Component type list, select MSNBC Components.
4. In the Choose a MSNBC component list, select the MSNBC component to add and click Finish.

The picture is added to the page. You can move it around like any other picture, though you should take care not to remove the hyperlink associated with it.

If you select the MSNBC weather component, you must also choose a city to associate with the component. MSNBC offers weather information for 14,000 cities.

When you add a weather component, FrontPage displays Seattle's forecast and temperature regardless of the city you have selected. To see the correct information, preview the page in a Web browser or click the Preview button at the bottom of the editing window.

Link Bars

Link bars, which were called navigation bars in FrontPage 2000, are related groups of hyperlinks that are represented as graphical buttons that are arranged vertically or horizontally.

Every FrontPage template uses link bars to provide links to the different pages in the Web.

Figure 20.4 shows a page in a customer support Web that uses a link bar. The bar, which runs vertically along the left edge of the page, includes links to six pages: What's New, Products, FAQ, Service Requests, Suggestions, and Catalogs/Manuals.

FIGURE 20.4

Navigating a Web using link bars.

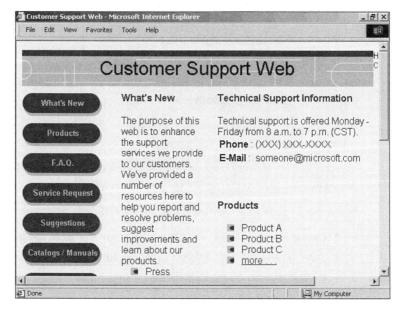

To add a link bar to a page:

1. Choose Insert, Navigation. The Insert Web Components dialog box is displayed with the Link Bars item selected.

2. In the Choose a bar type list, select the type of bar to add and click Finish.

There are three kinds of link bars: bars based on the navigational structure of your Web, bars that link to pages and Web addresses of your choosing, and back/next bars linking to pages in a sequence, such as pages in an online book.

It's easy to get lost when you're visiting the pages of a large site on the World Wide Web. One of the ways publishers make these Webs easier to use is through the use of link bars.

Most commercial news and sports sites have link bars that lead to the main topics they cover. A sports site such as ESPN.com has links to its NFL, NBA, NHL, and MLB pages on a navigation bar that's part of every page. If you dive down several links into ESPN's site while you're reading stories, you can get back to a starting point by using the navigation bar.

Link bars can be added to your own FrontPage 2002 Webs and placed in shared borders to make them appear on every page. There are four styles of bars:

- Vertical lists of graphic links
- Horizontal lists of graphic links
- Vertical lists of text links
- Horizontal lists of graphic links

When you are working with a link bar, you don't create any of the hyperlinks that it contains. Instead, these links are determined by the navigational structure you have created for the Web in the Navigation view.

After you have established the Navigation view for a Web, it will be used to determine which links appear on the Web's link bars.

You can edit an existing bar by double-clicking it in Page view. The Link Bar Properties dialog box opens (see Figure 20.5).

A link bar in FrontPage 2002 can display six different groups of hyperlinks:

- *Parent level*—Links to the parent of the current page and all its siblings
- *Same level*—Links to all pages that are siblings of the current page
- *Back* and *next*—Links to the siblings immediately to the left (back) and right (next) of the current page
- *Child level*—Links to all pages that are children of the current page
- *Global level*—Links to all pages that have no parents
- *Child pages under Home*—Links to all pages that have the Web's home page as a parent

FIGURE 20.5

Working on a link bar.

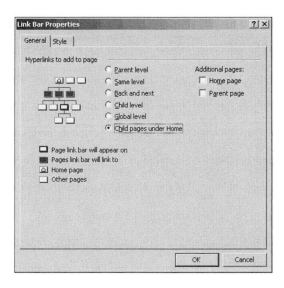

You also have the option of adding extra links for the Web's home page and the current page's parent, if these aren't already in the group.

The Link Bar Properties dialog box shown in Figure 20.5 contains a drawing of a Navigational view. As you choose the different hyperlink groups, this drawing changes to show the pages included in that group.

Two more things you can configure are a link bar's orientation (horizontal or vertical) and its appearance (buttons or text). Double-click the bar in editing view to open the Link Bar Properties dialog box and click the Style tab to bring it to the front (see Figure 20.6).

FIGURE 20.6

Configuring a bar's orientation and appearance.

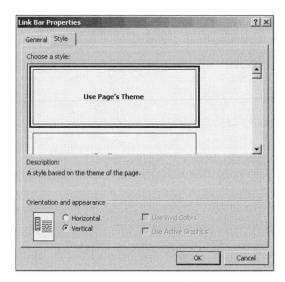

The selection that you make will be immediately reflected in the Web. You can easily experiment with the different styles until you find one that you like.

> If your Web does not have a theme applied to it, you will not see buttons on your link bar even if you select that option instead of text. FrontPage 2002 relies on themes to provide the buttons that are used on graphic link bars.

The Navigation view is used to provide the text that's associated with each hyperlink on a link bar. To change this text, right-click a page's icon in the Navigation view and select the Rename menu option.

This text appears on all link bars that link to the page, so it should be reasonably short to provide room for other links. It also is used on the page's banner—a FrontPage 2002 component displayed in the top shared border of any Web that uses FrontPage's built-in themes.

When you save or publish a Web, FrontPage 2002 creates pictures for each graphical page banner and link bar on your Web. The text is displayed over the component's background image.

Figure 20.7 shows the Navigation view for a newly created site that uses the Personal Web template.

FIGURE 20.7

Examining a Web's navigational structure.

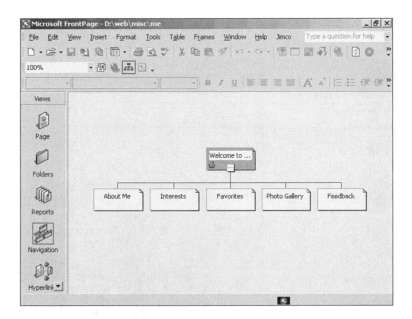

All five pages in the Personal Web are represented in the Navigation view.

The Navigation view establishes a parent-child relationship between the pages of a Web. In Figure 20.7, the page labeled Home Page is the parent of the other five pages: About Me, Interests, Favorites, Photo Gallery, and Feedback.

Pages are added to the Navigation view by dragging them from the Folders list.

When you drag a page onto the Navigation view, keep hold of it by holding your mouse button down. A dotted outline indicates the relationship that would be established if you dropped the page at that location. The outline changes depending on where you have dragged the page and which page it is closest to.

Figure 20.8 shows an outline around the cursor that shows a parent-child relationship between a page called Favorites page and a new page that hasn't been dropped. The cursor is closest to the Favorites page.

FIGURE 20.8

Dragging a new page into the Navigation view.

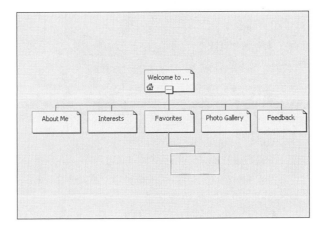

You can pick up pages in the Navigation view and drag them to new locations. The easiest way to get a feel for this view is to drag a new page around and drop it at several different places to see what relationship is established.

In general, a page dropped above another page becomes its parent. A page dropped below a page becomes its child. A page that's dropped beside a page is its sibling and shares the same parent.

An exception: Pages dropped above a Web's home page will be orphans—no lines will connect them to other pages. You can use this to start new parent-child groups that are completely unrelated to other pages of the Web.

In the Navigation view, a parent can have as many children as desired, but a child has only one parent.

20

> The one-parent rule is where the parent-child metaphor starts to get a little creepy. If you suspect something untoward is going on inside FrontPage 2002's Navigation view, think of these pages as paramecia. They also reproduce through a one-parent system that doesn't involve a stork.

Page Banners

Page banners are specified with all of FrontPage 2002's themes, so you should already have experience working with them. They look like giant link bars (if they're graphical) and provide a place to give a page a title.

To add a banner to a page, choose Insert, Page Banner. The Page Banner Properties dialog box opens (Figure 20.9).

FIGURE 20.9

Adding a banner to a page.

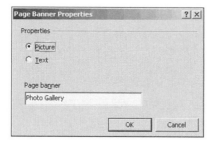

A page banner contains a single line of text and can have a graphical background. The picture used as the background is defined by the Web's theme—Webs without a theme cannot have graphical page banners.

The text of a page banner will be the same as its title in the Navigation view window. If the page isn't in the navigational structure of the Web yet, it must be added before a banner can be displayed.

To make changes to a banner, double-click it in the editing window. The Page Banner Properties dialog box opens.

All of this takes place behind the scenes, so you work with these components differently than you do with pictures.

Workshop: Create a FrontPage Family Tree

The parent-child relationships in the Navigation view can be thought of as a family tree.

If you're not familiar with the term, a *family tree* is a drawing that shows several generations of a family and how they are related to each other.

The Navigation view looks like one of these trees although, admittedly, the family's a little odder than most. You can use the view to determine which pages have children, which children have grandchildren, and so on. The home page sits on top as the grandsire of many descendants.

This hour's workshop is to put three generations of your own family into the Navigation view.

Do the following:

- Create a new Web with no pages in it
- Add a new page named after one of your grandparents
- Add pages named after each child of that grandparent
- Add pages named after you and each of your siblings

After this is done, you'll have several different pages with absolutely no connection to each other. Use the Navigational view to establish the correct parent, child, and sibling relationships among these pages.

When this is done, add a common link bar to the top of each page of the Web. This bar should contain only the children of the current page.

Add a second link bar to the right of every page that contains a link to all siblings and the parent.

Solution

Figure 20.10 shows a Navigation view family tree of the Bradfords from the 1970s TV drama *Eight Is Enough*. If you're familiar with the show, the names of Tom Bradford and his eight kids are probably familiar to you. Sandra Sue might not be—she's the infant daughter of Susan and Merle the Pearl.

The quickest way to add empty pages to a Web and save them is to click the New Page and Save buttons on the Standard toolbar. The Save As dialog box opens, enabling you to give the page a filename before saving it.

After all the pages have been created, you can drag them onto the Navigation view to establish the correct parent-child relationships. This view is also used to give each page a name, which you must do before the page's title will appear on link bars.

Shared borders are established through the Format, Shared Borders command. You can add top and right borders and apply the change to the entire Web, as described during Hour 6, "Create a Web Page."

20

FIGURE 20.10

Three generations of pages in the Navigation view.

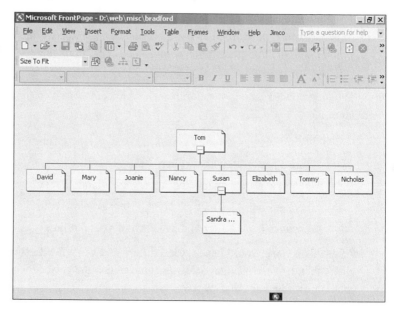

Link bars are added through the Insert, Navigation command. If you have applied a theme to the Web, you can use graphic buttons. Otherwise, all link bars will be displayed as text.

If you are creating Webs that have common groups of links on several different pages, the easiest way to handle this in FrontPage 2002 is through link bars.

Summary

One of the biggest selling points for FrontPage 2002 is the ability to create interesting Webs without a lot of work.

As you concentrate on the appearance of your Web and the information it contains, FrontPage uses HTML, CSS, and other Web technology behind the scenes to put every-thing together and make it work.

FrontPage Web components embody the same principle, making it easy to incorporate unusual things into your Web such as link bars, news and weather reports, page banners, and more than three dozen other offerings.

Because the Web changes at a fast pace, FrontPage 2002 enables you to keep up by find-ing new Web components on the World Wide Web.

To see what's available, choose Insert, Web Component, and then click the Find components on the Web hyperlink. You will be taken to Microsoft's Office Update Worldwide site, which describes the new components that have become available for FrontPage 2002 and the other programs in Office XP.

Q&A

Q In FrontPage 2000, I was able to create a navigation bar with text links instead of graphical buttons. Is this still possible?

A You can still use text instead of graphics, but the feature has moved. Choose Insert, Navigation to open the Insert Web Components dialog box with Link Bars selected in the Component Type list. Click Next, and then scroll in the Choose a bar style list box, select a style from the list, and then click Finish.

Several text link styles are available, including the style that was offered in the previous version of FrontPage.

Exercises

Challenge your knowledge of the FrontPage 2002 graphical user interface with the following exercises:

- In a personal Web you have created for yourself, add a vertical link bar to all pages that contains hyperlinks to the sites you visit most often on the World Wide Web.

- Add one of the MSNBC news headline pictures to a Web, publish it in a Web browser, and try it out over time to see how it is automatically updated.

For solutions to these exercises, visit the book's official Web site at http://www.cadenhead.org/frontpage/.

20

PART VI

Rounding Out Your FrontPage Expertise

Hour

HOUR 21

Create a Form by Hand

Forms gather information from the people who visit a Web. You can use forms to solicit feedback, conduct surveys, play games, and interact with an audience in ways that aren't possible with other media.

During Hour 8, "Communicate on Your Web with Forms," you used the Form Page Wizard, which is well suited to many forms. For the times it isn't, you can create a form manually by designing it on a Web page.

During this hour, you'll learn how to design a form by using textboxes, check boxes, option buttons, drop-down boxes, and more. You'll create these elements, add labels that describe their purposes, and limit the visitor's answers to a range of possible choices.

When the form is completed, you'll determine how to use the information it has collected—saving it to a text file, sending it as e-mail, or calling special Web server programs that can decode the form.

You'll also be able to modify existing forms, which is useful even if they were originally created by a wizard.

Create a Form by Hand

To add a form to a Web page, Choose Insert, Form, Form. A form will be added to the page with its boundaries marked by a dotted outline (see Figure 21.1).

FIGURE 21.1

Editing a newly added form on a page.

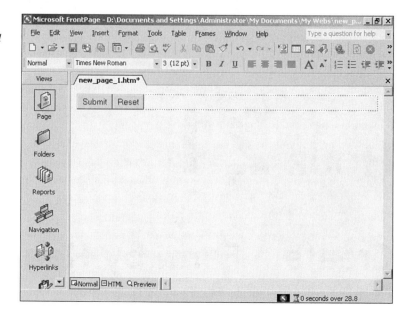

Forms are made up of the following elements:

- One-line textboxes
- Scrolling text areas
- Check boxes
- Option buttons
- Drop-down boxes
- Labels
- Push buttons
- Pictures
- Group boxes
- Advanced buttons

Figure 21.2 shows most of these elements on a Web page.

Every form element is added by using a command on the Insert, Form menu. To add an element to a form, place your cursor within the form in the editing window, then choose Insert, Form and the element you want to add.

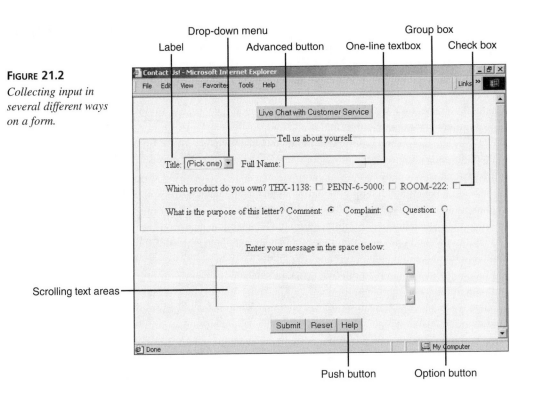

FIGURE 21.2
*Collecting input in
several different ways
on a form.*

Every form is added to a page with two built-in elements:

- A Submit button for transmitting the information collected on the form
- A Reset button for clearing out all answers on a form and starting over

These two buttons are placed at the bottom of a form, but you can move them anywhere within the form's border.

All information that is collected on a form must come from elements located within its border in Page view. This border is used only for that purpose, and it does not show up when the page is displayed in a browser.

Form elements can be arranged within a border, just like anything else on a Web page. You can put them into tables, add pictures, and other things, as long as the form elements stay within the border.

You can add additional forms to a page by adding form elements outside of a border. FrontPage 2002 will automatically border the elements and add Submit and Reset buttons.

Each element of a form can be added to a Web by choosing Insert, Form and picking the element. FrontPage 2002 offers a shortcut that's handy if you are working on a form with a lot of elements—a Form toolbar.

21

To open the Form toolbar, choose Insert, Form, then place your mouse at the top edge of the menu above all the elements. A four-pointed arrow will appear in place of your cursor, as shown in Figure 21.3. Click anywhere on the top edge and drag to open the Form toolbar.

Click and drag to open the Form toolbar

FIGURE 21.3

Viewing the Form toolbar.

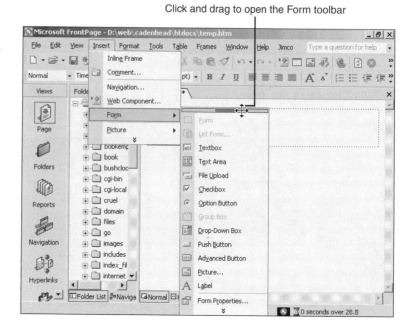

Add Textboxes and Text Areas

Textboxes and text areas enable the visitor to enter keyboard input on a Web page. A textbox can hold a single line of input, so it's convenient for things like a user's name, street address, and ZIP code. A text area can hold an unlimited number of lines, making it useful for longer input such as a user's comments about your site

Add a textbox to a form by choosing Insert, Form, Textbox, and remember to place the textbox within the form's border. FrontPage 2002 assigns it a default width that approximates the number of characters that can be displayed in the box. More characters can be entered, but they won't all appear within the box. Text areas also have a default number of lines that are displayed.

FrontPage gives each box a default name and value, just as it does with all other form elements. To change these things after the element has been added to a page, double-click the element to bring up the Textbox Properties dialog box, shown in Figure 21.4.

FIGURE 21.4

Editing a textbox.

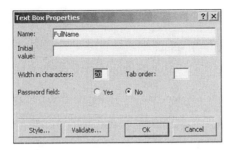

Every form element should be given a descriptive name that explains its purpose. This name will be used when the element's information is transmitted, and it also can be used by a scripting language such as JavaScript to get the element's value.

The name given to a form element should contain only alphanumeric characters and the underscore character ("_"). If you use anything else, such as spaces, FrontPage will warn you that the form might not work correctly in a browser.

If you give a textbox an initial value, that value will appear when the form is first loaded or the Reset button is clicked. This can be used to give the textbox a default value. For instance, the Internal Revenue Service could put a default value of 100 in the Percentage of Your Income to Pay This Year in Taxes textbox. Taxpayers would have to edit this initial value to pay less than 100 percent of their income in federal tax.

Select the password field option to hide all input entered into a one-line textbox. Asterisks will appear in place of what's really being typed as a way to protect against snoops, but the real text will be sent when the form is submitted.

Add a text area to a page by choosing Insert, Form, Text Area. A text area will be added that is two lines tall and roughly 20 characters wide—unlike a text box, a text area can receive more than one line of input from a user.

To change the size of the text area, double-click the element in the editing window to open the Text Area Box Properties dialog box.

Add Labels

A *label* is text that describes the purpose of another form element. Because elements are often used to answer questions, labels are used to actually ask the questions.

To add a label to a form, begin by typing the text for the label. This text should be on the same line as the form element it's associated with. Enter the text of a label next to a one-line text box, and then select both the text and the form element by dragging your mouse over the label and the element. Choose Insert, Form, Label. A border will appear around the text to indicate that it's now a label.

Turning text into a label makes it easier for people to use a form. In many cases, they can click the label in addition to the form element. Clicking a check box's label is the same as clicking the check box, for instance.

Labels provide assistance to Web users with non-visual browsers and other technology for differently abled people. Assistive software can use the label to explain the purpose of a form element. For example, a nonvisual Web browser could speak each label aloud before enabling the user to enter information into the form element that's associated with the label.

Add Option Buttons and Check Boxes

Option buttons and check boxes are form elements that have only two possible values: selected or not selected. You can set these elements to either value when the page is first loaded.

A check box appears with a check mark if it's selected and appears empty otherwise. Each box is given a name and a value—ON by default—that is sent for each selected check box when the form is transmitted. You can change the name and value by double-clicking the element to open a Properties dialog box.

There are two differences between check boxes and option buttons:

- They look different.
- Option buttons can be grouped together to prevent more than one of them from being selected at one time. Check boxes cannot.

One sample use for check boxes: Ask people what political parties they voted for in the past decade. If your audience is in the U.S., there could be check boxes for the Republican, Democratic, Libertarian, Green, and Reform parties. Between zero and five boxes could be checked, depending on how often the person jumped across party lines at the ballot box. An appropriate value for these boxes would be YES, because it's transmitted only for boxes that are selected.

An option button is a circle that has a dot in it if it's selected. You group option buttons together by giving each of them the same name, which should also contain only alphanumeric characters and underscores.

Add a check box and a series of option buttons to a form by choosing Insert, Form, Check Box and Insert, Form, Option Button, respectively. Only one option button can be selected in any group, so if you select one of them, the others will all be deselected.

The value given to an option button should describe what selecting the button means. Consider option buttons with the group name `CustomerSatisfaction` and the labels Ecstatic, Happy, Undecided, Displeased, and Enraged. These labels could also be used as values for the buttons—so if someone picks the Enraged button, `CustomerSatisfaction` will be transmitted with a value of "Enraged."

An option button is being edited in Figure 21.5.

FIGURE 21.5

Editing an option button.

Add Drop-down Boxes

Drop-down boxes serve a similar purpose to option buttons: They enable the user to choose from several possible responses. However, instead of these possible choices being divided into buttons, they're placed in a menu. Drop-down boxes also differ in another way—they can be configured to allow more than one choice to be selected.

When you add a drop-down box to a form, it doesn't have any possible responses. You add these responses by editing the menu. Double-click it to open the Drop-Down Box Properties dialog box, shown in Figure 21.6.

FIGURE 21.6

Editing a drop-down box.

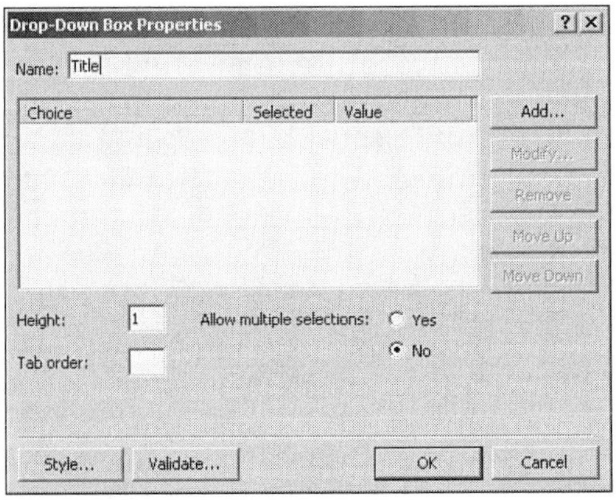

21

The Add button is used to add new responses to the menu. Each response has a Choice value that will appear on the menu, and the Selected value is transmitted with the form unless you specify an alternative.

The Add Choice dialog box is shown in Figure 21.7.

FIGURE 21.7

Adding choices to a drop-down box.

The default behavior of a drop-down box is to allow one choice to be selected and to display the menu on a single-line when it isn't being used. Both of these things can be changed in the Drop-Down Box Properties dialog box.

Change the Allow Multiple Selections option from No to Yes to enable users to enter more than one answer at a time. To change the number of lines that are displayed without scrolling, enter a different value in the Height text box.

Figure 21.8 shows a drop-down box being set up to ask a user to list her favorite sports. Up to five sports can be selected, and because the Height is set to 5, all five choices are displayed, avoiding the need for a drop-down arrow and scrollbar.

FIGURE 21.8

Creating a drop-down box that allows multiple selections.

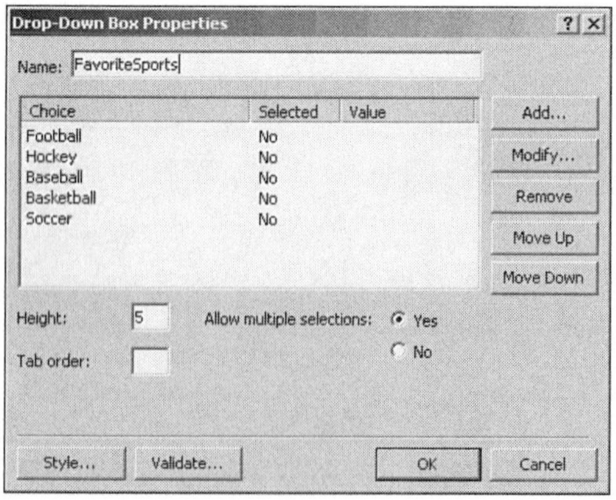

After you've added all possible responses to a drop-down box, you can rearrange them with the Move Up and Move Down buttons.

> The first choice in a drop-down box is sometimes used like a label. A value such as "(Pick one)" or "(Click here to select)" is used as the topmost choice. This has the added advantage of preventing the first real choice from being selected simply because it appears when the page is loaded.

Add Push Buttons and Pictures

Push buttons are form elements that look just like the Submit and Reset buttons incorporated into every FrontPage 2002 form.

If you delete the Submit and Reset buttons from a form, you can put them back by inserting a push button for each and editing its properties. Otherwise, there isn't a way to use a push button to transmit a value without writing your own interactive programs in a scripting language such as JavaScript.

Push buttons can be associated with hyperlinks, so you can add them to a form as links to other pages. One possible use: a Help button that loads a page describing how to use the form.

Pictures on a form, which are added by choosing Insert, Form, Picture, are used for two purposes:

- Replacing the Submit button with a graphical version
- Creating an imagemap that is handled by a Web server

A picture element is placed on a form as a FrontPage imagemap component. This component, unlike other imagemaps, requires a Web server that includes FrontPage Server Extensions.

When the picture is clicked, the form is submitted with some extra information: the exact location on the picture where it was clicked. Neither FrontPage 2002 nor its server extensions do anything with this location information. Because of that, the only thing you can do with a picture label is use it as an alternative Submit button—if your server has FrontPage extensions.

Receive Information from a Form

21

The last step in creating a form is deciding where to put all the information you've gathered. To set this up, right-click within a form's borders in the editing window, and then choose Form Properties. The Form Properties dialog box appears, as shown in Figure 21.9.

FIGURE 21.9

*Determining where
form data should be
sent.*

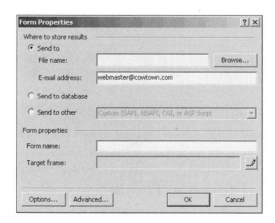

Your choices are the following:

- Send it in an e-mail to a specified address
- Store it as a file on your Web
- Send it to a database
- Send it to a form-handling program on your Web server

The first three options require a Web server that supports FrontPage Server Extensions. Form data that is mailed will arrive like any other e-mail. The name and value of each form element will be displayed in the body of the e-mail, as in the following:

```
FullName: Puddin N. Tane
Title: Mr.
THX-1138: Own
ROOM-222: Own
Purpose: Complaint
```

To save a form to a file, you specify the filename and folder where it should be stored. If this file doesn't exist when someone uses the form, it will be created.

If you don't restrict access to the form results file by using FrontPage 2002's security feature, everyone who visits your Web will be able to read the file by loading its address directly with their browser.

Sending form data to a database was covered during Hour 19, "Add a Database to Your Web."

The last way to handle forms is to call up a program on your Web server that can take in form data and do something with it. (Most of these programs simply e-mail the data to a specified address.)

Form-handling programs rely on the Common Gateway Interface (CGI), a protocol that determines how a Web server exchanges information with other programs on the same computer. CGI programs require special access to a Web server, and most Web hosting services don't grant it to their customers for security reasons. Some hosting services install CGI programs that can be shared by all customers.

If you have a CGI program that handles forms, all you need to do in FrontPage 2002 is specify the name and location of the program and its delivery method. The method is either POST or GET, and the documentation for the CGI program should specify which one to use.

Figure 21.10 shows how this information is configured in FrontPage 2002.

FIGURE 21.10

Calling a CGI program to handle a form.

Workshop: Create a Feedback Form

Anyone who believes that there's no such thing as a stupid question, as I do, should get a chance to test that theory with the hour's workshop. Your project is to create the world's most intrusive Web feedback form.

Many sites on the World Wide Web include a form for sending feedback to the publisher. They ask for your name, e-mail address, and some comments about the site. Some might ask other questions, such as the subject of your message, but usually the requests are kept to a minimum.

With this in mind, take one of the Webs you've created and add a new feedback page to it. Instead of relying on the Form Page Wizard or the Feedback Form template, add it as a blank page and develop the form by hand. Ask for as much personal information you can possibly think to ask: name, e-mail address, mailing address, phone number, birthday, birthplace, mother's maiden name, blood type, weight, height, allergies, gender, current net worth, most painful childhood memory, number of past broken bones, phobias, and so on.

21

Try to add questions that require every one of the form elements, except pictures—it isn't easy to intrude on someone's personal life with a question that requires an imagemap.

Also, give every form element (except for labels) a name that describes its purpose. This will make it easier to decipher form results that are mailed to you or published as a Web page.

When you're done, save the form responses using a method that's supported by your Web hosting server, and then publish the Web. If you're hosting Webs on a server that supports FrontPage Server Extensions, have the form results mailed to an e-mail address.

Solution

Figure 21.11 shows a Web form that includes every element but pictures.

FIGURE 21.11

An intrusive Web form.

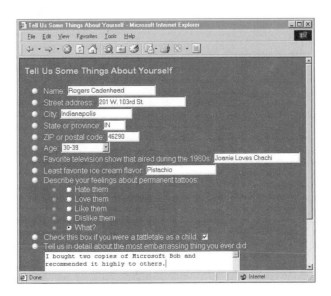

Creating this form took the following steps:

- Text was added to a Web page for use as a label.
- A form element was added adjacent to the text.
- The form element was double-clicked and given a name using its Properties dialog box.

An extra step was involved in the creation of the option buttons—all these buttons were given the same group name.

After the drop-down menu was placed on the form, items were added to it by double-clicking the menu and using its Properties dialog box.

If the form shown in Figure 21.11 were submitted to an e-mail address, it would arrive looking like the following:

```
************************************************************************
Name:                        Rogers Cadenhead
StreetAddress:               201 W. 103rd St.
City:                        Indianapolis
StateOrProvince:             IN
ZipOrPostalCode:             46290
Age:                         30-39
Favorite80sTVShow:           Joanie Loves Chachi
LeastFavoriteIceCreamFlavor: Pistachio
Tattoo:                      What?
Tattletale:                  ON
EmailAddress:                frontpage24@prefect.com

MostEmbarrasingThing:

I bought two copies of Microsoft Bob and recommended it
highly to others.
```

Summary

Forms are an essential feature of the World Wide Web because they immediately connect a publisher with the people who visit a Web.

You can create forms quickly with FrontPage 2002's Form Page Wizard. You also can take more control over a form by adding its elements to a Web page directly.

By using textboxes, check boxes, option buttons, and other parts of a form, you can ask questions in a variety of different ways. A multiple-choice question can be limited to a single answer with option buttons or multiple answers on a drop-down box. More open-ended answers can be typed in as one or more lines of text.

After spending two hours on the subject of Web forms, you should be able to ask the visitors to your FrontPage 2002 Webs anything. Getting them to actually *answer* is another matter.

21

Q&A

Q FrontPage saves form data to a .csv file, but GeoCities won't let me publish it. How can I fix this?

A GeoCities and some other hosting providers limit the file extensions that can be used on their server for security reasons. In the Form Properties dialog box, change the file extension from .csv to .txt.

A CSV file is a text file containing data that is separated by commas. Using .txt as the extension instead of .txt does not change the contents of the file in any way.

Q Why would an imagemap be a form element?

A There are a number of useful purposes for a picture on the World Wide Web that tells a form handler where it was clicked. One of the most common is a street map that can be clicked to center the map at a new location.

There also are games in which visitors must click a specific place in a large picture to win a prize. Because the imagemap handler is on the Web server, the contest organizers can successfully hide the location. Using these imagemaps requires CGI programs and special Web server access.

Exercises

Challenge your knowledge of FrontPage 2002 forms with the following exercises:

- Create a form that a visitor can use to send e-mail to you, including elements for the sender's name, e-mail address, subject, and comments.

- Add a Help button to the form you created during this hour's workshop. Use it to either apologize to people in advance or simply to help them understand how to use the form.

For solutions to these exercises, visit the book's official Web site at http://www.cadenhead.org/frontpage/.

HOUR 22

Divide a Page into Separate Frames

A few years after the creation of HTML and the World Wide Web, Netscape introduced a new feature for sites called *frames*. Frames divide a browser window into smaller sections, each holding its own Web page, which enables you to view two pages simultaneously.

During this hour, you'll learn how to create frames and place pages into them. You'll discover how to resize a frame, hide its scrollbar, and convert existing Webs into frames.

Create a Frame

Frames divide a browser window into two or more separate windows. You can configure frames in several ways:

- Frames can be set to a specific size
- Frames can be resized when site visitors change the size of their browsers
- Frames can have vertical and horizontal scrollbars or no scrollbars at all

The simplest framed page contains two frames—either top and bottom or left and right. Figure 22.1 contains a Web page with two frames beside each other.

FIGURE 22.1

A Web page with left and right frames.

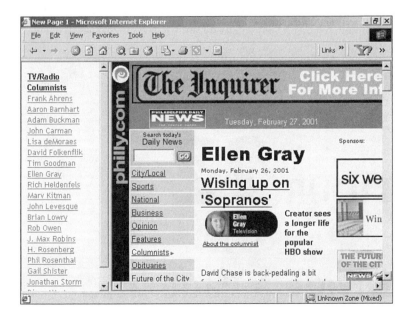

When you're working with frames, a hyperlink in one frame can open in that frame or any other frame on the page. It also can open in a new window or fill the entire Web browser window. The frame in which the linked document loads is called the *target frame*.

In Figure 22.1, the frame on the left contains a list of hyperlinks to newspaper columnists who cover television and radio. The target frame is the one on the right, so when one of the columnist's names is clicked, his column opens in the right frame.

You can determine the target frame of a hyperlink in two different ways:

- Set up the hyperlink so that it includes a reference to a target frame.
- Set up the page containing the hyperlink so that it has a default target frame for all hyperlinks.

Add Framed Pages to a Web

Choose File, New, Page or Web. The New Page or Web task pane opens (see Figure 22.2).

FIGURE 22.2

Choosing what kind of page to create.

Page Templates link

22

In the New Page or Web task pane, click Page Templates. The Page Templates dialog box is displayed.

Click the Frames Pages tab to view 10 different templates for framed pages you can add to your Web.

This dialog box can be used to find out more about each frame template before you choose one.

In Figure 22.3, the Contents template preview is displayed in the Frame Pages tab of the Page Templates dialog box. It contains a thin frame on the left and a larger frame on the right.

FIGURE 22.3

Selecting a frame template.

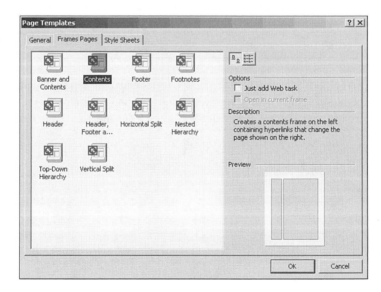

The Web page displayed in Figure 22.1 was created with the Contents template.

The Page Templates dialog box displays the approximate size and alignment of the different frames.

Table 22.1 lists the frame templates that are available.

TABLE 22.1   Frame Page Templates

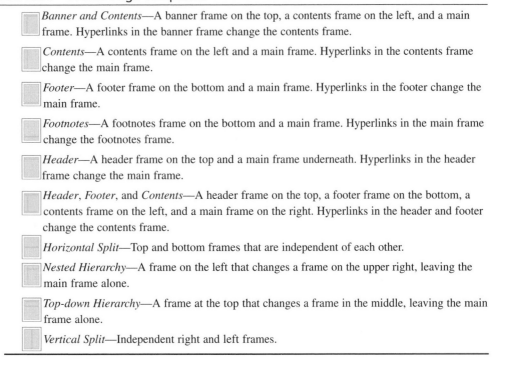

Banner and Contents—A banner frame on the top, a contents frame on the left, and a main frame. Hyperlinks in the banner frame change the contents frame.

Contents—A contents frame on the left and a main frame. Hyperlinks in the contents frame change the main frame.

Footer—A footer frame on the bottom and a main frame. Hyperlinks in the footer change the main frame.

Footnotes—A footnotes frame on the bottom and a main frame. Hyperlinks in the main frame change the footnotes frame.

Header—A header frame on the top and a main frame underneath. Hyperlinks in the header frame change the main frame.

Header, Footer, and *Contents*—A header frame on the top, a footer frame on the bottom, a contents frame on the left, and a main frame on the right. Hyperlinks in the header and footer change the contents frame.

Horizontal Split—Top and bottom frames that are independent of each other.

Nested Hierarchy—A frame on the left that changes a frame on the upper right, leaving the main frame alone.

Top-down Hierarchy—A frame at the top that changes a frame in the middle, leaving the main frame alone.

Vertical Split—Independent right and left frames.

To select a frames template, choose its icon and click the OK button. FrontPage 2002 creates a framed Web page by placing some unusual items in the editing window: two or more empty frames, each with Set Initial Page and New Page buttons (see Figure 22.4).

Use the New Page button to create a page and place it in the frame. A new blank page opens in the frame for immediate editing.

FIGURE 22.4

Setting up a new Web page with frames.

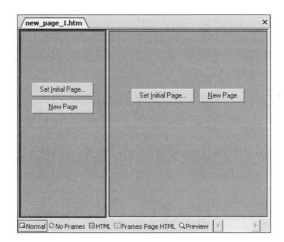

Use the Set Initial Page button to load an existing Web page in the frame. It opens the Insert Hyperlink dialog box, which is used to select a page in the current Web or any page on the World Wide Web (see Figure 22.5).

FIGURE 22.5

Opening a Web page in a frame.

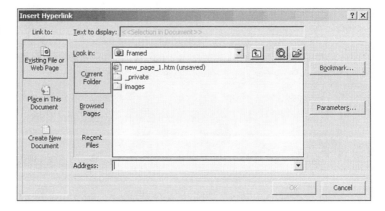

If you link to a page on the World Wide Web, the frame uses that page rather than storing a copy of it in your Web. Although the page loads in FrontPage 2002's editing window and you can make changes, your editing won't show up when the page is previewed or published.

A framed page requires one Web page for each frame and an extra page that is used to configure the frames. The extra page sets up the frames at the desired height or width, determines whether scrollbars are displayed, and either allows or disallows a user to move the frame borders around.

When you save a group of pages that are placed within frames, you must save the extra page also.

Create a New Frame from a Template

With the techniques that have been covered up to this point, you can add a framed page to a Web and pick the pages that will be contained in each frame.

This hour's first project is a FrontPage Web that serves as a directory to popular news, sports, and business Web sites.

Before you do anything involving frames, create a new Web to work on:

1. Choose File, New, Page or Web. The New Page or Web task pane opens alongside the editing window.

2. Click the Web Site Templates link in the task pane. The Web Site Templates dialog box opens, listing the kinds of Webs you can create.

3. Choose the Empty Web template. In the Specify the location of the new Web drop-down list, choose a folder on your system for the new Web, and then click OK. FrontPage creates the Web and opens it for editing.

   You need to add one page that will be associated later with a frame.

4. Choose File, New, Page or Web, and then click the Blank Page link in the task pane. A new page opens for editing.

5. Choose File, Save. In the File name box, give the page the name sections.htm and then click Save.

   Now that you have a Web, you're ready to add a framed page to it.

6. Click File, New, Page or Web to open the New Page or Web task pane.

7. Click the Page Templates link to open the Page Templates dialog box, and then click the Frames Pages tab to bring it to the front.

   The Contents template, which displays a thin frame to the left of a wider one, is used for this project.

8. Choose the Contents icon and click OK. The editing window opens with two empty frames containing Set Initial Page and New Page buttons, which is the same view shown in Figure 22.4.

9. In the left frame, click Set Initial Page to open the Insert Hyperlink dialog box. Choose the page sections.htm and click OK to associate it with the frame.

10. In the right frame, click Set Initial Page, choose the Web address `http://www.iht.com`, and then click OK. The home page of the *International Herald Tribune* is loaded.

11. To save the page, choose File, Save and give it the name `index.htm`. Figure 22.6 shows what the page looks like in Internet Explorer 5.

FIGURE 22.6

Viewing the Web page with two frames.

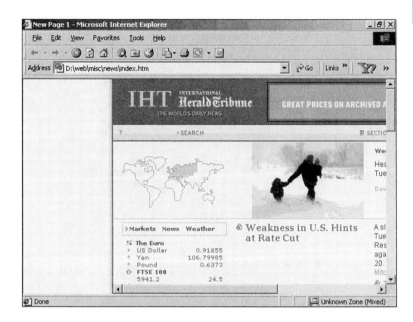

Later this hour, you will finish this project by adding content to the left frame.

Modify a Frame

Because frames are created from standard templates, you will probably need to make adjustments as you're working on a frame-based page.

To make changes to a frame, right-click anywhere within its boundaries to display a shortcut menu (see Figure 22.7).

FIGURE 22.7

Modifying a frame.

Select Frame Properties from the shortcut menu. The Frame Properties dialog box, shown in Figure 22.8, is used to configure the frame. You can change its size, add or remove scrollbars, and make other changes.

Every frame is given a name by default, and this name is referred to by hyperlinks that load pages into the frame.

You can adjust a frame's width or row height, but not both. Vertical frames are measured according to their width, and horizontal frames are measured according to their row height.

FIGURE 22.8

Changing a frame's size, name, and other features.

These measurements can be specified in three ways:

- Pixels
- A percentage
- A relative value

Pixel measurements are the most exact, of course. If you set a frame to 100 pixels in width, it will be displayed at that size whenever possible.

Percentages indicate how much of the browser window will be taken up by the frame.

Relative values are arbitrary numbers that have meaning only when compared to the relative values of other frames. For example, consider a Web page containing two frames, one with a relative value of 2 and the other with a relative value of 8. The first frame will be four times as small as the other frame because its relative value is four times as small.

Because the placement of frames can greatly affect a Web page's appearance, many Web designers prevent frame borders from being resized.

To load the `index.htm` page you created for the news directory Web and modify the left frame:

1. Right-click anywhere in the left frame.
2. Choose Frame Properties.
3. Deselect the Resizeable in Browser check box, and then click OK.

Create an Alternative to Frames

Although frames were introduced by Netscape in late 1995, people who use text-based browsers and old versions of popular browsers won't be able to use a Web that's reliant on frames. Also, frames have been one of the more widely criticized aspects of Web design—some users find them confusing and difficult to use.

For these reasons, some Web developers create a frame and a non-frame way to view their Webs.

In FrontPage 2002, when you are editing frames, two extra buttons appear at the bottom edge of the editing window: No Frames and Frames Page HTML, as shown in Figure 22.9.

FIGURE 22.9

Choosing different options in the editing window.

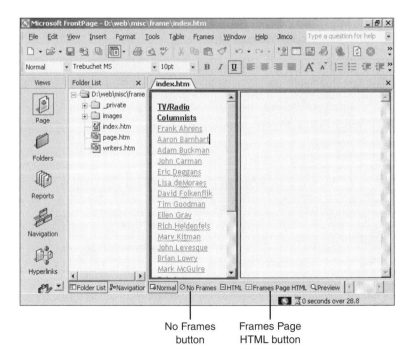

No Frames button

Frames Page HTML button

Click the No Frames button to edit the Web content that will appear in browsers that do not support frames. The default is to display the text, "This page uses frames, but your browser doesn't support them."

You can use the No Frames window to link to a separate version of your FrontPage Web that does not require frames.

 Depending on how a frame page has been designed, you might be able to use it in a Web's non-frame alternative. Its suitability will depend on whether it has hyperlinks of its own rather than relying on another frame page's links.

Open Linked Pages into Frames

When you're using hyperlinks on a page displayed in a frame, you can load the linked page in four places:

- The same frame
- A different frame on the same page
- The entire Web browser window, replacing the frames
- A second browser window

The place where the linked page loads is called the *target frame*. You can designate a target frame whenever you create or edit a hyperlink.

To edit a hyperlink, right-click the link and choose Edit Hyperlink from the shortcut menu. The Edit Hyperlink dialog box is displayed (see Figure 22.10).

Target Frame button

FIGURE 22.10

Editing a hyperlink to add a target frame.

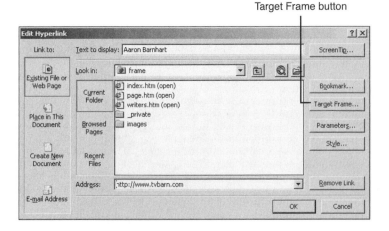

The Edit Hyperlink dialog box displays the link in the Address text box. To add a target frame, click the Target Frame button. The Target Frame dialog box is displayed (see Figure 22.11).

FIGURE 22.11

Selecting a hyperlink's target frame.

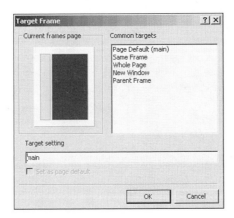

You can specify the target frame by name or use one of five alternatives:

- *Page Default*—The frame that all hyperlinks open into when no target frame has been specified
- *Same Frame*—The same frame as the page containing the hyperlink
- *Whole Page*—A new page takes up the entire browser window
- *New Window*—A new page in a new browser window, leaving the existing browser window alone
- *Parent Frame*—The page that contains the hyperlink's frame and any others created at the same time

These alternative targets are useful when you want to break out of the currently displayed frames in some way, either to open new frames or to open a page that doesn't contain any frames at all.

The Target Frame dialog box also can be used to visually choose the target. Click a frame in the Current frames section of the dialog box.

All the frame templates in FrontPage 2002 set a default target for each page contained in a frame. You can change the default target by editing one of the properties of that framed page.

To choose a new default frame for a page, right-click an empty area in the frame and choose Page Properties from the shortcut menu that appears. The Page Properties dialog box is displayed (see Figure 22.12).

Target Frame button

FIGURE 22.12
Choosing a target frame.

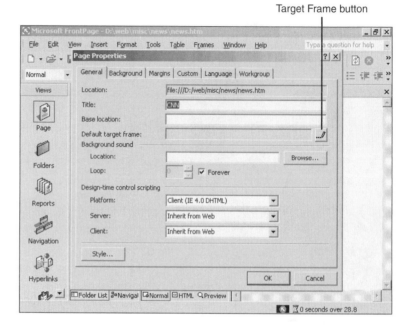

If a default target has been set for the page, its name will be displayed in the Default target frame text box. To set a default, click the Change Target Frame button shown in Figure 22.12.

> You can use most of these target frame options with any hyperlink, regardless of whether your Web contains frames. The Whole Page target is useful when you want to make sure that a page in your Web is displayed in a full browser window (rather than in an existing frame). The New Window option opens a separate browser window.

Add an Inline Frame

FrontPage 2002 adds support for inline frames, which are frames located entirely within another Web page.

Inline frames are supported in Internet Explorer versions 4.0 and later and in Netscape Navigator version 6.0 and later. If you have set up a FrontPage Web to work with earlier versions of those browsers, you won't be able to add inline frames to it.

If you're unclear about where inline frames might be useful, a good example is a software download page in which a user must agree to the terms of a licensing agreement. The agreement could be put in an inline frame with its own vertical scrollbar, saving users the trouble of loading it on a separate page.

22

To add an inline frame to a page, open the page and choose Insert, Inline Frame. A frame will open in the page with Set Initial Page and New Page buttons (see Figure 22.13).

FIGURE 22.13

Editing a new inline frame on a Web page.

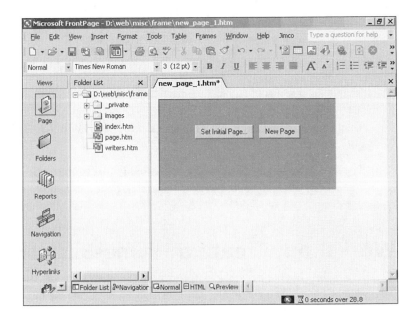

Use these buttons to choose the page to display in the frame. After the page has been loaded, you can edit the frame to change its appearance.

Click the top edge of the frame to select it, right-click an empty area within the frame, and then click Inline Frame Properties from the shortcut menu. The Inline Frame Properties dialog box is displayed (see Figure 22.14).

The Inline Frame Properties dialog box can be used to change the height and width of the frame and add or remove borders and scrollbars.

Because the default size for inline frames is pretty small in FrontPage 2002, you will probably resize most of the ones you work with.

FIGURE 22.14

Changing inline frame properties.

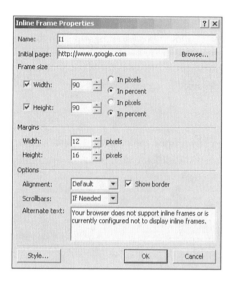

To change a frame's size, click the check box next to Width or Height and change its numeric value (as shown in Figure 22.14).

The size of an inline frame can be expressed in pixels or as a percentage of the page that contains it. Choose the In Pixels or In percent option to indicate what the numeric value represents.

Workshop: Create a Frame-Based Web

Earlier this hour, you created a Web with a frame that links to the newspaper site of the *International Herald Tribune*. The other frame displayed the page sections.htm.

For this hour's workshop, you will extend that project by creating two new Web pages that contain links to news and business sites. Links to these pages will be added to sections.htm.

Your Web should contain each of the following:

- A new page called news.htm that links to the *International Herald Tribune* (http://www.iht.com) and two other news sites.

- A new page called business.htm that links to three business- or stock-related sites.

- Hyperlinks on the sections.htm page that link to the two new pages you created.

- Hyperlinks on news.htm and business.htm that link back to sections.htm. Associate these links with the word Home.

The Web should also follow these guidelines:

- The news, business, and sections pages in your Web should open in the left frame, which is named contents.

- The news and business sites you link to should open in the right frame named main.

Solution

You can create the news.htm and business.htm pages with links to any of your favorite Web sites.

Two news sites you could use along with the *International Herald Tribune* are ABC News (http://www.abcnews.com) and Obscure Store (http://www.obscurestore.com), a lesser-known site that links to some of the most unusual stories in the daily press.

Three business sites you could use are the Wall Street Journal (http://public. wsj.com), ClearStation (http://www.clearstation.com), and Christopher Byron's column in the *New York Observer* (http://www.nyobserver.com/pages/envelope.asp).

To create a hyperlink for a news or business site:

1. Open the page that contains the site's name (either news.htm or business.htm).

2. Highlight the name in the editing window and click the Hyperlink button in the toolbar. The Insert Hyperlink dialog box is displayed.

3. Enter the news or business Web site's address in the Address text box and click the Target Frame button. The Target Frame dialog box is displayed.

4. In the Target setting text field, enter main, the name of the right frame. Click OK in this dialog box and OK in the Insert Hyperlink dialog box to save your change to the hyperlink.

Follow the same first three steps to create the "Home" hyperlinks on news.htm and business.htm. The word "Home" should be linked to the page sections.htm, which opens in the contents frame. For step 4 in the Target Frame dialog box (shown earlier in Figure 22.11), choose Same Frame in the Common targets list.

Figure 22.15 shows what this Web looks like in Internet Explorer 5.

22

FIGURE 22.15

Browsing a news portal using frames.

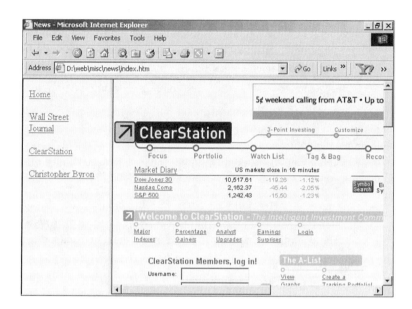

To try out this Web, visit the book's Web site at `http://www.cadenhead.org/frontpage` and open the Hour 22 page.

Summary

Frames are a great example of how FrontPage 2002 can simplify Web development. Working with frames by directly editing HTML tags on a Web page can be cumbersome, especially if your Web contains frames contained within other frames and other complex arrangements.

During this hour, you added frames to a Web, opened links in different frames, and edited frames by adding and removing scrollbars.

You also worked with inline frames—frames that are located entirely within another Web page.

Frames take up a lot of real estate on a browser window and are unpopular with some World Wide Web users because they can be more confusing than Webs that do not employ frames.

If you decide to employ them on a Web, FrontPage's frame templates make it easy to add 10 different frame layouts to a page.

Q&A

Q Why aren't frames created using cells, as tables are?

A Unlike tables, frames must be defined strictly in one direction: horizontal or vertical. It's a different way to subdivide a rectangular area than tables use, but it can be
just as effective.

Unless you start with a frames page template, you will create a page with multiple
frames one frame at a time. The first two-page frame is loaded, one of those frames
splits into two, and so on, until all frames have been developed.

**Q I created a Web with frames. When I preview it in Internet Explorer, the
Address bar does not change when I load different pages in my Web. What's
wrong?**

A The Address bar of a Web browser is not supposed to change as you load pages
into different frames. This prevents a user from bookmarking a page contained
within a frame rather than loading all the frames.

To get a better understanding of why this is important, open the Web you finished
during this hour's workshop. Preview the `index.htm` page in a browser and then
preview the `sections.htm` page.

The only way for the Web to work correctly is if `index.htm` is loaded. Loading one
of the other pages causes the Web to be displayed without any frames.

Exercises

Challenge your knowledge of FrontPage 2002 frames with the following exercises:

- Create a Web page that contains a list of search engine links on a single line.
  Put an inline frame on the page and make it the target frame of those links.

- Add a `sports.htm` page to the workshop Web with three links to sports Web
  sites such as ESPN.com (`http://espn.go.com`), CBS SportsLine (`http://www.
  sportsline.com`), and *The Hockey News* (`http://www.thehockeynews.com`).

For solutions to these exercises, visit the book's official Web site at `http://www.
cadenhead.org/frontpage/`.

Hour 23

Create and Edit Web Pages Using HTML

All World Wide Web pages are created using Hypertext Markup Language (HTML), a set of formatting commands that are added to text documents. These formatting commands, which are called *tags*, turn normal text into headings, hyperlinks, paragraphs, images, and anything else you can put on a Web page.

When you work on a page in FrontPage 2002 and apply formatting to part of the page, FrontPage marks that section with the corresponding HTML tags. This takes place behind the scenes: You don't ever have to see how FrontPage uses HTML to format and present the document. As you edit a page, you see how it's going to look in a browser and can avoid learning HTML entirely.

Well, almost entirely.

There are times when you might need to add something to your FrontPage Web using HTML tags rather than your own editing. For example, if you host banner ads on your Web, the service delivering the ads might provide HTML-tagged text that presents them.

During this hour, you'll learn how to add HTML text to a Web page, view the markup tags that make up a document, and use FrontPage 2000 to create and edit Web pages with HTML.

Tag a Page with HTML Commands

A Web document is actually an ordinary text file that you can load with any text editor, such as Windows Notepad. HTML tags are added to the text to achieve different effects, such as the following:

- Creating a hyperlink
- Turning text into a heading
- Making several lines of text into a list
- Displaying a picture of your 1970 Dodge Dart

All HTML tags begin with the < character and end with the > character. The following tag adds a horizontal line to a Web page:

```
<hr>
```

The text "hr" stands for "horizontal rule." You can place an <hr> tag on a Web page anywhere you want a line to appear.

There are two kinds of tags: opening tags and closing tags. An *opening tag* indicates where some kind of formatting should begin. A *closing tag* indicates where it should end.

Consider the following marked-up text from a Web page:

```
<h1>Today's Top Story</h1>
```

This text uses the HTML tag <h1> to turn the text "Today's Top Story" into a size 1 heading. There also are <h2>, <h3>, <h4>, <h5>, and <h6> tags for headings with five additional sizes.

There are two HTML tags in this example: the opening tag, <h1>, and its closing tag, </h1>. The names of all closing tags are preceded by the slash character (/).

Most HTML tags require opening and closing tags in order to function correctly. For headings, you must use both tags to show where the heading begins and where it ends.

The <hr> tag is one of several opening tags that do not require a corresponding closing tag. The horizontal line appears on a page exactly where the <hr> opening tag is placed.

HTML tags aren't case sensitive, so you could place `<H1>`, `</H1>`, and `<HR>` on a Web page and achieve the same effects as `<h1>`, `</h1>`, and `<hr>`.

An HTML tag begins with the < character and the name of the tag. It also may contain extra information to control two things:

- How the tag is displayed on a page
- What the tag can be used to do

All this extra information is placed before the > character at the end of a tag, as in the following example:

```
<hr width="50%">
```

This `<hr>` tag has the added text `width="50%"`. This is a tag attribute that causes the horizontal line to be displayed 50 percent as wide as it would appear normally. A tag can have more than one attribute as long as they're set apart from each other by blank spaces.

After you understand the way HTML tags are structured, it becomes easier to understand what they're being used to accomplish. Even if this is your first exposure to HTML, you might be able to figure out what the following tagged text accomplishes:

```
<a href="http://www.mcp.com/sams">Visit Sams Publishing</a>
```

In this example, HTML turns the text "Visit Sams Publishing" into a hyperlink pointing to `http://www.mcp.com/sams`, the address of Sams Publishing's Web site. The `<a>` tag stands for "anchor"—hyperlinks are also called *anchors*—and the `href` attribute is short for "Hypertext Reference."

Work with HTML in Page View

The normal editing mode in FrontPage 2002 is to convert what you do in Page view into HTML. For this reason, if you typed the text `<hr>` on a page, FrontPage would assume that you wanted to display that text `<hr>` rather than a horizontal line. To add a horizontal line to a page you are editing, choose Insert, Horizontal Line.

To work directly with HTML in FrontPage, open a Web document and click the HTML button at the bottom of the FrontPage editing window, as shown in Figure 23.1.

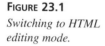

FIGURE 23.1
*Switching to HTML
editing mode.*

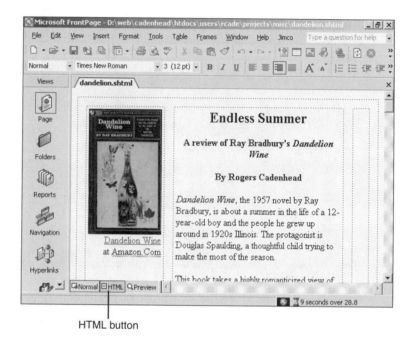

HTML button

The buttons along the bottom edge of the FrontPage editing window enable you to shift between three different modes:

- *Normal*—See how the document looks as you work on it, letting FrontPage write its own HTML behind the scenes.

- *HTML*—See the HTML is used to create the document and make changes using markup tags.

- *Preview*—See how the document will appear in a Web browser. You cannot edit the document while it is in this mode.

As you are working on a Web document, you can click the HTML button at any time to edit the HTML used to create the document. Figure 23.2 shows what FrontPage 2002 looks like in HTML editing mode.

If you're looking at the HTML of a page that was created in FrontPage 2002, don't expect to make much sense of it unless you're experienced with HTML. The software uses some complex HTML to produce the presentation, formatting, and effects that you have learned about in the past 22 hours.

The easiest way to experiment with HTML in FrontPage is to try it out on a new Web with no theme.

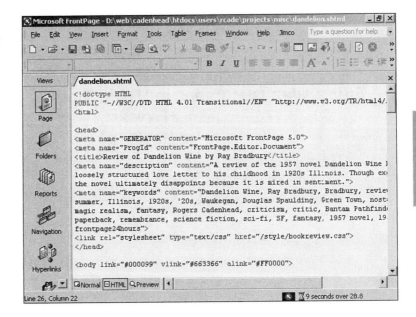

FIGURE 23.2

Viewing a Web page's HTML formatting.

FrontPage 2002 starts every Web page with a minimal amount of HTML formatting:

- <html> tags to show where the Web page begins and ends (in other words, the entire document).
- <head> tags to indicate the page's header—information about the page that isn't displayed in the main browser window.
- <title> tags to give the page a title in the browser's title bar.
- <body> tags to indicate the page's body—the area that will show up in the main browser window.

FrontPage also uses several <meta> tags in the header of the page that describe the document and how it was created.

> One of these tags shows that "Microsoft FrontPage 5.0" is the Web editing software being used to work on the page. This is an internal version number—FrontPage 2002 is the fifth major release of the software.

You can change the title of a page by editing the text between the opening and closing <title> tags. The text will appear on the title bar of the Web browser when the page is loaded.

Anything you want to display on a Web page should be placed between the existing <body> tags.

Paragraphs of text are formatted with the <p> tag.

Edit a Web Document in HTML Mode

Your first project today is to add text to a Web page in HTML mode. To get started, create a new One Page Web in FrontPage 2002:

1. Choose File, New, Page or Web. The New Page or Web task pane opens with a list of pages and Webs you can create.

2. Click the Web Site Templates link. The Web Site Templates dialog opens with the One Page Web icon selected.

3. Click OK. The new Web is created.

4. Double-click the Web document index.htm in the Folder List to open it in Page view.

5. Click the HTML button to edit the page in HTML mode.

   Figure 23.3 shows what index.htm looks like when you first open it for editing in HTML mode.

FIGURE 23.3

Editing a One Page Web in HTML mode.

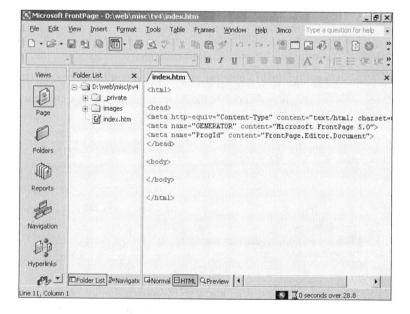

In a new One Page Web, the file index.htm contains <html> tags around the entire document, <head> tags around the header information, and <body> tags around the contents of the page.

One line defines the title of the page:

`<title>Home Page</title>`

You can change the title by editing the text between the <title> and </title> tags.

6. Make the title of index.htm the text Television. With the document open in HTML mode, edit the line so that it becomes the following:

`<title>Television</title>`

When a Web document is loaded by a browser, its title is displayed in the browser's title bar along the top edge of the browser window.

The contents of the page are located within the <body> and </body> tags. There's nothing within these tags when index.htm is first created in a One Page Web.

Listing 23.1 contains several paragraphs that have been formatted using the <p> tag.

7. Place your cursor between the <body> and </body> tags in the index.htm page, and type in each line of the listing. Press Enter at the end of each line.

> The line numbers at the beginning of each line should not be typed in. They're used for reference in this book, to make it easier to explain what's going on in a listing.

LISTING 23.1   The Paragraphs to Add to index.htm

```
1: <p>For years, researchers and politicians have been saying
2: that the amount of violence on television causes people to
3: behave more violently in real life.</p>
4:
5: <p>I've been watching around 7-10 hours of TV every day for
6: the past 15 years.</p>
7:
8: <p>When someone says that TV makes you violent, it
9: makes me so angry I could hit someone.</p>
```

Paragraphs in HTML are formatted using the <p> tag. The blank lines after each paragraph will be ignored when the document is displayed in a Web browser—HTML tags control all the formatting.

8. After you have added these paragraphs to index.htm, save the page and click the Preview in Browser button on the toolbar to see the result (see Figure 23.4).

FIGURE 23.4
*Paragraphs of text on
a Web page.*

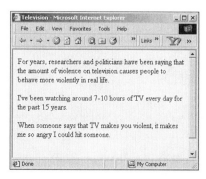

The text added to index.htm is displayed like the paragraphs you've been working with in FrontPage's Normal editing mode. Text fills the available space and moves around if you resize the browser window.

You can switch back and forth between normal and HTML editing modes in Page view, making changes to the page in both views.

A good way to discover things about HTML is to create a simple page in HTML mode, make a change to it in Normal mode, and switch back to HTML mode so that you can see what was changed.

With index.htm open, switch to Normal mode and make the following changes, using the techniques you have learned about in previous hours of the book:

1. Add a hyperlink to the word television that links to the Web address
   http://www.teevee.org.

2. Highlight the text 7-10 hours of TV every day and make it boldface.

3. Highlight the word angry and choose Format, Font to open the Font dialog. Change the color of the word to red, and then click OK.

Switch to HTML mode to see the changes FrontPage 2000 has made to the page. The text of the page should be the same as Listing 23.2 (or something close to it).

LISTING 23.2   The HTML of index.htm

```
1: <html>
2:
3: <head>
4: <meta http-equiv="Content-Type" content="text/html; charset=windows-1252">
5: <meta http-equiv="Content-Language" content="en-us">
6: <title>Television</title>
7: <meta name="GENERATOR" content="Microsoft FrontPage 5.0">
8: <meta name="ProgId" content="FrontPage.Editor.Document">
```

```
 9: </head>
10:
11: <body>
12: <p>For years, researchers and politicians have been saying
13: that the amount of violence on
    ➥<a href="http://www.teevee.org">television</a> causes people to
14: behave more violently in real life.</p>
15:
16: <p>I've been watching around <b>7-10 hours of TV every day</b> for
17: the past 15 years.</p>
18:
19: <p>When someone says that TV makes you violent, it
20: makes me so <font color="#FF0000">angry</font> I could hit someone.</p>
21: </body>
22:
23: </html>
```

Appendix A, "HTML 4.01 Quick Reference," describes each tag in HTML 4.01 and its attributes. You can use it to better understand how FrontPage 2002 implements HTML.

Modify How FrontPage Uses HTML

When Web designers evaluate Web publishing software, one of the most important features they look for is whether the program will leave existing HTML alone when a document is edited.

This feature, which is often called "round-trip HTML," is supported in FrontPage 2002.

The reason this is important is because of quirks in how browsers render HTML tags.

To see an example of this, two Web pages are displayed by Microsoft Internet Explorer 5 in Figure 23.5.

FIGURE 23.5

Two Web pages created with the same HTML tags.

The two pages in Figure 23.5 display a group of five images that are pushed together. The goal is to make them look like a single image—a television playing a movie. Dividing images this way is a common technique used by professional Web designers when they are creating a complex, visually appealing page.

The TV on the left in Figure 23.5 was created with this HTML:

```
<p><center><img src="tvtop.gif" width=239 height=18
align=bottom><br><img src="tvleft.gif" width=15 height=120
align=bottom><img src="tvscreen.gif" width=160
height=120><img src="tvright.gif" width=64 height=120
align=bottom><br><img src="tvbottom.gif" width=239 height=30
align=bottom></center></p>
```

The TV on the right was created with this HTML:

```
<p>
<center>
<img SRC="tvtop.gif" ALIGN="bottom" width="239" height="18">
<br>
<img SRC="tvleft.gif" ALIGN="bottom" width="15" height="120">
<img SRC="tvscreen.gif" width="160" height="120">
<img SRC="tvright.gif" ALIGN="bottom" width="64" height="120">
<br>
<img SRC="tvbottom.gif" ALIGN="bottom" width="239" height="30">
</center>
</p>
```

Both of these televisions are displayed using the same HTML tags in the same order, but only one of them is displayed correctly. The TV on the right contains white lines around the movie, making it obvious that the television is made up of five separate images.

The only difference between these pages is that one of them puts each HTML tag on its own line, and the other does not. The placement of tags on different lines often leads to display glitches like this in Internet Explorer, Netscape Navigator, and other browsers.

For this reason, when a designer finally gets the HTML tags on a page to produce the desired effect, editing tools such as FrontPage 2002 can be configured to leave tags alone when the document is edited.

FrontPage also can be set up to rearrange HTML tags to make them more readable when the page is viewed in HTML editing mode.

To configure how HTML tags are formatted, choose Tools, Page Options. The Page Options dialog opens with several tabs: General, AutoThumbnail, Default Font, HTML Source, Color Coding, and Compatibility.

Click the HTML Source tab to make changes to how HTML is formatted in FrontPage. The settings on this tab, which is shown in Figure 23.6, apply to all Web documents you edit.

HTML Source tab

FIGURE 23.6

Changing how HTML is handled by FrontPage.

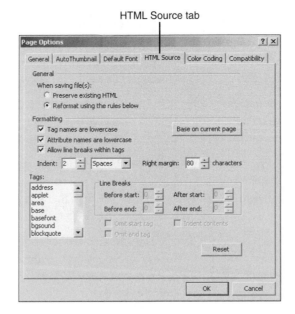

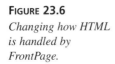

If you want FrontPage 2002 to leave existing HTML alone, click the Preserve existing HTML radio button. This is the safest choice, especially if you often work with Web documents created using publishing software other than FrontPage.

To make FrontPage format HTML tags according to its own rules, click Reformat using the rules below, and then make other choices in the dialog box to set up how FrontPage should format the tags you use on a document.

There are check boxes you can choose to make FrontPage convert tag and attribute names to lowercase. This makes the HTML tags in a Web document more readable and does not affect the presentation of Web pages.

With the other options on the HTML Source page of the dialog box, you can customize how tags are indented, set a right margin, and choose different formatting rules individually for each HTML tag.

Click the OK button to make your changes permanent. They will be in effect for all documents you edit, even if you close one Web and open another.

As you might have noticed when editing in HTML mode, FrontPage uses different colors for text, HTML tags, attributes, and other elements on a page. To customize the colors that are used, choose Tools, Page Options, and then click the Color Coding tab. Pick the colors you want, and then click OK to make your changes permanent.

Workshop: Add a Hit Counter Using HTML

It's possible to use FrontPage 2002 entirely as an HTML editor. You can take advantage of its Web management and maintenance features while marking up pages strictly in HTML mode, as if you were using Windows Notepad or another plain-text word processor.

However, it doesn't take a psychic friend to figure out that most FrontPage 2002 users will be content to let the software write its own HTML. If you're one of these people, the main reason you need the HTML editing mode is to add HTML-tagged text to a page.

The World Wide Web has numerous services that can enhance your FrontPage Web, including free hit counters, guest books, and banner advertising exchanges. Many of these programs offer their services through HTML tags that you must place on your pages.

One of these services is FastCounter, one of the free services offered by Microsoft bCentral, a site catering to small-business owners promoting their companies on the Web. FastCounter is a hit counter that you can place on any Web page to count the number of times the page is visited. The service is free in exchange for a hyperlink to FastCounter's Web site.

Full details on how to join FastCounter are at `http://www.fastcounter.com`. When you sign up, you receive HTML-tagged text that must be placed where you want the counter to appear on a page.

For this hour's workshop, join FastCounter and add a hit counter to a page on one of your FrontPage Webs.

Solution: Try Out Your Hit Counter

After you sign up for FastCounter, you will be asked a few questions in order to set up the counter:

- The address of the Web page you're putting the counter on
- The starting count
- The appearance of the counter (there are 10 styles to choose from)

After you answer these questions, you will be presented with a Web page that contains the HTML-tagged text of your counter, as shown in Figure 23.7.

FIGURE 23.7

*Getting the HTML text
of a FastCounter.*

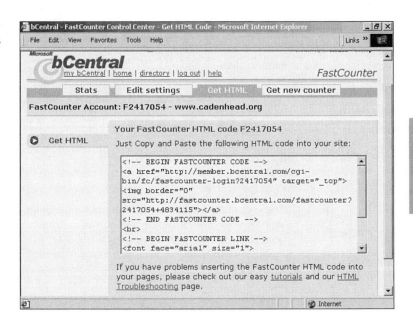

The specific HTML tags for FastCounter will be different depending on the account ID you receive when you sign up. (LinkExchange might also have altered the HTML tags by the time you try the service.) The following is an example of FastCounter HTML for a counter associated with account number 2355643:

```
<!-- BEGIN FASTCOUNTER CODE -->
<a href="http://member.bcentral.com/cgi-bin/fc/fastcounter-login?2355643"
➥ target="_top">
<img border="0" src="http://fastcounter.bcentral.com/fastcounter?2355643
➥+4711293"></a>
<!-- END FASTCOUNTER CODE -->
<br>
<!-- BEGIN FASTCOUNTER LINK -->
<font face="arial" size="1">
<a href="http://fastcounter.bcentral.com/fc-join" target="_top">FastCounter by
➥ bCentral</a>
</font><br>
<!-- END FASTCOUNTER LINK -->
```

The HTML text for FastCounter is presented in a text box so that you can copy-and-paste it to your Web. To do this:

1. Click in the text box to place your cursor there, and then press Ctrl+A. All the text will be highlighted.

2. Press Ctrl+C to copy the text to the Windows Clipboard.

3. In FrontPage 2002, open the Web page that will contain the counter.

4. Switch to HTML editing mode, and place your cursor at the spot on the page where the counter should appear. This text can be placed anywhere on a Web page. It's often put at the bottom, right above the `</body>` tag that closes out the page's visible contents.

5. Press Ctrl+V to paste the text from the Windows Clipboard to the page.

After you place the counter, you can highlight it in Normal editing mode and use the Align Left, Center, and Align Right toolbar buttons to move it around. You can also place it in a table cell.

If you have trouble finding the right place to put the counter, switch to Normal editing mode before pasting the counter from the Clipboard. Click your cursor exactly where you want the counter to be placed, and then switch back to HTML mode. Your cursor will be at the same place you clicked.

Figure 23.8 shows a Web page with account number 2355643's FastCounter placed at the bottom.

FIGURE 23.8

Counting hits using FastCounter.

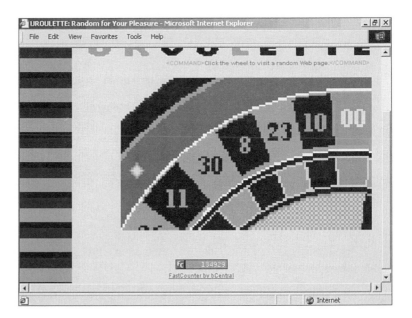

You can see this counter on the World Wide Web at http://www.uroulette.com, a site published by the author of this book.

> FrontPage 2002 also offers a wizard for adding a FastCounter and other Microsoft bCentral services to the page you are currently editing. Choose Insert, Web Component, and then click bCentral Web Components on the dialog box that appears. FastCounter is one of the listed components. Click it to begin setting up a counter.

23

Summary

It doesn't take long to become an old fogey, by World Wide Web standards. If FrontPage 2002 is your first experience creating Webs, you'll probably hear some "in my day, things were different" stories about HTML.

Before the development of software like FrontPage 2002, all Webs were created by marking up text with HTML tags in simple text editors such as Windows Notepad. Many developers still prefer working directly with HTML because of perceived limitations in software that creates these tags for you. They feel that you get more control over the finished product by coding it yourself.

You can be both old-fashioned and newfangled with FrontPage 2002. You can view the HTML when you want to, and hide it when you use the software's graphical user interface to design Webs. You also can use FrontPage 2002 to avoid HTML entirely.

No matter how you do it, things are a lot easier than they were in my day way back in 1995. As an old fogey myself, I should point out that we worked on our HTML while walking uphill 20 miles both to and from school in driving snow, without any of that fancy GORE-TEX insulated coat-lining, and we etched our Web pages onto rusty shovels with sharp rocks.

And we liked it.

Q&A

Q Why doesn't any of the text from a shared border show up in HTML mode?

A FrontPage 2002 saves the contents of shared borders separately from the rest of each page in a Web. The border elements are saved to their own Web pages in the Web's _borders folder. Everything is combined when you publish.

You can't normally get to the _borders folder within FrontPage—it's one of several folders that won't show up when folders and files are listed. To make these folders appear, choose Tools, Web Settings, click the Advanced tab, and then select the Show hidden files and folders check box. The _borders folder will contain one page for each border you are using: top.htm, left.htm, right.htm, and bottom.htm. You can open and edit these pages like any other pages in your Web.

Q Is there any reason I should work directly with HTML instead of using FrontPage 2002 to create the HTML for me?

A One of the main purposes of software like FrontPage 2002 is to make it easier to create Web pages. Many people who don't have a technical background will find it easier to develop Web pages if they don't have to learn the tags and syntax of HTML.

The main advantage of learning and using HTML is that you can implement everything in the language as it's introduced. FrontPage 2002 supports most features that are currently implemented by Netscape Navigator and Microsoft Internet Explorer, but as new features are introduced by the World Wide Web Consortium and browser developers, you might need to rely on HTML to implement them.

Exercises

Challenge your knowledge of FrontPage 2002 HTML editing with the following exercises:

- Create a Web page in HTML editing mode that contains a short review of a Web site you visit frequently. Add a hyperlink to the site somewhere in the text of your page.
- In Normal editing mode, create a list of items using the Numbering toolbar button and another list using the Bullets toolbar button. View the page in HTML editing mode to see if you can figure out how the <OL>, <UL>, and <LI> tags are used.

For solutions to these exercises, visit the book's official Web site at http://www.cadenhead.org/frontpage/.

HOUR 24

Format Your Web Through Cascading Style Sheets

The biggest push in World Wide Web design today is to separate the appearance of a page—its fonts, colors, and alignment—from the information it offers.

This change makes a Web publisher's life much easier when the site needs to be redesigned.

It also makes a Web more adaptable to the diverse audience that will view it. Although Netscape Navigator and Microsoft Internet Explorer users constitute more than 90 percent of Web surfers today, many other types of browsing software will be used to visit a public Web—text-only browsers, nonvisual browsers, personal digital assistants, and lesser-known browsers such as Opera.

Earlier, you learned about themes, which are a way to define a Web's visual appearance in FrontPage 2002. During this hour, you'll take that principle one step further by using a Web technology called Cascading Style Sheets.

Using style sheets, you can modify the appearance of a Web in dramatic ways and save all this information to a single file. Changing the file changes everything in the Web that links to the style sheet.

During this hour, you learn how to create new styles and modify some existing ones. You can extend the visual appeal of your FrontPage 2002 Webs in ways that are not possible through standard HTML.

Define Styles on the Web

Most popular word processors today have a feature called *styles*. They enable you to define the kinds of information that will appear in a document—such as headlines, body text, and pictures—and then give each of them its own specific formatting.

For example, you could establish a style making all body text in your document 12-point Courier that is indented .25 inches from the left margin. After you have set up this rule for body text, every paragraph in the document that has been defined as body text will be displayed in 12-point Courier font and indented .25 inches along the left. Later, if you decide to pick a different font or font size, you can modify the body text style instead of changing each paragraph in the document directly.

This idea has been introduced to the World Wide Web through *Cascading Style Sheets (CSS)*, a language that specifies how the contents of a Web page should be presented. Cascading Style Sheets are an extension of HTML, rather than a replacement.

A *style sheet* is a set of commands that define how a Web document will be presented. A Web page can incorporate a style sheet in two ways:

- Placing the style sheet on the page along with HTML tags
- Storing the style sheet separately in its own file

Currently there are three versions of CSS, which started to be supported in version 3.0 of Internet Explorer and version 4.0 of Navigator. CSS 1.0 is most widely supported in current browsers, and it contains commands to set the fonts, colors, and formatting of text, hyperlinks, and other parts of a page.

"Most widely supported" is a far cry from "fully supported" when it comes to Cascading Style Sheets. Neither Microsoft nor Netscape has implemented all of the CSS 1.0 standard in its current browser, and there are incompatibilities between the two implementations.

Use Styles Instead of FrontPage 2002 Themes

FrontPage 2002 includes a feature that enables you to choose an entire Web's appearance at one time—*themes*. You can modify parts of a theme, such as a text font, and all selected Web pages will be updated to reflect the change.

Themes are similar to Cascading Style Sheets, but are much more limited. They are used only to define some overall aspects of a page's presentation: the color and font of text, hyperlinks, and headings, the background of each page, the appearance of navigation buttons and bullets. Everything you use a theme for can be handled manually within Page view. You can set the background, establish all fonts, and create your own link bar graphics.

Unlike themes, Cascading Style Sheets can be used for techniques that are completely impossible in HTML. Take a look at Figure 24.1.

24

FIGURE **24.1**

A Web page that uses Cascading Style Sheets.

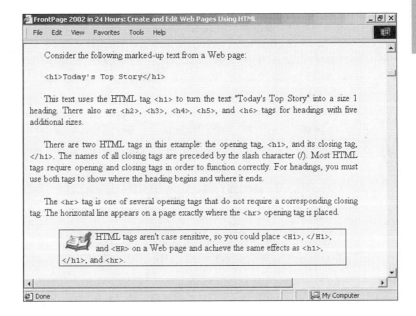

This Web page uses CSS to do several unusual things:

- Indent the start of each paragraph
- Justify paragraphs along the right margin
- Give one paragraph its own border edge and background color

Style sheets enable you to take control over formatting decisions that have been automatically handled by the Web browser until now, such as the background color of each paragraph. They also give you many more options for determining the appearance of the different page elements.

One of the things you can do with CSS is apply a theme. If you choose not to apply a theme using CSS, FrontPage 2002 will apply the graphics, fonts, and colors of a theme using standard HTML. CSS can produce the same effects.

> CSS can't be used to apply a theme if you're targeting a browser audience with anything earlier than Internet Explorer 3.0 or Navigator 4.0. Style sheets are not supported by WebTV or older browsers.

Create a Style Sheet

Style sheets can be implemented as part of a Web page or on a separate document that's linked to the page. The second technique is better because you can attach the same style sheet to other pages, establishing a common style for them all.

To create a style sheet:

1. Choose File, New, Page or Web. The New Page or Web task pane opens.

2. In the New Page or Web task pane, click the Page Templates link (see Figure 24.2). The Page Templates dialog box is displayed.

    The Page Templates dialog box displays different Web pages you can create.

FIGURE 24.2
Choosing the page to create.

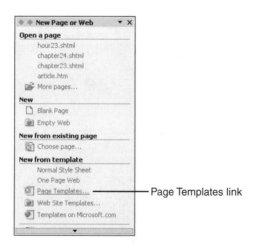

Page Templates link

3. Click the Style Sheets tab to bring it to the top, and then choose the Normal Style Sheet icon (see Figure 24.3).

4. Click OK to create the style sheet.

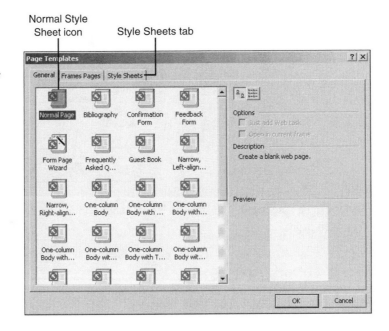

FIGURE 24.3

Creating a blank style sheet.

As you can see in Figure 24.3, several of the style sheets you can choose have the same names as themes, and they define many of the same fonts, colors, and heading styles. (Cascading Style Sheets don't define navigational buttons or page banners, however.) Choosing a Normal style sheet gives you an empty file to add styles to.

Style sheets should be saved with the `.css` filename extension. You can place them in the main folder of your Web or any of its subfolders, such as the `images` subfolder.

> Themes don't mix well with style sheets, especially when you're working on them for the first time. For the Webs you create during this hour, remove all themes before linking any style sheets.

Edit a Style

The Style dialog box is displayed, as shown in Figure 24.4.

FIGURE 24.4

Creating and modify-ing styles on a style sheet.

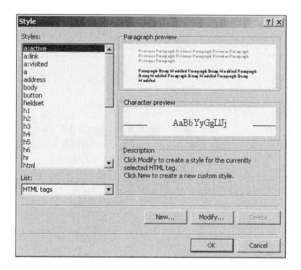

Styles can be associated with specific HTML tags, which alter how the tag is displayed on a Web page.

The style will be displayed only when the page is loaded by a Web browser that supports Cascading Style Sheets. Other browsers will display the page as if no styles were applied to it.

Styles also can be defined separately from existing HTML tags.

One of the most popular uses of style sheets is to display text that is justified along the right margin. Browsers are not able to support this formatting without style sheets.

Open a blank style sheet and choose the Format, Style command to open the Style dialog box.

To modify the style for paragraphs, scroll the Styles list until you find the p tag. Choose this tag and click the Modify button to display the Modify Style dialog box.

The Modify Style dialog box displays a preview of what text will look like when the style is applied to it. Because no changes have been made yet, there's nothing to see.

Changes are made to a style by clicking the Format button, which causes a drop-down menu to appear, as shown in Figure 24.5.

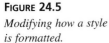

FIGURE 24.5

Modifying how a style is formatted.

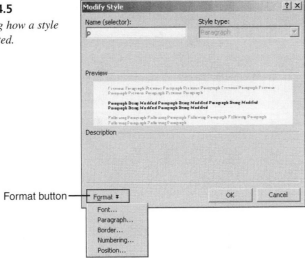

Format button ——

You can use the Format button on the Modify Style dialog box to make the following changes to how a tag is displayed on a Web page:

- *Font*—The font, size, color, and other attributes of text
- *Paragraph*—The spacing and indentation of paragraphs containing this text
- *Border*—The border and shading that appear
- *Numbering*—The way lists of this text are numbered and indented and the icons used with each item
- *Position*—The placement of the item in relation to other items that are either adjacent or overlapping on the Web

These formatting changes can be applied to any element of a Web, although several options are best suited to text.

To change the style for paragraphs, click the Format button in the Modify Style dialog box and choose Paragraph. The Paragraph dialog box opens.

In the Paragraph dialog box, the Alignment drop-down list box is used to choose how paragraphs are aligned in the style you are editing. Click this box and choose the Justify option, as shown in Figure 24.6, and then click the OK button.

Figure 24.6

Setting a new style for paragraphs.

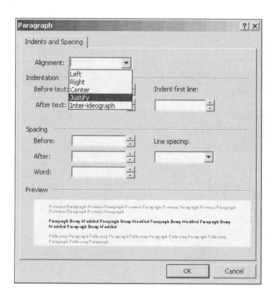

After you have defined a style, the Modify Style dialog box displays a new description for p tags:

```
text-align: justify
```

This is a Cascading Style Sheets formatting command. FrontPage 2002 creates these commands for you, so you don't have to learn the particulars of the CSS language to make use of it on your Webs.

Click the OK button to exit this dialog box, and then click the OK button to exit the Style dialog box.

When you modify a style by editing a .css page, FrontPage 2002 displays that style using the Cascading Style Sheets language in Page view. Don't edit this document manually unless you're familiar with CSS—instead, click Format, Style to open the Style dialog box and make changes.

The Style dialog box can be used to display all HTML tags or just user-defined styles— HTML tags that have new styles applied to them and new styles that aren't associated with a tag.

Save the style sheet you have created in a folder that contains one of your FrontPage Webs. Give it the filename mainstyle.css. If you don't have the Web open, FrontPage opens it automatically after the style sheet has been saved.

Apply a Modified Style to a Page

At this point, you have worked with style sheets by saving them in a separate file. You can also edit a style sheet while editing a Web page, which causes the style to apply only to that page.

Editing styles in a `.css` file enables you to make changes that apply to all Web pages linked to the style sheet.

To link a style sheet to a page, open the page for editing, and then choose Format, Style Sheet Links. The Link Style Sheet dialog box is displayed (see Figure 24.7).

FIGURE 24.7

Adding a style sheet to a page.

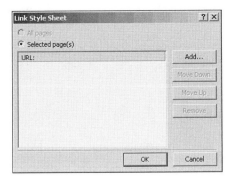

The Link Style Sheet dialog box can be used to add a style sheet to the current page or all pages in a Web. For now, choose the Selected page(s) option, and then click Add. A Select Style Sheet dialog box will open.

The Select Style Sheet dialog box enables you to find the folder that contains the style sheet you want to add—in this case, `mainstyle.css`. Find the folder, choose the filename, and then click OK (see Figure 24.8).

FIGURE 24.8

Choosing the style sheet to add.

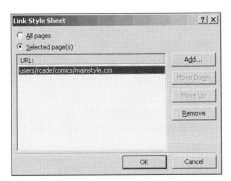

After you choose the style sheet, it will appear in the Link Style Sheet dialog box. You can add additional style sheets at this point—a page can be linked to more than one sheet.

Click the OK button to exit the Link Style Sheet dialog box. The changes you made to the HTML <P> tag will be reflected immediately in the Web page.

Match Tags with FrontPage 2002 Features

Style sheets use HTML tags to identify elements of a Web. If you're not familiar with HTML, you might not know how these tags are used on a Web.

When you choose Format, Font to add a special effect, the following HTML tags are used:

- `blink`: Blink effect
- `cite`: Citation effect
- `code`: Code effect
- `dfn`: Definition effect
- `em`: Emphasis effect
- `kbd`: Keyboard effect
- `samp`: Sample effect
- `strike`: Strikethrough effect
- `strong`: Strong effect
- `sub`: Subscript effect
- `sup`: Superscript effect
- `u`: Underline effect
- `var`: Variable effect

Several buttons on the Formatting toolbar can be used to format text. They're associated with the following HTML tags:

- `b` is associated with the Boldface button
- `i` is associated with the Italics button
- `u` is associated with the Underline button
- `blockquote` is associated with the Increase Indent button

The Formatting toolbar also has a pull-down menu with several formatting options that apply to entire paragraphs. They use the following HTML tags:

- p: Normal
- pre: Formatted
- address: Address
- h1–h6: Heading 1–Heading 6
- ol: Before and after a numbered list
- ul: Before and after a bulleted list
- dir: Before and after a directory list
- menu: Before and after a menu list
- li: For each item in a numbered, bulleted, directory, or menu list
- dl: Before and after a definition list
- dt: For each term in a defined term list
- dd: For each definition in a definition list

There are other HTML tags that FrontPage 2002 uses as you create a Web, including a for hyperlinks, img for pictures, and applet for Java applets.

To determine the tags that are being used by FrontPage, create a new page that contains nothing but a single Web element. Switch to HTML mode for that page and you'll see the tag—or tags—used to create it.

Create a New Style

A style sheet can contain new styles that aren't directly associated with an existing HTML tag. These styles often are used to create styles that have been slightly modified from existing tags, as in the following styles you could include on a sheet:

- p: A normal paragraph
- p.quote: A paragraph that contains a quotation
- p.author: A paragraph that identifies the author of the text
- p.contact: A paragraph that indicates how to contact the author

You can give each of these styles a different appearance as a way to distinguish them from each other.

Open the mainstyle.css file, created earlier in this hour, in FrontPage to add these new styles.

24

To create a new style:

1. Choose Format, Style, and then click the New button. The New Style dialog box is displayed, as shown in Figure 24.9.

FIGURE 24.9

Creating a new style.

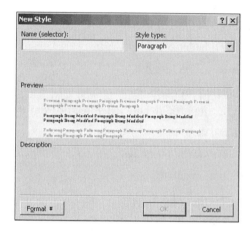

2. Enter the name of the style in the Name text box. Because you are basing the style on an existing HTML tag, the first part of the name should be the tag the style is based on.

3. Follow this with a period and a name that describes what the style is used for. The p.quote, p.author, and p.contact styles are examples of this.

4. Choose one of two options in the Style type list: Paragraph or Character. The style type indicates whether the style applies to an entire paragraph (the Paragraph option) or a portion of a paragraph (the Character option).

   If you apply a paragraph type style to text in a paragraph, the entire paragraph will be formatted according to the rules of that style.

For this tutorial, after you enter the name of the style (p.quote, p.author, or p.contact), the Style type list box will have the Paragraph type selected and will be grayed out so that you cannot change it. These styles are based on the HTML paragraph tag, which must have a style type of Paragraph.

5. After you have named a style, you can format it by clicking the Format button, as you did earlier this hour. Your new style will show up in the Style dialog box on the list of user-defined styles like any HTML tag you've customized. You can modify how a style is formatted by choosing it and then clicking the Format button.

Workshop: Create and Use New Styles

For this hour's workshop, add all three styles (`p.quote`, `p.author`, and `p.contact`) to `mainstyle.css` using these specifications:

- `p.quote`: The paragraph should be italicized and indented 15 pixels on the left margin
- `p.author`: The paragraph should be bold with no indentation
- `p.contact`: The paragraph should use the 8-point Times New Roman text and be surrounded by a black border

Solution

To create each of these new styles, follow these steps:

1. Open the style sheet `mainstyle.css`, created in this hour, in FrontPage 2002.
2. Choose Format, Style to open the Style dialog box (shown earlier in Figure 24.4)
3. Click the New button to open the New Style dialog box (see Figure 24.10).
4. Enter the name of the style in the Name text box.
5. Click the Format button, and then choose one of the options that appears in the drop-down menu to set up how the style is formatted.

    - To make `p.quote` italicized, click Format, Font to open the Font dialog box. One of the options in the Font style list box is Italic.

      To indent the left margin 15 points, click Format, Paragraph to open the Paragraph dialog box. Enter 15 in the Before Text box.

    - To make `p.author` bold, click Format, Font, then choose Bold in the Font style list box.

    - To make `p.contact` 8-point Times New Roman, click Format, Font, then choose Times New Roman in the Font list and `8pt` in the Size list.

      To place a border around it, click Format, Border. The Borders and Shading dialog box is displayed. Click the Box setting, as shown in Figure 24.10.

24

FIGURE 24.10

Choosing a border for a style.

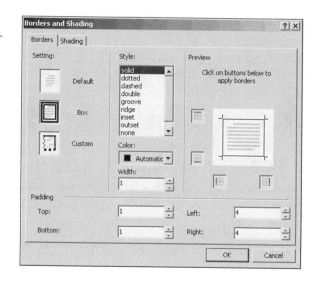

After you link a stylesheet to a document, all the styles it contains will show up in the Style drop-down list on the Formatting toolbar along with the other options to format a paragraph.

Figure 24.11 shows the Style drop-down list with the new styles at the end: author, contact, and quote. FrontPage leaves off the first part of a style name in this list.

FIGURE 24.11

Choosing a style for a paragraph.

Summary

Twenty-four hours ago, give or take, you had a copy of FrontPage 2002 somewhere in the vicinity of your computer. After finishing all the hour-long lessons in this book, you should have quite a bit of FrontPage 2002 knowledge in the vicinity of your brain.

FrontPage 2002, like most programs in the Office productivity suite, offers hundreds of advanced features that most users will never even try to use. This book focused on its essential features, including themes, templates, wizards, views, components, scripting, access control, and publishing.

You've taken a barnstorming tour of World Wide Web development, learning about HTML, Dynamic HTML, Cascading Style Sheets, Java, ActiveX, JavaScript, VBScript, and Active Server Pages.

All this stuff is taking up space in your brain along with things such as sports trivia, the Magna Carta, restaurant tip mathematics, and the cast members of television sitcoms from the '70s. Make the most of that real estate by using FrontPage 2002 to publish your own Webs.

Your pages will be at home on the World Wide Web, regardless of whether the things you're interested in are significant, silly, or psychotic. It's the second-largest repository of useful and useless information in the world.

As the author of this book and a longtime FrontPage user, I'm always eager to see what readers are doing with the software. When you publish your FrontPage Web, tell me about it by visiting this book's official Web at `http://www.cadenhead.com/frontpage/`.

—Rogers Cadenhead

Q&A

Q I've created a new style based on the keyboard tag. How do I apply this style to a Web page?

A FrontPage 2000 did not display all user-defined styles in the Formatting menu. The only styles that showed up were the ones that have a `Paragraph` style type. This made it difficult to use any of the `Character` styles you created, because there was no place in FrontPage from which you could select those styles.

FrontPage 2002 displays all styles you create in the Formatting menu. `Paragraph` styles are displayed next to a paragraph icon and `Character` styles are displayed with an underlined "a" icon, as shown in Figure 24.15.

Exercises

Challenge your knowledge of FrontPage 2002 style sheets with the following exercises:

- Create a new style for hyperlinks that makes them stand out more from other text.
- Copy the text of a news article to a Web page and create different styles for the headline, author's name, and text of the article.

For solutions to these exercises, visit the book's official Web site at `http://www.cadenhead.org/frontpage/`.

Part VII
Appendixes

APPENDIX A

HTML 4.01 Quick Reference

All World Wide Web documents are created using Hypertext Markup Language, also called HTML. This language enables you to create Web documents by "marking up" a document with hidden tags. These HTML tags determine the presentation, structure, and interactivity of a Web document and are surrounded by the < and > characters. Some examples:

- <P>—A tag that denotes the beginning of a paragraph
-
—A tag that represents a line break
- <IMG>—A tag for the presentation of an image file

Although you don't see any of these tags when a Web document is loaded into a browser, you see all the effects they create on the document.

This appendix describes the tags in HTML 4.01. You can use it to learn more about how FrontPage 2002 marks up the documents you create for presentation on the Web.

Working with HTML

For the most part, you'll probably create Web pages in FrontPage 2002 without ever looking at the HTML tags used on the page. Many people find it easier to work with an editor such as FrontPage 2002 because it works with HTML behind the scenes, hiding the complexities of the language.

To see the HTML tags being used to create a FrontPage 2002 Web document, open the document in Page view, and then click the HTML button at the bottom edge of the FrontPage editor, as shown in Figure A.1.

FIGURE A.1

Viewing a Web document's HTML tags.

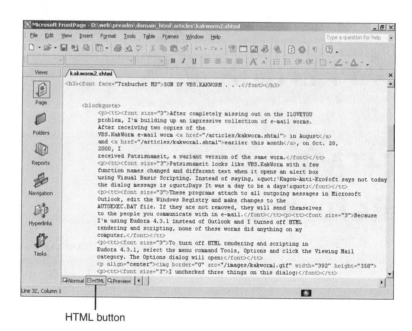

HTML button

This appendix provides a quick way to look up the purpose and function of any HTML tag that you encounter in a document. It covers HTML 4.01, the current version of the language according to the World Wide Web Consortium.

The World Wide Web Consortium, also called the W3C, created HTML in the early 1990s. The organization continues to shepherd the language and all future developments related to it. For a full HTML 4.01 specification, visit the following Web page: http://www.w3.org/MarkUp/.

The following terms are used throughout this appendix:

- A URL is a *Uniform Resource Locator*, which identifies the location of a resource on the World Wide Web. In other words, this is the address of a Web page or another type of document on the Web. An example of a URL is `http://www.cnn.com`, the address of the TV news channel CNN.

- *Metadata* is information that describes a document rather than being part of that document.

- A *deprecated element* is something introduced in a prior version of HTML that has been replaced with a better alternative as of HTML 4.01.

Common Attributes

Many of the tags in HTML 4.01 have the same attributes. The following list describes the most commonplace ones:

- `accesskey="character"`—On form controls and anchors, a single character that can be entered to access the document element.

- `align="text"`—The alignment of information in a section of a document.

- `alt="text"`—Alternative text that describes images, forms, objects, and other parts of a document.

- `char="character"`—The character that acts as an axis of alignment when the contents of a table are being lined up.

- `charoff="number"`—The number of spaces to offset the axis character when you're aligning table contents.

- `class="text"`—One or more class names to assign to the document element, separated by blank spaces.

- `dir="text"`—The direction of text and tables—either `"ltr"` (left-to-right) or `"rtl"` (right-to-left).

- `disabled`—An attribute that disables a control on a form so that it cannot handle user input.

- `id="text"`—The name to give the document element.

- `lang="text"`—The language used in a document element's attributes and its enclosed text.

- `name="text"`—A name for the document element.

- `onblur="script"`—An event that occurs when a document element loses the user input focus.

A

- onchange="*script*"—An event that occurs when a document element loses the user input focus and its value was changed while it had the focus.

- onclick="*script*"—An event that occurs when the user clicks the mouse on the document element.

- ondblclick="*script*"—An event that occurs when the user double-clicks the mouse over the document element.

- onfocus="*script*"—An event that occurs when a document element receives the user input focus.

- onkeydown="*script*"—An event that occurs when a key is pressed.

- onkeypress="*script*"—An event that occurs when a key is pressed and released.

- onkeyup="*script*"—An event that occurs when a key is released.

- onload="*script*"—An event that occurs when an entire document or all frames within a frameset have been loaded.

- onmousedown="*script*"—An event that occurs when the user clicks the mouse while the cursor is over the document element.

- onmouseout="*script*"—An event that occurs when a cursor that is over a document element moves away from that element.

- onmouseover="*script*"—An event that occurs when a mouse cursor is moved over a document element.

- onmousemove="*script*"—An event that occurs when a mouse cursor is moved while over a document element.

- onmouseup="*script*"—An event that occurs when the user releases the mouse button while the cursor is over the document element.

- onreset="*script*"—An event that occurs when all controls on a form have been reset.

- onselect="*script*"—An event that occurs when text in a text-editing user control has been selected.

- ="*script*"—An event that occurs when a form is submitted.

- onunload="*script*"—An event that occurs when a document has been unloaded from a window or frame.

- readonly—An attribute indicating that the value in a form control cannot be edited.

- style="*text*"—Style information for this individual document element.

- tabindex="*number*"—The place in the tab order of the document element.

- target="*text*"—The name of the frame in which a document should be opened.

- title="*text*"—Explanatory text about a document element.
- usemap="*URL*"—The URL of an imagemap to associate with the document element, which must match the name attribute of an existing <MAP> element.
- valign="*text*"—The vertical alignment of information within table cells.

Tags

Each of the following sections defines a tag that's a part of the HTML 4.01 specification for the language.

> The tags are listed here using uppercase letters. Although traditionally the case of tags has been irrelevant, it seems that the W3C's future specifications might require most tags to use only lowercase letters (<!DOCTYPE> being the only exception listed here). What this means is that if you find yourself coding HTML, be sure that you are using lowercase tags or you could find yourself having to change them a few years from now.

<!DOCTYPE...>

- **Purpose**: This tag appears as the first line of a document and declares the HTML version that it uses.
- **Start Tag**: Required
- **End Tag**: Not allowed
- **Attributes**: None
- **Deprecated Attributes**: None
- **Other Attributes**: None

One of the following three <!DOCTYPE> tags is used:

```
<!DOCTYPE HTML PUBLIC "-//W3C//DTD HTML 4.01//EN"
    "http://www.w3.org/TR/REC-html40/strict.dtd">

<!DOCTYPE HTML PUBLIC "-//W3C//DTD HTML 4.01 Transitional//EN"
    "http://www.w3.org/TR/REC-html40/loose.dtd">

<!DOCTYPE HTML PUBLIC "-//W3C//DTD HTML 4.01 Frameset//EN"
    "http://www.w3.org/TR/REC-html40/frameset.dtd">
```

Each of these tags contains a URL. The filenames of these URLs are strict.dtd, loose.dtd, and frameset.dtd, respectively. These names describe the level of HTML 4.01 support in the document, as follows:

A

- **Strict**: Document doesn't use anything that has been deprecated and doesn't use frames.
- **Loose**: Document uses some deprecated elements of the language that involve visual presentation.
- **Frameset**: Document uses the same deprecated elements as the preceding level and also contains frames.

Ideally, the strict `<!DOCTYPE>` should be declared because it is fully compliant with HTML 4.01. The main reason to use the loose `<!DOCTYPE>` is because some presentation-related elements of HTML 4.01—such as style sheets—are not fully adopted by Web browser developers yet.

`<A>...</A>`

- **Purpose**: This tag encloses an anchor—a part of a document that is associated with another resource on the World Wide Web. It also can be used to create an association between two sections of the same document.
- **Start Tag**: Required
- **End Tag**: Required
- **Special Attributes**:

  `coords="text"`—The coordinates of the geometric shape of an imagemap area associated with the anchor

  `name="text"`—The name of the anchor

  `href="URL"`—A resource on the Web, specified by its URL, that the anchor should be associated with

  `hreflang="text"`—The language of the resource identified by an `href` attribute

  `type="name"`—Advice on the content type expected at the associated resource on the Web

  `rel="link_types"`—The relationship of the current document to the associated resource on the Web

  `rev="link_types"`—The relationship of the associated resource on the Web to the current document

  `shape="text"`—The geometric shape of an imagemap area associated with the anchor

  `charset="text"`—The character set of the associated resource on the Web

- **Deprecated Attributes**: None
- **Other Attributes**: `accesskey`, `class`, `dir`, `id`, `lang`, `onblur`, `onclick`, `ondblclick`, `onfocus`, `onkeydown`, `onkeypress`, `onkeyup`, `onmousedown`, onmousemove, onmouseout, onmouseover, onmouseup, `style`, `tabindex`, `target`, `title`

`<ABBR>...</ABBR>`

- **Purpose**: This tag encloses text that is an abbreviation.
- **Start Tag**: Required
- **End Tag**: Required
- **Special Attributes**: None
- **Deprecated Attributes**: None
- **Other Attributes**: `class`, `dir`, `id`, `lang`, `onclick`, `ondblclick`, `onkeydown`, onkeypress, onkeyup, onmousedown, onmousemove, onmouseout, onmouseover, onmouseup, `style`, `title`

`<ACRONYM>...</ACRONYM>`

- **Purpose**: This tag encloses text that is an acronym.
- **Start Tag**: Required
- **End Tag**: Required
- **Special Attributes**: None
- **Deprecated Attributes**: None
- **Other Attributes**: `class`, `dir`, `id`, `lang`, `onclick`, `ondblclick`, `onkeydown`, onkeypress, onkeyup, onmousedown, onmousemove, onmouseout, onmouseover, onmouseup, `style`, `title`

`<ADDRESS>...</ADDRESS>`

- **Purpose**: This tag encloses contact information about the author of an entire document or a specific section of a document. Most Web browsers display this information in a different manner than other text.
- **Start Tag**: Required
- **End Tag**: Required
- **Special Attributes**: None
- **Deprecated Attributes**: None
- **Other Attributes**: `class`, `dir`, `id`, `lang`, `onclick`, `ondblclick`, `onkeydown`, onkeypress, onkeyup, onmousedown, onmousemove, onmouseout, onmouseover, onmouseup

A

\<APPLET\>

- **Purpose**: This tag has been deprecated. Most browsers today support the `<OBJECT>` tag for Java applets. In the case of the Java Plug-In, one would use the `<EMBED>` tag just as one would for any other plug-in.

\<AREA\>

- **Purpose**: This tag indicates an area on an imagemap that should be associated with a link.
- **Start Tag**: Required
- **End Tag**: Not allowed
- **Special Attributes**:

  `href="URL"`—A URL that the imagemap area should be associated with

  `shape="text"`—The geometric shape of the area, which may be `"default"`, `"circle"`, `"poly"`, or `"rect"`

  `coords="text"`—The coordinates of the geometric shape

  `nohref`—This attribute indicates that the area has no link associated with it

- **Deprecated Attributes**: None
- **Other Attributes**: `accesskey`, `alt`, `class`, `dir`, `id`, `lang`, `name`, `onblur`, `onclick`, `ondblclick`, `onfocus`, `onkeydown`, `onkeypress`, `onkeyup`, `onmousedown`, `onmousemove`, `onmouseout`, `onmouseover`, `onmouseup`, `style`, `tabindex`, `target`, `title`

\<B\>...\</B\>

- **Purpose**: This tag encloses text that should be displayed in boldface. Although it has not been deprecated, the HTML 4.01 specification advises that style sheets are a better alternative.
- **Start Tag**: Required
- **End Tag**: Required
- **Special Attributes**: None
- **Deprecated Attributes**: None
- **Other Attributes**: `class`, `dir`, `id`, `lang`, `onclick`, `ondblclick`, `onkeydown`, `onkeypress`, `onkeyup`, `onmousedown`, `onmousemove`, `onmouseout`, `onmouseover`, `onmouseup`, `style`, `title`

<BASE>

- **Purpose**: This tag is used to explicitly define the base URL for the document. This base URL will be combined with each relative URL in the document to form a full address to a resource on the Web.
- **Start Tag**: Required
- **End Tag**: Not allowed
- **Special Attributes**:

  href="*URL*"—The base URL of the document.
- **Deprecated Attributes**: None
- **Other Attributes**: target

<BASEFONT>...</BASEFONT>

- **Purpose**: This tag has been deprecated.

<BIG>...</BIG>

- **Purpose**: This tag encloses text that should be displayed in a larger-than-normal font. Although it has not been deprecated, the HTML 4.01 specification advises that style sheets are a better alternative.
- **Start Tag**: Required
- **End Tag**: Required
- **Special Attributes**: None
- **Deprecated Attributes**: None
- **Other Attributes**: class, dir, id, lang, onclick, ondblclick, onkeydown, onkeypress, onkeyup, onmousedown, onmousemove, onmouseout, onmouseover, onmouseup, style, title

<BLOCKQUOTE>...</BLOCKQUOTE>

- **Purpose**: This tag encloses a block of quoted text, which will be indented and displayed in its own paragraph when the document is viewed. A shorter quote can be enclosed within the <Q> tag.
- **Start Tag**: Required
- **End Tag**: Required
- **Special Attributes**:

  cite="*URL*"—The address of a document containing information about the source of the quotation.

A

- **Deprecated Attributes**: None
- **Other Attributes**: `class, dir, id, lang, onclick, ondblclick, onkeydown, onkeypress, onkeyup, onmousedown, onmousemove, onmouseout, onmouseover, onmouseup, style, title`

The `<BLOCKQUOTE>` tag commonly is used to indent a block of text even if it's not a quotation. This usage has been deprecated in HTML 4.01, in favor of using style sheets to achieve the same effect.

`<BODY>...</BODY>`

- **Purpose**: This tag encloses the content of the document, which should be displayed when it's loaded by a program such as a Web browser. Several popular presentation attributes have been deprecated, in favor of using the `<STYLE>` tag to accomplish the same task.
- **Start Tag**: Optional
- **End Tag**: Optional
- **Special Attributes**: None
- **Deprecated Attributes**: `alink, background, bgcolor, link, text, vlink`
- **Other Attributes**: `class, dir, id, lang, onclick, ondblclick, onkeydown, onkeyup, onkeypress, onload, onmousedown, onmousemove, onmouseout, onmouseover, onmouseup, onunload, style, title`

`<BR>`

- **Purpose**: This tag inserts a line break in a document, causing subsequent text and other elements to be displayed on a new line.
- **Start Tag**: Required
- **End Tag**: Not allowed
- **Special Attributes**: None
- **Deprecated Attributes**: `clear`
- **Other Attributes**: `class, id, style, title`

`<BUTTON>...</BUTTON>`

- **Purpose**: This tag adds a button control to a form.
- **Start Tag**: Required
- **End Tag**: Required

- **Special Attributes**:

    name="*text*"—The name of the button

    value="*text*"—The initial value of the button

    type="*text*"—The type of button to add to the form

- **Deprecated Attributes**: None
- **Other Attributes**: accesskey, class, dir, disabled, id, lang, onblur, onclick, ondblclick, onfocus, onkeydown, onkeyup, onkeypress, onmousedown, onmousemove, onmouseout, onmouseover, onmouseup, style, tabindex, title

<CAPTION>...</CAPTION>

- **Purpose:** This tag encloses a short description of a table. The <CAPTION> tag must immediately follow a <TABLE> tag, and a table can have only one caption.
- **Start Tag:** Required
- **End Tag:** Required
- **Special Attributes**: None
- **Deprecated Attributes**: align
- **Other Attributes**: class, dir, id, lang, onclick, ondblclick, onkeydown, onkeyup, onkeypress, onload, onmousedown, onmousemove, onmouseout, onmouseover, onmouseup, onunload, style, title

<CENTER>...</CENTER>

- **Purpose**: This tag has been deprecated.

<CITE>...</CITE>

- **Purpose**: This tag encloses a citation or some other kind of reference to another source.
- **Start Tag**: Required
- **End Tag**: Required
- **Special Attributes**: None
- **Deprecated Attributes**: None
- **Other Attributes**: class, dir, id, lang, onclick, ondblclick, onkeydown, onkeypress, onkeyup, onmousedown, onmousemove, onmouseout, onmouseover, onmouseup, style, title

A

<CODE>...</CODE>

- **Purpose**: This tag encloses text that reprints source code from a computer programming language or similar information.
- **Start Tag**: Required
- **End Tag**: Required
- **Special Attributes**: None
- **Deprecated Attributes**: None
- **Other Attributes**: class, dir, id, lang, onclick, ondblclick, onkeydown, onkeypress, onkeyup, onmousedown, onmousemove, onmouseout, onmouseover, onmouseup, style, title

<COL>

- **Purpose**: This tag encloses a column in a table so that it can be structured.
- **Start Tag**: Required
- **End Tag**: Not allowed
- **Special Attributes**:

  span="*number*"—The number of columns in the column group

  width="*number*"—The default width for columns in the column group
- **Deprecated Attributes**: None
- **Other Attributes**: align, char, charoff, class, dir, id, lang, onclick, ondblclick, onkeydown, onkeypress, onkeyup, onmousedown, onmousemove, onmouseout, onmouseover, onmouseup, style, title, valign

<COLGROUP>...</COLGROUP>

- **Purpose**: This tag encloses a group of columns in a table so that they can be structured at the same time.
- **Start Tag**: Required
- **End Tag**: Optional
- **Special Attributes**:

  span="*number*"—The number of columns in the column group

  width="*number*"—The default width for columns in the column group
- **Deprecated Attributes**: None
- **Other Attributes**: align, char, charoff, class, dir, id, lang, onclick, ondblclick, onkeydown, onkeypress, onkeyup, onmousedown, onmousemove, onmouseout, onmouseover, onmouseup, style, title, valign

<DEL>...</DEL>

- **Purpose**: This tag encloses a section of a document that has been deleted since a previous edition of the document. Text within this tag often is displayed by using strikethrough characters.
- **Start Tag**: Required
- **End Tag**: Required
- **Special Attributes**:

  cite="*URL*"—The address of a document containing information about the inserted section

  datetime="*date_and_time*"—The time and date that the insertion was made
- **Other Attributes**: class, dir, id, lang, onclick, ondblclick, onkeydown, onkeypress, onkeyup, onmousedown, onmousemove, onmouseout, onmouseover, onmouseup, style, title

<DD>...</DD>

- **Purpose**: This tag encloses a block of text that provides a definition for a term, which itself is enclosed within a <DD> tag. A list of terms and definitions is enclosed within a <DL> tag.
- **Start Tag**: Required
- **End Tag**: Optional
- **Special Attributes**: class, dir, id, lang, onclick, ondblclick, onkeydown, onkeypress, onkeyup, onmousedown, onmousemove, onmouseout, onmouseover, onmouseup, style, title

<DFN>...</DFN>

- **Purpose**: This tag encloses text that's either a definition or something that's being defined.
- **Start Tag**: Required
- **End Tag**: Required
- **Special Attributes**: None
- **Deprecated Attributes**: None
- **Other Attributes**: class, dir, id, lang, onclick, ondblclick, onkeydown, onkeypress, onkeyup, onmousedown, onmousemove, onmouseout, onmouseover, onmouseup, style, title

A

`<DIR>...</DIR>`

- **Purpose**: This tag has been deprecated.

`<DIV>...</DIV>`

- **Purpose**: This tag encloses a section of a document into its own block. It's used as a way to organize the content internally and can be used with attributes to affect the presentation of the section.
- **Start Tag**: Required
- **End Tag**: Required
- **Special Attributes**: None
- **Deprecated Attributes**: align
- **Other Attributes**: class, dir, id, lang, onclick, ondblclick, onkeydown, onkeypress, onkeyup, onmousedown, onmousemove, onmouseout, onmouseover, onmouseup, style, title

`<DL>...</DL>`

- **Purpose**: This tag encloses a list of terms and their definitions. The terms and definitions are enclosed within `<DT>` and `<DD>` tags, respectively.
- **Start Tag**: Required
- **End Tag**: Required
- **Special Attributes**: class, dir, id, lang, onclick, ondblclick, onkeydown, onkeypress, onkeyup, onmousedown, onmousemove, onmouseout, onmouseover, onmouseup, style, title

`<DT>...</DT>`

- **Purpose**: `<DT>` defines a block of text as a single term in a definition type list. A collection of terms and definitions are enclosed within a `<DL>` tag.
- **Start Tag**: Required
- **End Tag**: Optional
- **Special Attributes**: class, dir, id, lang, onclick, ondblclick, onkeydown, onkeypress, onkeyup, onmousedown, onmousemove, onmouseout, onmouseover, onmouseup, style, title

`<EM>...</EM>`

- **Purpose**: This tag encloses text that needs a special emphasis. Most Web browsers will display this text in italics. For a stronger emphasis, use the `<STRONG>` tag.

- **Start Tag**: Required
- **End Tag**: Required
- **Special Attributes**: None
- **Deprecated Attributes**: None
- **Other Attributes**: `class`, `dir`, `id`, `lang`, `onclick`, `ondblclick`, `onkeydown`, `onkeypress`, `onkeyup`, `onmousedown`, `onmousemove`, `onmouseout`, `onmouseover`, `onmouseup`, `style`, `title`

<FIELDSET>...</FIELDSET>

- **Purpose**: This tag encloses a group of related controls on a form.
- **Start Tag**: Required
- **End Tag**: Required
- **Special Attributes**: None
- **Deprecated Attributes**: `align`
- **Other Attributes**: `accesskey`, `class`, `dir`, `id`, `lang`, `onclick`, `ondblclick`, `onkeydown`, `onkeypress`, `onkeyup`, `onmousedown`, `onmousemove`, `onmouseout`, `onmouseover`, `onmouseup`, `style`, `title`

<FONT>...</FONT>

- **Purpose**: This tag has been deprecated.

<FORM>...</FORM>

- **Purpose**: This tag encloses a group of related controls that take information from the person browsing the document.
- **Start Tag**: Required
- **End Tag**: Required
- **Special Attributes**:

  `action="`*URL*`"`—The URL that will receive and process the results of the form.

  `method="`*text*`"`—The method that will be used to transmit the form results.

  `name="`*text*`"`—The name of the image, which can be used by style sheets or scripts. The preferred attribute to use for this purpose is `id`.

  `enctype="`*text*`"`—The content type used to transmit the form results.

  `accept-charset="`*text*`"`—One or more character sets, separated by commas, that must be accepted in the form results.

A

accept="*text*"—One or more content types, separated by commas, that can be transmitted successfully by using the form.

- **Deprecated Attributes**: None
- **Other Attributes**: class, dir, id, lang, onclick, ondblclick, onkeydown, onkeypress, onkeyup, onmousedown, onmousemove, onmouseout, onmouseover, onmouseup, onreset, onsubmit, style, target, title

<FRAME>

- **Purpose**: This tag encloses a frame and establishes its appearance.
- **Start Tag**: Required
- **End Tag**: Not allowed
- **Special Attributes**:

  name="*text*"—The name of the frame.

  longdesc="*URL*"—The URL to a document that contains a long description of the frame.

  src="*URL*"—The URL of a document that contains the contents of the frame.

  noresize—An attribute that indicates the frame cannot be resized.

  scrolling="*text*"—How scrolling is handled for the frame.

  frameborder="*number*"—Whether a border exists around the frame.

  marginwidth="*number*"—The space between the frame's contents and its left and right borders.

  marginheight="*number*"—The space between the frame's contents and its top and bottom borders.

- **Deprecated Attributes**: None
- **Other Attributes**: class, id, style, target, title

<FRAMESET>...</FRAMESET>

- **Purpose**: This tag encloses information that establishes the arrangement of frames in a document. It's used in place of the <BODY> tag and should immediately follow the document's header.
- **Start Tag**: Required
- **End Tag**: Required

- **Special Attributes**:

  rows="*list*"—The height of each vertical frame in the frameset, with values separated by commas.

  cols="*list*"—The width of each horizontal frame in the frameset, with values separated by commas.

- **Deprecated Attributes**: None
- **Other Attributes**: class, id, onload, onunload, style, title

\<HEAD\>...\</HEAD\>

- **Purpose**: This tag encloses header information that describes a document, such as its title and a description of its content. The information inside this tag is not displayed when the page is shown in a browser.
- **Start Tag**: Optional
- **End Tag**: Optional
- **Special Attributes**:

  profile="*URL*"—The address of a document containing information about the metadata that can be defined in the header.

- **Deprecated Attributes**: None
- **Other Attributes**: lang, dir

\<H1\>...\</H1\>, \<H2\>...\</H2\>, \<H3\>...\</H3\>, \<H4\>...\</H4\>, \<H5\>...\</H5\>, and \<H6\>...\</H6\>

- **Purpose**: Each of these tags encloses a heading—also called a *headline*—that is presented on a document. These headings range from \<H1\> (most prominent) to \<H6\> (least prominent).
- **Start Tag**: Required
- **End Tag**: Required
- **Special Attributes**: None
- **Deprecated Attributes**: align
- **Other Attributes**: class, dir, id, lang, onclick, ondblclick, onkeydown, onkeypress, onkeyup, onmousedown, onmousemove, onmouseout, onmouseover, onmouseup, style, title

<HR>

- **Purpose**: This tag causes a horizontal line—also called a *rule*—to be displayed as part of a document.
- **Start Tag**: Required
- **End Tag**: Not allowed
- **Special Attributes**: None
- **Deprecated Attributes**: `align`, `noshade`, `size`, `width`
- **Other Attributes**: `class`, `dir`, `id`, `lang`, `onclick`, `ondblclick`, `onkeydown`, `onkeypress`, `onkeyup`, `onmousedown`, `onmousemove`, `onmouseout`, `onmouseover`, `onmouseup`, `style`, `title`

<HTML>...</HTML>

- **Purpose**: This tag encloses an HTML document in its entirety.
- **Start Tag**: Optional
- **End Tag**: Optional
- **Special Attributes**: None
- **Deprecated Attributes**: `version`
- **Other Attributes**: `lang`, `dir`

<I>...</I>

- **Purpose**: This tag encloses text that should be italicized. Although it hasn't been deprecated, the HTML 4.01 specification advises that style sheets are a better alternative.
- **Start Tag**: Required
- **End Tag**: Required
- **Special Attributes**: None
- **Deprecated Attributes**: None
- **Other Attributes**: `class`, `dir`, `id`, `lang`, `onclick`, `ondblclick`, `onkeydown`, `onkeypress`, `onkeyup`, `onmousedown`, `onmousemove`, `onmouseout`, `onmouseover`, `onmouseup`, `style`, `title`

<IFRAME>...</IFRAME>

- **Purpose**: This tag encloses a frame that is inserted into a document in the same manner as images and other objects.
- **Start Tag**: Required

- **End Tag**: Required
- **Special Attributes**:

  `frameborder="number"`—Whether a border exists around the frame.

  `longdesc="URL"`—The URL of a document containing a long description of the frame.

  `marginheight="number"`—The space between the frame's contents and its top and bottom borders.

  `marginwidth="number"`—The space between the frame's contents and its left and right borders.

  `name="text"`—The name of the frame.

  `scrolling="text"`—How scrolling is handled for the frame.

  `src="URL"`—The URL of a document that contains the contents of the frame.

  `width="number"`—The width of the frame.

  `height="number"`—The height of the frame.

- **Deprecated Attributes**: None
- **Other Attributes**: `align, class, id, name, style, target, title`

`<IMG>`

- **Purpose**: This tag encloses an image file that's displayed as part of the document. The `<OBJECT>` tag also can be used to display image files.
- **Start Tag**: Required
- **End Tag**: Not allowed
- **Special Attributes**:

  `height="number"`—The height of the image.

  `hspace="number"`—The amount of whitespace to insert in a document between the image and the other information to the left and right of it.

  `ismap`—An attribute that indicates the image is a server-side imagemap.

  `name="text"`—The name of the image, which can be used by style sheets or scripts. The preferred attribute to use for this purpose is `id`.

  `src="URL"`—The URL of the image file.

  `longdesc="URL"`—The URL of a comprehensive description of the image and any imagemaps it contains.

  `vspace="number"`—The amount of whitespace to insert in a document between the image and the other information above and below it.

  `width="number"`—The width of the image.

- **Deprecated Attributes**: align, border
- **Other Attributes**: alt, class, dir, id, lang, onclick, ondblclick, onkeydown, onkeypress, onkeyup, onmousedown, onmousemove, onmouseout, onmouseover, onmouseup, style, title, usemap

\<INPUT\>

- **Purpose**: This tag encloses a control that is part of a form.
- **Start Tag**: Required
- **End Tag**: Not allowed
- **Special Attributes**:

  accept—A list of content types, separated by commas, that can be transmitted successfully by the server that's processing the form.

  name="*text*"—The name of the control.

  type="*text*"—The type of control to include on the form.

  value="*text*"—The initial value of the control.

  size="*number*"—The size of the control's input area.

  maxlength="*number*"—The maximum number of characters that can be entered into a control's text input area.

  checked—This attribute indicates that a radio or check box control should be selected when the form is first displayed.

  src="*URL*"—The URL of an image to display as a Submit button.

  ismap—An attribute that indicates the tag is used with a server-side imagemap.

- **Deprecated Attributes**: None
- **Other Attributes**: accesskey, align, alt, class, dir, disabled, id, lang, onblur, onchange, onclick, ondblclick, onfocus, onkeydown, onkeypress, onkeyup, onmousedown, onmouseover, onmousemove, onmouseout, onmouseup, onselect, readonly, style, tabindex, title, usemap

\<INS\>...\</INS\>

- **Purpose**: This tag encloses a section of a document that has been inserted since a previous edition of the document.
- **Start Tag**: Required
- **End Tag**: Required

- **Special Attributes**:

  `cite="URL"`—The address of a document containing information about the inserted section.

  `datetime="date_and_time"`—The time and date that the insertion was made.

- **Other Attributes**: `class`, `dir`, `id`, `lang`, `onclick`, `ondblclick`, `onkeydown`, `onkeypress`, `onkeyup`, `onmousedown`, `onmousemove`, `onmouseout`, `onmouseover`, `onmouseup`, `style`, `title`

\<ISINDEX\>

- **Purpose**: This tag has been deprecated.

\<KBD\>...\</KBD\>

- **Purpose**: This tag encloses text that should be entered by a user in a computer program or similar information.
- **Start Tag**: Required
- **End Tag**: Required
- **Special Attributes**: None
- **Deprecated Attributes**: None
- **Other Attributes**: `class`, `dir`, `id`, `lang`, `onclick`, `ondblclick`, `onkeydown`, `onkeypress`, `onkeyup`, `onmousedown`, `onmousemove`, `onmouseout`, `onmouseover`, `onmouseup`, `style`, `title`

\<LABEL\>...\</LABEL\>

- **Purpose**: This tag is used to provide a label for form controls that don't already have them.
- **Start Tag**: Required
- **End Tag**: Required
- **Special Attributes**:

  `for="text"`—The ID name of the control that this label is associated with.

- **Deprecated Attributes**: None
- **Other Attributes**: `accesskey`, `class`, `dir`, `id`, `lang`, `onblur`, `onclick`, `ondblclick`, `onfocus`, `onkeydown`, `onkeypress`, `onkeyup`, `onmousedown`, `onmousemove`, `onmouseout`, `onmouseover`, `onmouseup`, `style`, `title`

A

<LEGEND>...</LEGEND>

- **Purpose**: This tag provides a caption for a group of controls that have been associated with each other using the <FIELDSET> tag. This tag must be enclosed within the <FIELDSET> tag.
- **Start Tag**: Required
- **End Tag**: Required
- **Special Attributes**: None
- **Deprecated Attributes**: align
- **Other Attributes**: accesskey, class, dir, id, lang, onclick, ondblclick, onkeydown, onkeypress, onkeyup, onmousedown, onmousemove, onmouseout, onmouseover, onmouseup, style, title

<LI>...</LI>

- **Purpose**: This tag encloses a list of items that will be individually numbered. Each item in the list is identified by the <LI> tag. To display a list without numbering, use the <UL> tag.
- **Start Tag**: Required
- **End Tag**: Optional
- **Special Attributes**: None
- **Deprecated Attributes**: compact, type, value
- **Other Attributes**: class, dir, id, lang, onclick, ondblclick, onkeydown, onkeypress, onkeyup, onmousedown, onmousemove, onmouseout, onmouseover, onmouseup, style, title

<LINK>

- **Purpose**: This tag defines a link—a relationship between this document and other resources. More than one of these relationships can be defined, but <LINK> can be used only in the header section of a document.
- **Start Tag**: Required
- **End Tag**: Not allowed
- **Special Attributes**:

  name="text"—The name of the anchor.

  href="URL"—A resource on the Web, specified by its URL, that the anchor should be associated with.

  hreflang="text"—The language of the resource identified by an href attribute.

media="*text*"—The intended medium of style sheet information.

type="*name*"—The content type of the associated resource on the Web.

rel="*link_types*"—The relationship of the current document to the associated resource on the Web.

rev="*link_types*"—The relationship of the associated resource on the Web to the current document.

charset="*text*"—The character set of the associated resource on the Web.

- **Deprecated Attributes**: None
- **Other Attributes**: accesskey, class, dir, id, lang, onclick, ondblclick, onkeydown, onkeypress, onkeyup, onmousedown, onmousemove, onmouseout, onmouseover, onmouseup, style, tabindex, target, title

<MAP>...</MAP>

- **Purpose**: This tag encloses a client-side imagemap that associates areas on an object with links.
- **Start Tag**: Required
- **End Tag**: Required
- **Special Attributes**:

  name="*text*"—The name of the imagemap.

- **Deprecated Attributes**: None
- **Other Attributes**: class, dir, id, lang, onclick, ondblclick, onkeydown, onkeypress, onkeyup, onmousedown, onmousemove, onmouseout, onmouseover, onmouseup, style, title

<MENU>...</MENU>

- **Purpose**: This tag has been deprecated.

<META>

- **Purpose**: This tag defines a metadata property for the document, which can contain several different properties.
- **Start Tag**: Required
- **End Tag**: Not allowed
- **Special Attributes**:

  name="*text*"—The name of the property.

  content="*text*"—The value of the property.

http-equiv="*text*"—The name of an HTTP Response Header that will be set to this tag's value (http-equiv is used as an alternative to the name attribute).

scheme="*text*"—Additional information that describes how the content attribute has been used.

- **Deprecated Attributes**: None
- **Other Attributes**: lang, dir

<NOFRAMES>...</NOFRAMES>

- **Purpose**: This tag encloses content that is an alternative to frames in the same document. Browsers that don't support frames will display this alternative content instead. The <NOFRAMES> tag should be used within a <FRAMESET> tag.
- **Start Tag**: Required
- **End Tag**: Required
- **Special Attributes**: None
- **Deprecated Attributes**: None
- **Other Attributes**: class, dir, lang, id, onclick, ondblclick, onkeydown, onkeypress, onkeyup, onmousedown, onmousemove, onmouseout, onmouseover, onmouseup, style, title

<NOSCRIPT>...</NOSCRIPT>

- **Purpose**: This tag encloses content that is displayed when a script is not executed, either because the browsing software doesn't handle scripts or because it doesn't handle the script language being used.
- **Start Tag**: Required
- **End Tag**: Required
- **Special Attributes**:

src="*URL*"—The URL of a document containing the script.

type="*text*"—The scripting language being used.

defer—This attribute indicates that the script doesn't add any content to the document.

- **Deprecated Attributes**: language
- **Other Attributes**: class, dir, id, lang, onclick, ondblclick, onkeydown, onkeypress, onkeyup, onmousedown, onmousemove, onmouseout, onmouseover, onmouseup, style, title

<OBJECT>...</OBJECT>

- **Purpose**: This tag encloses an object that is presented as part of the document. Objects can be files, interactive programs, and other HTML documents.
- **Start Tag**: Required
- **End Tag**: Required
- **Special Attributes**:

  classid="*URL*"—The URL of an object's implementation, which can be used in place of the data attribute or in conjunction with it, depending on the type of object.

  codebase="*URL*"—The base URL for other URLs specified as attributes of the object.

  codetype="*text*"—The content type of the data identified by the classid attribute.

  data="*URL*"—The URL of the data associated with the object.

  height="*number*"—The height of the object.

  hspace="*number*"—The amount of whitespace to insert in a document between the object and the other information to the left and right of it.

  width="*number*"—The width of the object.

  type="*text*"—The content type of the data identified by the data attribute.

  archive="*text*"—A list of URLs—separated by spaces—of any archive files that contain classid and data for faster downloading.

  declare—An attribute that indicates this object is being declared but should not be presented until a subsequent <OBJECT> tag does so.

  standby="*text*"—A message that should be displayed while the object is being downloaded.

  vspace="*number*"—The amount of whitespace to insert in a document between the image and the other information above and below it.

- **Deprecated Attributes**: align, border
- **Other Attributes**: class, dir, id, lang, name, onclick, ondblclick, onkeydown, onkeypress, onkeyup, onmousedown, onmousemove, onmouseout, onmouseover, onmouseup, style, tabindex, title, usemap

<OL>...</OL>

- **Purpose**: This tag encloses a list of items that will be individually numbered. Each item in the list is identified by the <LI> tag. To display a list without numbering, the <UL> tag is used.

- **Start Tag**: Required
- **End Tag**: Required
- **Special Attributes**: None
- **Deprecated Attributes**: compact, start, type
- **Other Attributes**: class, dir, id, lang, onclick, ondblclick, onkeydown, onkeypress, onkeyup, onmousedown, onmousemove, onmouseout, onmouseover, onmouseup, style, title

<OPTION>...</OPTION>

- **Purpose**: This tag adds a choice to a menu control on a form.
- **Start Tag**: Required
- **End Tag**: Optional
- **Special Attributes**:

  selected—This attribute indicates that this option should be selected when the menu is first displayed.

  value="text"—The initial value of the option.

  label="text"—A shorter label of the option that can be used as an alternative.

- **Deprecated Attributes**: None
- **Other Attributes**: class, dir, disabled, id, lang, onclick, ondblclick, onkeydown, onkeypress, onkeyup, onmousedown, onmousemove, onmouseover, onmouseout, onmouseup, style, title

<OPTGROUP>...</OPTGROUP>

- **Purpose**: This tag encloses a group of menu options on a form.
- **Start Tag**: Required
- **End Tag**: Required
- **Special Attributes**:

  label="text"—The label for the option group.

- **Deprecated Attributes**: None
- **Other Attributes**: class, dir, disabled, id, lang, onblur, onchange, onclick, ondblclick, onkeydown, onkeypress, onkeyup, onmousedown, onmousemove, onmouseout, onmouseover, onmouseup, onfocus, style, title

\<P\>...\</P\>

- **Purpose**: This tag encloses a paragraph of text.
- **Start Tag**: Required
- **End Tag**: Optional
- **Special Attributes**: None
- **Deprecated Attributes**: align
- **Other Attributes**: class, dir, id, lang, onclick, ondblclick, onkeydown, onkeypress, onkeyup, onmousedown, onmousemove, onmouseout, onmouseover, onmouseup, style, title

Many HTML authors use one or more \<P\> tags without any text as a way to insert white-space into a document. This is discouraged in the HTML 4.01 specification, which says that HTML browsing software should ignore repeated \<P\> tags without any text.

\<PARAM\>

- **Purpose**: This tag establishes a parameter—a value that will be provided to an object before it's presented as part of a document. More than one parameter can be used, but all of them should be enclosed within the related \<OBJECT\> tag.
- **Start Tag**: Required
- **End Tag**: Not allowed
- **Special Attributes**:

  name="*text*"—The name of the parameter.

  value="*text*"—The value of the parameter, which can be a string of text, an object, or a URL to a resource where one or more values are stored.

  valuetype="*text*"—The type of information stored as the parameter's value.

  type="*text*"—The content type of the URL specified in value.

- **Deprecated Attributes**: None
- **Other Attributes:** id

\<PRE\>...\</PRE\>

- **Purpose**: This tag encloses text that should not be formatted in the same manner as other HTML text. Most Web browsers will display this preformatted text in a monospace font with all whitespace intact, rather than ignoring repeated space characters as HTML normally does. Word-wrapping also might not occur, causing text to flow outside the right margin of the browser window.

A

- **Start Tag**: Required
- **End Tag**: Required
- **Special Attributes**: None
- **Deprecated Attributes**: `width`
- **Other Attributes**: `class`, `dir`, `id`, `lang`, `onclick`, `ondblclick`, `onkeydown`, `onkeypress`, `onkeyup`, `onmousedown`, `onmousemove`, `onmouseout`, `onmouseover`, `onmouseup`, `style`, `title`

`<Q>...</Q>`

- **Purpose**: This tag encloses a short amount of quoted text, which will be displayed with quotation marks around it when the document is viewed. Unlike a longer quotation enclosed within the `<BLOCKQUOTE>` tag, this text will not be set apart from other content by paragraph breaks.
- **Start Tag**: Required
- **End Tag**: Required
- **Special Attributes**:

  `cite="URL"`—The address of a document that contains information about the source of the quotation.
- **Deprecated Attributes**: None
- **Other Attributes**: `class`, `dir`, `id`, `lang`, `onclick`, `ondblclick`, `onkeydown`, `onkeypress`, `onkeyup`, `onmousedown`, `onmousemove`, `onmouseout`, `onmouseover`, `onmouseup`, `style`, `title`

`<S>...</S>`

- **Purpose**: This tag has been deprecated.

`<SAMP>...</SAMP>`

- **Purpose**: This tag encloses text that reprints output from a computer program, a script, or another similar process.
- **Start Tag**: Required
- **End Tag**: Required
- **Special Attributes**: None
- **Deprecated Attributes**: None
- **Other Attributes**: `class`, `dir`, `id`, `lang`, `onclick`, `ondblclick`, `onkeydown`, `onkeypress`, `onkeyup`, `onmousedown`, `onmousemove`, `onmouseout`, `onmouseover`, `onmouseup`, `style`, `title`

<SCRIPT>...</SCRIPT>

- **Purpose**: This tag places an executable script within a document.
- **Start Tag**: Required
- **End Tag**: Required
- **Special Attributes**:

  src="*URL*"—The URL of a document containing the script.

  type="*text*"—The scripting language being used.

  defer—This attribute indicates that the script doesn't add any content to the document.
- **Deprecated Attributes**: language
- **Other Attributes**: charset

<SELECT>...</SELECT>

- **Purpose**: This tag adds a menu control to a form.
- **Start Tag**: Required
- **End Tag**: Required
- **Special Attributes**:

  name="*text*"—The name of the button.

  size="*number*"—The number of items to display in a menu, presented as a scrolling list box.

  multiple—This attribute indicates that more than one item can be selected from the menu.
- **Deprecated Attributes**: None
- **Other Attributes**: class, dir, disabled, id, lang, onclick, ondblclick, onkeydown, onkeyup, onkeypress, onmousedown, onmousemove, onmouseout, onmouseover, onmouseup, style, tabindex, title

<SMALL>...</SMALL>

- **Purpose**: This tag encloses text that should be displayed in a smaller-than-normal font. Although it has not been deprecated, the HTML 4.01 specification advises that style sheets are a better alternative.
- **Start Tag**: Required
- **End Tag**: Required
- **Special Attributes**: None

A

- **Deprecated Attributes**: None
- **Other Attributes**: class, dir, id, lang, onclick, ondblclick, onkeydown, onkeypress, onkeyup, onmousedown, onmousemove, onmouseout, onmouseover, onmouseup, style, title

<SPAN>...</SPAN>

- **Purpose**: This tag encloses a small section of a document into its own block. Like <DIV>, it's used to organize the content internally and can be used with attributes to change the presentation of the section.
- **Start Tag**: Required
- **End Tag**: Required
- **Special Attributes**: None
- **Deprecated Attributes**: None
- **Other Attributes**: align, class, dir, id, lang, onclick, ondblclick, onkeydown, onkeypress, onkeyup, onmousedown, onmousemove, onmouseout, onmouseover, onmouseup, style, title

<STRIKE>...</STRIKE>

- **Purpose**: This tag has been deprecated.

<STRONG>...</STRONG>

- **Purpose**: This tag encloses text that needs a strong emphasis. Most Web browsers display this text in bold. You can place a lesser emphasis on text with the <EM> tag.
- **Start Tag**: Required
- **End Tag**: Required
- **Special Attributes**: None
- **Deprecated Attributes**: None
- **Other Attributes**: class, dir, id, lang, onclick, ondblclick, onkeydown, onkeypress, onkeyup, onmousedown, onmousemove, onmouseout, onmouseover, onmouseup, style, title

<STYLE>...</STYLE>

- **Purpose**: This tag establishes style sheet rules in the header of a document.
- **Start Tag**: Required
- **End Tag**: Required

- **Special Attributes**:

  type="*text*"—The style sheet language being used.

  media="*text*"—The intended medium on which this style sheet will be displayed.

- **Deprecated Attributes**: None
- **Other Attributes**: dir, lang, title

_{...}

- **Purpose**: This tag encloses text that is a subscript.
- **Start Tag**: Required
- **End Tag**: Required
- **Special Attributes**: None
- **Deprecated Attributes**: None
- **Other Attributes**: class, dir, id, lang, onclick, ondblclick, onkeydown, onkeypress, onkeyup, onmousedown, onmousemove, onmouseout, onmouseover, onmouseup, style, title

^{...}

- **Purpose**: This tag encloses text that is a superscript.
- **Start Tag**: Required
- **End Tag**: Required
- **Special Attributes**: None
- **Deprecated Attributes**: None
- **Other Attributes**: class, dir, id, lang, onclick, ondblclick, onkeydown, onkeypress, onkeyup, onmousedown, onmousemove, onmouseout, onmouseover, onmouseup, style, title

<TABLE>...</TABLE>

- **Purpose**: This tag encloses information that has been organized into a table containing rows and columns of rectangular cells.
- **Start Tag**: Required
- **End Tag**: Required
- **Special Attributes**:

  border="*number*"—The width of the border around the table, or "0" if the border should not be displayed.

A

`cellpadding="number"`—The amount of space between the contents of a table cell and its borders.

`cellspacing="number"`—The amount of space between cells in the table.

`frame="text"`—The sides of a frame surrounding the table that are visible, if any.

`summary="text"`—A summary of the purpose and structure of the table, for the benefit of nonvisual Web browsing software.

`rules="text"`—The rules (lines) that will appear between cells in a table, if any.

`width="number"`—The desired width of the table, expressed in either pixels or as a percentage of the space available in the browser.

- **Deprecated Attributes**: `align`, `bgcolor`
- **Other Attributes**: `class`, `dir`, `frame`, `id`, `lang`, `onclick`, `ondblclick`, `onkeydown`, `onkeypress`, `onkeyup`, `onmousedown`, `onmousemove`, `onmouseout`, `onmouseover`, `onmouseup`, `style`, `title`

<TBODY>...</TBODY>

- **Purpose**: This tag encloses one or more rows of a table's cells—the actual body of the table. If a table contains either a `<THEAD>` or a `<TFOOT>` row, the `<TBODY>` tag must be used to hold the body of the table. A table's body must contain the same number of columns as its header and footer.
- **Start Tag**: Optional
- **End Tag**: Optional
- **Special Attributes**: None
- **Deprecated Attributes**: None
- **Other Attributes**: `align`, `char`, `charoff`, `class`, `dir`, `id`, `lang`, `onclick`, `ondblclick`, `onkeydown`, `onkeypress`, `onkeyup`, `onmousedown`, `onmousemove`, `onmouseout`, `onmouseover`, `onmouseup`, `style`, `title`, `valign`

<TD>...</TD>

- **Purpose**: This tag encloses a cell in a table that doesn't contain header information.
- **Start Tag**: Required
- **End Tag**: Optional
- **Special Attributes**:

`headers="text"`—The header cells that provide information about the current cell, with the `id` attributes of the different cells separated by spaces.

`scope="text"`—The set of table cells that this header cell provides information about.

`abbr="text"`—An abbreviated version of the cell's content.

`axis="categories"`—A list of categories, separated by commas, that the cell belongs to.

`rowspan="number"`—The number of rows occupied by the cell, or `"0"` if the cell should span all rows from the current row to the end of the current table section (defined using `<THEAD>`, `<TBODY>`, or `<TFOOT>`).

`colspan="number"`—The number of columns occupied by the cell, or `"0"` if the cell should span all columns from the current column to the end of the current column group (defined using `<COLGROUP>`).

- **Deprecated Attributes**: `bgcolor`, `nowrap`, `height`, `width`
- **Other Attributes**: `align`, `char`, `charoff`, `class`, `dir`, `id`, `lang`, `onclick`, `ondblclick`, `onkeydown`, `onkeypress`, `onkeyup`, `onmousedown`, `onmousemove`, `onmouseout`, `onmouseover`, `onmouseup`, `style`, `title`, `valign`

`<TEXTAREA>...</TEXTAREA>`

- **Purpose**: This tag adds a text input area control to a form.
- **Start Tag**: Required
- **End Tag**: Required
- **Special Attributes**:

  `name="text"`—The name of the control.

  `rows="number"`—The number of rows in the text area.

  `cols="number"`—The number of columns in the text area.

- **Deprecated Attributes**: None
- **Other Attributes**: `class`, `dir`, `disabled`, `id`, `lang`, `onblur`, `onchange`, `onclick`, `ondblclick`, `onfocus`, `onkeydown`, `onkeypress`, `onkeyup`, `onmousedown`, `onmousemove`, `onmouseout`, `onmouseover`, `onmouseup`, `onselect`, `readonly`, `style`, `tabindex`, `title`

`<TFOOT>...</TFOOT>`

- **Purpose**: This tag encloses a table row that appears as a footer below all other rows of the table. Like the `<THEAD>` tag, this footer can be used to provide information about the specific columns in the table. It must contain the same number of columns as the `<TBODY>` and `<TFOOT>` table rows it is associated with. A table's footer must appear before any `<TBODY>` tags in that table.

- **Start Tag**: Required
- **End Tag**: Optional
- **Special Attributes**: None
- **Deprecated Attributes**: None
- **Other Attributes**: `align`, `char`, `charoff`, `class`, `dir`, `id`, `lang`, `onclick`, `ondblclick`, `onkeydown`, `onkeypress`, `onkeyup`, `onmousedown`, `onmousemove`, `onmouseout`, `onmouseover`, `onmouseup`, `style`, `title`, `valign`

`<TH>...</TH>`

- **Purpose**: This tag encloses a cell in a table that contains header information.
- **Start Tag**: Required
- **End Tag**: Optional
- **Special Attributes**:

  `headers="text"`—The header cells that provide information about the current cell, with the `id` attributes of the different cells separated by spaces.

  `scope="text"`—The set of table cells that this header cell provides information about.

  `abbr="text"`—An abbreviated version of the cell's content.

  `axis="categories"`—A list of categories, separated by commas, that the cell belongs to.

  `rowspan="number"`—The number of rows occupied by the cell.

  `colspan="number"`—The number of columns occupied by the cell.
- **Deprecated Attributes**: `bgcolor`, `nowrap`, `height`, `width`
- **Other Attributes**: `align`, `char`, `charoff`, `class`, `dir`, `id`, `lang`, `onclick`, `ondblclick`, `onkeydown`, `onkeypress`, `onkeyup`, `onmousedown`, `onmousemove`, `onmouseout`, `onmouseover`, `onmouseup`, `style`, `title`, `valign`

`<THEAD>...</THEAD>`

- **Purpose**: This tag encloses a table row that appears as a header above all other rows of the table. Like the `<TFOOT>` tag, this header can be used to provide information about the specific columns in the table. It must contain the same number of columns as the `<TBODY>` and `<THEAD>` table rows it's associated with. A table's header must appear before any `<TBODY>` tags in that table.
- **Start Tag**: Required
- **End Tag**: Optional

- **Special Attributes**: None
- **Deprecated Attributes**: None
- **Other Attributes**: align, char, charoff, class, dir, id, lang, onclick, ondblclick, onkeydown, onkeypress, onkeyup, onmousedown, onmousemove, onmouseout, onmouseover, onmouseup, style, title, valign

<TITLE>...</TITLE>

- **Purpose**: This tag encloses the title of the document. In most Web browsers, the title is displayed in the browser window's title bar.
- **Start Tag**: Required
- **End Tag**: Required
- **Special Attributes**: None
- **Deprecated Attributes**: None
- **Other Attributes**: lang, dir

<TR>...</TR>

- **Purpose**: This tag encloses a row of cells in a table.
- **Start Tag**: Required
- **End Tag**: Optional
- **Special Attributes**: None
- **Deprecated Attributes**: None
- **Other Attributes**: align, char, charoff, class, dir, id, lang, onclick, ondblclick, onkeydown, onkeypress, onkeyup, onmousedown, onmousemove, onmouseout, onmouseover, onmouseup, style, title, valign

<TT>...</TT>

- **Purpose**: This tag encloses text that should be displayed in a monospace or teletype font. Although this tag hasn't been deprecated, the HTML 4.01 specification advises that style sheets are a better alternative.
- **Start Tag**: Required
- **End Tag**: Required
- **Special Attributes**: None
- **Deprecated Attributes**: None
- **Other Attributes**: class, dir, id, lang, onclick, ondblclick, onkeydown, onkeypress, onkeyup, onmousedown, onmousemove, onmouseout, onmouseover, onmouseup, style, title

A

<U>...</U>

- **Purpose**: This tag has been deprecated.

<UL>...</UL>

- **Purpose**: This tag encloses a list of items that won't be individually numbered. Each item in the list is identified by the <LI> tag. Most Web browsers display these unordered lists with a bullet character preceding each item. A numbered list requires the <OL> tag.
- **Start Tag**: Required
- **End Tag**: Required
- **Special Attributes**: None
- **Deprecated Attributes**: compact, type
- **Other Attributes**: class, dir, id, lang, onclick, ondblclick, onkeydown, onkeypress, onkeyup, onmousedown, onmousemove, onmouseout, onmouseover, onmouseup, style, title

<VAR>...</VAR>

- **Purpose**: This tag encloses text that represents a variable name or a command-line argument for a computer program.
- **Start Tag**: Required
- **End Tag**: Required
- **Special Attributes**: None
- **Deprecated Attributes**: None
- **Other Attributes**: class, dir, id, lang, onclick, ondblclick, onkeydown, onkeypress, onkeyup, onmousedown, onmousemove, onmouseout, onmouseover, onmouseup, style, title

APPENDIX B

Installing FrontPage 2002

Microsoft FrontPage 2002 uses an Installation Wizard that guides you through the process of setting up FrontPage and the other programs in the Office productivity suite.

The software setup process is relatively simple. After asking 6–8 questions about how you would like to set up the software, the wizard will begin installing FrontPage 2002 on your system.

The software also has a diagnostic feature that makes it easy to fix any installation errors that occur—FrontPage can detect when files it needs are missing and prompt you to reinsert the installation CD to correct the problem.

This appendix offers some guidance for any problems that you might encounter as you install FrontPage.

Getting Started with FrontPage 2002

Microsoft FrontPage 2002 is available as a standalone product and as part of the Office XP suite of programs. The following minimum system requirements have been recommended by Microsoft:

- A Pentium processor with 32MB of memory
- A CD-ROM drive
- A VGA monitor (although a Super VGA, 256-color monitor is preferred)
- A Microsoft-compatible mouse
- Windows 95, 98, Me, NT, or 2000
- A 28,800-baud or faster modem

Installing the whole Office suite, which includes FrontPage 2002, requires approximately 320MB of hard drive space. You can reduce this amount during installation by choosing not to install some Office programs.

Server Extensions

Among the optional features you can use with FrontPage 2002 are FrontPage Server Extensions and Office Server Extensions. These programs extend a Web server's capabilities to support interactive features such as a feedback form, search engine, and a discussion forum. Office Server Extensions are an enhanced version of FrontPage Server Extensions that enable additional Web functionality in Office 2002 programs.

Office Server Extensions require the Windows NT or 2000 operating system and one of two servers: Microsoft Internet Information Server 4.0 (Windows NT Server 4.0) or Personal Web Server 4.0 (Windows NT Workstation 4.0).

FrontPage Server Extensions have the same requirements, but they're also available for other servers, such as Apache, which is widely used on Linux systems. You need either Office Server Extensions or FrontPage Server Extensions to use some Web publishing features in FrontPage 2002:

- Remote management of a Web
- Form submission using a FrontPage 2002 component instead of a CGI program
- Working directly with a Microsoft Access 2002 database on a Web
- Use of other FrontPage 2002 components

FrontPage Server Extensions are supported by the Personal Web Server that can be installed with Windows 98. These extensions are also supported on some Web hosting services. Check with your service provider to make sure that extensions are supported before you use these features in your Webs.

Most FrontPage 2002 features that require server extensions will work on a Web host that is configured to work with FrontPage 2000. However, if you make use of new features such as server log analysis and expanded access control, you must host your Web on a server that has been upgraded to FrontPage 2002 Server Extensions.

Self-Repairing Application

One of the features of FrontPage 2002 is its capability to repair itself. When the program is launched, it will make sure that all essential files and program libraries are present on your system. If any of these files or libraries is not found, a dialog box will appear that enables you to reinstall the missing elements.

Users who have installed FrontPage 2002 from a network might not have to do anything to cause the software to repair itself. Network administrators have the option of placing these files on the network for use during self-repair.

If FrontPage 2002 was installed from CD-ROM, you'll need to keep those CDs handy in case the self-repair feature is ever needed.

This self-repair function is a part of all Microsoft Office 2002 products.

Conflicts with Previous Editions

By default, FrontPage 2002 will be installed in place of any version of FrontPage that's already on your system. The software is backward-compatible, so you'll be able to load Webs created with FrontPage 2000 and earlier versions of the software.

However, you should back up all existing Webs before you install the new version to make sure that they're not overwritten during the upgrade.

If you want to keep a previous edition of FrontPage on your system, you must choose the Typical, Complete, or Custom option during installation, as shown in Figure B.1.

B

FIGURE B.1

Choosing how to install FrontPage.

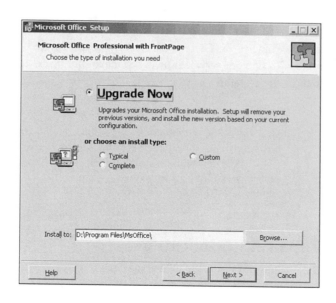

If you choose a custom installation, you'll be able to make the following configuration choices:

- The drive and folder where the software should be installed
- Whether to save previous versions of the software or to delete them during installation

You'll also be able to choose where specific elements of the software are stored. By default, most programs and files related to FrontPage 2002 are stored on your hard drive. One exception is a group of additional FrontPage 2002 themes.

During a customized installation, you can choose which elements of the software to save to your hard drive, which elements to run from the CD-ROM, and which elements to install only when they're first requested by a user.

The additional FrontPage 2002 themes fall into the third category. They won't be installed unless you choose to open the Install Additional Themes dialog box when you're defining a theme within the FrontPage editor.

If you have enough hard drive space on your system, you'll find it more convenient to keep the default options and install most of the program onto your hard drive.

Figure B.2 shows an installation dialog box where you can choose whether to replace existing Office applications, remove them, or leave them on your computer. If you're installing the standalone version of FrontPage 2002 instead of Office XP, you won't be asked about other Office applications by the installation wizard.

FIGURE B.2

Deciding what programs to replace or remove.

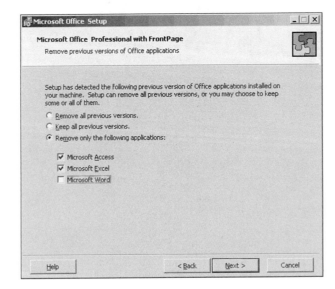

B

APPENDIX C

FrontPage Internet Resources

According to the World Wide Web search engine AltaVista, there are more than 170,000 Web pages that mention Microsoft FrontPage in some manner. Unless you have a few decades to kill, or an available pool of cheap labor, you might not want to sift through all those pages individually to find useful FrontPage sites.

This appendix covers the best Internet resources currently available for Microsoft FrontPage. You can find tips, bug-troubleshooting help, discussion forums, and many other useful bits of information that aren't in the official Microsoft FrontPage 2002 documentation. You'll also come across some good examples of Webs designed with FrontPage.

Although many of these resources are devoted to earlier editions of FrontPage, they might have been expanded to cover FrontPage 2002 as well by the time you read this.

Web Sites, Discussion Groups, and Mailing Lists

The most important resource, as far as this book is concerned, is this book's official World Wide Web site:

`http://www.cadenhead.org/frontpage`

Visit this Web site for the latest details on corrections, clarifications, and other information that supplements this book. You also can use it to send e-mail to author Rogers Cadenhead.

Web Sites

Microsoft FrontPage: `http://www.microsoft.com/frontpage/`

Microsoft's official home page for FrontPage 2002 and past versions of the software (see Figure C.1). Go here first for product specifications, technical support, and online ordering. You can search through Microsoft's database for information on bug fixes related to FrontPage, find out about free offers that you're eligible for, and subscribe to *Microsoft FrontPage Bulletin*, a monthly e-mail newsletter.

FIGURE C.1

Microsoft's official FrontPage site.

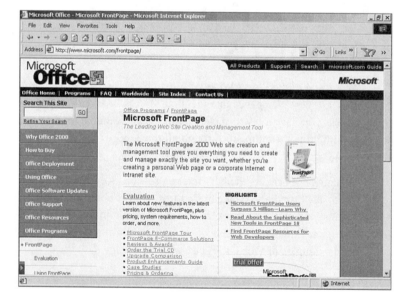

Chris's FrontPage Info Web: `http://www.webworkshop.org/frontpage/`

If you'd like the perspective of an experienced FrontPage Web designer, try Chris Calabrese's FrontPage Info Web site. A FrontPage user since January 1997, Calabrese has compiled quick tips, problem solutions, and a guide to Internet resources for FrontPage users.

FIGURE C.2

Chris Calabrese's FrontPage Info Web site.

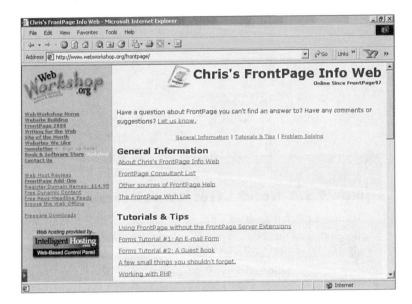

Dynamic Net FrontPage Support: `http://dynamicnet.net/support/frontpage.htm`

Although it's not as extensive as some of the other FrontPage Web sites, Dynamic Net's FrontPage Support site offers links to useful documents published by Microsoft, tips on newsgroups, Web sites, and books related to the software, and other information. It's one of the only sites that focuses on Active Server Pages in addition to FrontPage.

C

FIGURE C.3

*Dynamic Net's
FrontPage support site.*

FIGURE C.3

*Dynamic Net's
FrontPage support site.*

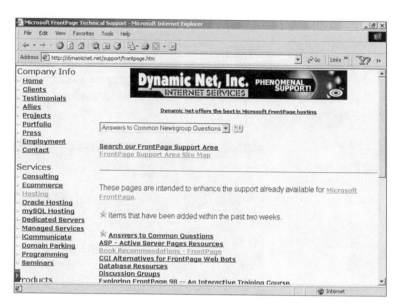

FrontPage World: `http://www.frontpageworld.com`

A guide to FrontPage that's published by Paul Colligan, one of the editors of the previous edition of this book. There's a guide to books, sites, and training programs available for FrontPage 2002, as well as an exclusive newsletter. Colligan's site was one of the first to offer information on FrontPage 2002.

FIGURE C.4

*Paul Colligan's
FrontPage World site.*

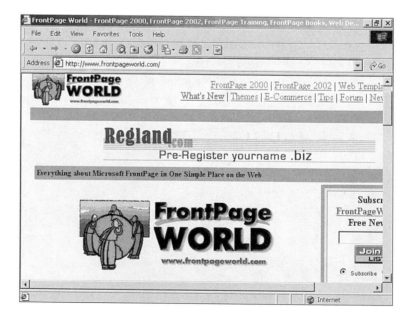

FrontPage 2000 in the Classroom: `http://www.actden.com/fp2000`

This is a 12-unit tutorial on FrontPage 2000 intended for teachers in grades kindergarten through 12 who want to use the software in their classrooms. The tutorial, created by ACT360 Media in conjunction with Microsoft, uses two animated characters from the year 2200 to explain the basics of using FrontPage 2000 to publish on the Web. There are quizzes at the end of each unit and a version of the tutorial you can print out.

FIGURE C.5

ACT360 Media's FrontPage 2000 in the Classroom tutorial.

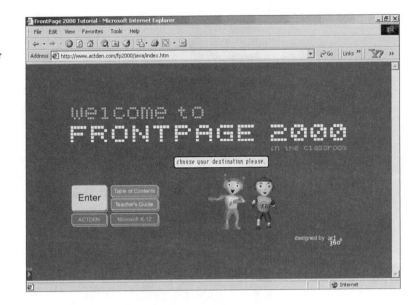

Web Hosting Providers That Support FrontPage: `http://www.microsoftwpp.com/wppsearch/`

A database of Web hosting providers that support FrontPage 2002 and previous versions of the software. This can be viewed by state or in alphabetical order, and there's an associated database for international providers. More than a dozen providers offer free hosting, which is useful when you're experimenting with the software. These companies include Yahoo! GeoCities, Angelfire, Tripod, and Talk City.

C

FIGURE C.6

Microsoft's directory of Web hosting providers that support FrontPage.

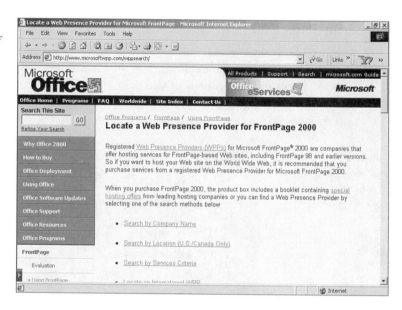

Acme Internet: `http://www.acmeinfo.com/`

Acme Internet, a Web hosting provider in Minneapolis, MN, is the first company that offered FrontPage 2000 hosting and a longtime specialist in Microsoft Web hosting. It's experienced with the issues that can arise in hosting and publishing FrontPage Webs.

FIGURE C.7

The home page of the Acme Internet hosting service.

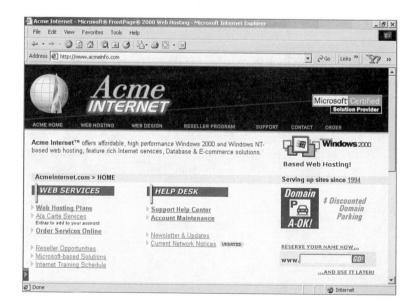

Mailing Lists and Discussion Forums

Microsoft FrontPage Client Newsgroup: `news://microsoft.public.frontpage.client`

If you can handle the large number of messages posted each day, this Usenet newsgroup is a great way to get personal support from other FrontPage users. If you don't have access to a news server that carries Microsoft newsgroups like this one, you can read it on the Google Web site at `http://groups.google.com`.

FrontPage Mailing List at St. John's

St. John's University hosts an active FrontPage mailing list that includes up to 40 messages a day from users of the software. To receive subscription information via e-mail, send a message to `listserv@maelstrom.stjohns.edu` with the text "info frontpage" as the body of your message.

C

INDEX

Hey, you've got enough worries.

Don't let IT training be one of them.

Get on the fast track to IT training at InformIT,
your total Information Technology training network.

 | **www.informit.com** | **SAMS**

■ Hundreds of timely articles on dozens of topics ■ Discounts on IT books
from all our publishing partners, including Sams Publishing ■ Free, unabridged
books from the InformIT Free Library ■ "Expert Q&A"—our live, online chat
with IT experts ■ Faster, easier certification and training from our Web- or
classroom-based training programs ■ Current IT news ■ Software downloads
■ Career-enhancing resources

InformIT is a registered trademark of Pearson. Copyright ©2001 by Pearson.
Copyright ©2001 by Sams Publishing.

SAMS
Teach Yourself
in 24 Hours

When you only have time for the answers™

Sams Teach Yourself in 24 Hours *gets you the results you want—fast! Work through 24 proven 1-hour lessons and learn everything you need to know to get up to speed quickly. It has the answers you need at the price you can afford.*

Sams Teach Yourself Java 2 in 24 Hours

Rogers Cadenhead
ISBN 0-672-32036-3
$24.99 US/$37.95 CAN

Other Sams Teach Yourself in 24 Hours Titles

Photoshop 6
Carla Rose
ISBN 0-672-31955-1
$24.99 US/$37.95 CAN

Macromedia Dreamweaver
Betsy Bruce
ISBN 0-672-32042-8
$24.99 US/$37.95 CAN

GoLive 5
Adam Pratt
ISBN 0-672-31900-4
$24.99 US/$37.95 CAN

Paint Shop Pro 7
T. Michael Clark
ISBN 0-672-32030-4
$19.99 US/$29.95 CAN

HTML & XHTML
Dick Oliver
ISBN 0-672-32076-2
$24.99 US/$37.95 CAN

CGI
Rafe Colburn
ISBN 0-672-31880-6
$24.99 US/$37.95 CAN

JavaScript
Michael Moncur
ISBN 0-672-32025-8
$24.99 US/$37.95 CAN

Flash 5
Phillip Kerman
ISBN 0-672-31892-X
$24.99 US/$37.95 CAN

All prices are subject to change.

SAMS

www.samspublishing.com